IN TAR AND PAINT AND STONE

This book takes its title from emigrant Charles Glass Grey's 1849 diary entry describing the names on Independence Rock: "Many ambitious mortals have immortalized themselves in tar & stone & paint."

IN TAR AND PAINT AND STONE

The Inscriptions at Independence Rock and Devil's Gate

LEVIDA HILEMAN

with a foreword by Randall A. Wagner

HIGH PLAINS PRESS

FIRST PRINTING

10 9 8 7 6 5 4 3 2 1

Library of Congress Cataloging-in-Publication Data

Hileman, Levida
In tar and paint and stone : the inscriptions at
Independence Rock and Devil's Gate /
Levida Hileman ; with a foreword by Randall A. Wagner
p. cm.
Includes bibliographical references and index.
ISBN 0-931271-61-4 (trade paper)
ISBN 0-931271-62-2 (cloth)
1. Independence Rock (Wyo.)--History.
2. Devil's Gate (Wyo.)--History.
3. Oregon National Historic Trail--History.
4. Pioneers--Oregon National Historic Trail--History.
5. Pioneers--Oregon National Historic Trail--Biography.
6. Incriptions--Wyoming--Independence Rock.
7. Incriptions--Wyoming--Devil's Gate.
8. Overland journeys to the Pacific.
I. Title.

F767.I38 H54 2001
978.7'02--dc21   2001020419

HIGH PLAINS PRESS
539 CASSA ROAD
GLENDO, WY 82213
WWW.HIGHPLAINSPRESS.COM
ORDERS: 1-800-552-7819

For my children

I am deeply grateful to my husband, Brock, without whom this book would never have been written. He supported me in every way, during six years of survey and research. He believed in me, even when I didn't, as I struggled with uncertainties and doubts. More importantly, he endured my quirks, whims, and odd fancies as I immersed myself with the people in this book. He traveled many miles with me, ever in the background, but always my constant source of strength and inspiration. In effect, he is my "rock."

CONTENTS

A little heap of dust,
A little streak of rust,
A stone without a name—
Lo! hero, sword, and fame.

— AMBROSE BIERCE

FOREWORD

INDEPENDENCE ROCK was a special landmark for most of the hundreds of thousands of emigrants who passed its imposing granite mass while traveling on the Oregon, California, and Mormon Trails. It remains a special place for all Wyoming residents who are aware of their state's rich history, as well as for western emigrant trails buffs worldwide.

Independence Rock was one of only a handful of natural landmarks that attracted the full attention of virtually every mountain man, trapper, trader, explorer, missionary, pioneer emigrant, and soldier who followed the great Platte River –South Pass trails from the early 1820s through the early 1860s. Only the landmarks between the last crossing of the North Platte River and Great South Pass carry this distinction because only here did all the Trails merge.

Chimney Rock, often considered the signature landmark of the Trails, was a distant feature for the considerable number of travelers using the trails on the north side of the North Platte. These emigrants, who originated their overland journey at Council Bluffs or Winter Quarters, found Chimney Rock's unique shape blending almost imperceptibly with the same-colored bluffs behind it. Scott's Bluff didn't become a major landmark until the trails were re-routed to Mitchell Pass in the 1850s. Fort Laramie, the dominant rest, re-supply, and military outpost on the trail system throughout the period of fur trade and emigration, does not qualify as a natural landmark. Laramie Peak and the surrounding mountains, known as the Black Hills by the emigrants, were too distant and massive to be useful in measuring pioneer progress.

Only after the emigration routes all came together on the west side of the North Platte River (in the vicinity of present-day Casper) did the landmarks take on a special significance. Now the entire emigration in any given year was following, if not the same track, at least the same travel corridor. Every passing pioneer witnessed the same scenes from almost the same viewpoint.

Of all these landmarks — Red Butte, Rock Avenue, Prospect Hill, Independence Rock, Devil's Gate, Split Rock, and the Oregon Buttes — it was Independence Rock that was the most anticipated. Here the emigrants met the Sweetwater River, the fresh, clean, and cool mountain stream that would lead them to South Pass and Oregon Country. Here, in most years, they found plentiful grass for their livestock and a pleasant place to camp. Here they could also check their schedule. Arrival at the Rock on or before the Fourth of July meant they would beat the autumn snowstorms in the far western mountains.

The anticipation of arrival at Independence Rock was enhanced by widely told tales of the Rock's early significance to the native populations, the explorers, and the fur trade. Several versions of how the Rock was named, and who did the naming, added to the mystique. Oregon and California emigrants knew this landmark as a milepost. They were nearing the midpoint of their seemingly endless journey.

Modern highway travelers cannot appreciate the drama of the approach to the landmark. It is only from the perspective of the Trail that Independence Rock completely dominates the landscape ahead, an apparent barrier to further progress. It is no wonder that this massive granite outcrop became the Trail's most significant billboard and message center. It practically forced travelers to stop, stay awhile, and leave word of their passing.

Levida Hileman has spent countless hours exploring every square inch of Independence Rock's complex surface in search of every remaining record of those who came this way. She spent more time introducing the Rock to other interested historians, and much more time researching every existing historic record of Independence Rock and every remaining pioneer diary entry to gain a firsthand, first-person impression of the experience of arriving at, staying near, and passing beyond this major western landmark.

In this book, Levida Hileman presents an account of that work in an interesting, easily readable format. *In Tar and Paint and Stone* brings Independence Rock and nearby Devil's Gate back to life at their most historic of times.

Many years ago, when I was very young, I rode a motorcycle to the top of Independence Rock. I started a love affair with the Rock, the Sweetwater River Valley, and the surrounding wild, rugged Wyoming countryside that day. The affair led to a lifelong fascination with the western emigrant trails. Levida Hileman's book has added to my knowledge, understanding, and appreciation in a most enjoyable way.

RANDALL A. WAGNER, PRESIDENT-ELECT
OREGON-CALIFORNIA TRAILS ASSOCIATION

PREFACE

THIS BOOK STARTED out as an interesting short-term project launched by Wyoming's Natrona County Historical Society and the Wyoming Chapter of the Oregon-California Trails Association, who saw the need to re-survey the inscriptions at Independence Rock and Devil's Gate. This was in the fall of 1994. I had retired in 1993 and, with my husband still working, had ample time to help with the survey. Little did I know that this "short-term project" would literally take over my life and lead me on a long quest for information resulting in meeting hundreds of people. Searching out the inscriptions can be an almost addictive activity, and I have been pulled back time after time to explore the secrets waiting to be uncovered at Independence Rock and Devil's Gate. Six years later I still feel that strong affinity with both locations. Over the years I have become intimately associated with many of the emigrants who left their long-ago inscriptions. Some of the names seem like friends or family to me, and I still feel the urge to trace their familiar inscriptions with my fingertips. At times I have felt, and I'm sure my husband has felt, that Independence Rock has taken over my life. I am often asked, "Why did you take on the Independence Rock study?" My answer is simple: "I did not choose Independence Rock so much as it chose me."

Much of the information I gathered has come from hours of reading manuscripts and diaries. I spent additional long

Early sketch of Independence Rock. The artist is unknown; however comparison of the handwriting on this sketch with Caspar Collins's sketches suggests this could possibly be a Collins sketch. The notation of "I.T." for Idaho Territory supports this premise. (Wyoming Department of Cultural Resources)

hours studying emigrant lists from various sources and comparing them to the names on Independence Rock. The Internet has been a very valuable resource, enabling me to obtain many of the emigrant and early census lists. Some of these were not alphabetized; therefore the process was tedious.

By far the most rewarding sources of information have been the numerous emigrant descendants I have corresponded with or talked to personally. Along with the surveying and research, my husband and I have spent five summers, more than one thousand hours, as volunteer docent interpreters at Independence Rock. With the permission of the Wyoming Department of Cultural Resources and Historic Sites, we spend our free time manning a simple information booth at the rest area at

Independence Rock. In this way, we meet many descendants who come to visit the Rock. These hundreds of descendants have been very helpful to me. I cannot begin to thank them all. I hope there are ways I have helped them in return.

Our favorite time to be at Independence Rock is over the Fourth of July holiday. Just as this date had meaning to many of the pioneers at Independence Rock, so it has meaning to many visitors today, for we see a great influx on this weekend. Independence Day celebrations were held over the years by the hundreds who passed by here long ago, and their diaries record how they displayed our nation's flag on those occasions. In 1998 Miles Hartung, a state employee at the Independence Rock Historic Site, raised a large American flag from a thirty-foot pole on top of the Rock's north end. This was an unforgettable sight. Proudly flying from atop this historic site, the flag honored all of those early people who considered this a milestone on their journey westward.

I have frequently been asked if my own inscription is on Independence Rock. I reply, "If I have left my name with the hundreds of others, it is in a spot very hard to find." I am certainly familiar with the secret places. However, a clue might be found in the often-quoted remark made by Rufus Sage in 1841: "if there remains no other mode of immortalizing myself, I will be content to descend to the grave, unhonored and unsung."

LEVIDA HILEMAN

PART ONE

THE
GREAT REGISTER
OF THE DESERT

THE EXPERIENCE OF
INDEPENDENCE ROCK

How this large granite rock came to be left out here all alone, miles from those of its kind, wise men may attempt to explain. At any rate here it is, defying wind and weather, a permanent land mark for the weary traveler.

Charles Ross Parke, *Dreams to Dust*

WEARY, DUSTY TRAVELERS, on their long journey across these plains, found this a place of rest during the trail years. Today hundreds of highway travelers find the inviting green grass of the rest area at Independence Rock a welcome stop along their journey. Just like their early predecessors, many take time to stop and marvel at the grandeur of Independence Rock. It is well worth the visit. This is the story of the people who came here long ago. A few of these were well-known even then, or history has since made then famous. However, the majority of the travelers who passed by Independence Rock and Devil's Gate were common, ordinary people toiling across long burdensome miles, hoping for a better life:

> If they are for the most part obscure individuals, if they rarely lead but are rather found among the crowd of the led, if failure and disappointment loom larger in their experience than adventure and success, they are for these very reasons more fittingly the mouthpiece of otherwise voiceless thousands. Of

This aerial view of Independence Rock shows the north end in foreground. Trail swales can be seen in upper portion of photo. (Author's Photo)

such men and women were the rank and file of the pioneers who made American tradition.

Elizabeth Page, *Wagons West*

Independence Rock is a solitary, smooth, rounded mass of granite jutting up from the plains of Wyoming's Sweetwater Valley. From a distance of even a few miles it seems rather insignificant, dwarfed by the jagged peaks of the surrounding Granite Mountains. In 1850 John Birney Hill described it this way: "When you are ten miles east of it, it looks like a kettle, bottom up minus the legs, or like an Indian mound that you read of."[1] The magic and the grandeur of Independence Rock does not really strike visitors until they are almost upon it. So it must have seemed to the emigrants on their long road west, for after seeing Chimney Rock and Court House Rock, many were expecting something grander in size and appearance. The altitude of the Independence Rock vicinity is 6,028 feet. Because of this altitude most emigrants noticed the cold nights and mornings, even in summer. The Rock stands adjacent to the curving Sweetwater River, surrounded by undulating plains. The highest point of the Rock is 136 feet above the surrounding terrain, about the height of a twelve-story building, and the mass of the Rock itself covers an area of approximately twenty-five acres. The distance around its base is almost one and one-fourth miles. Name-seekers can take a nice leisurely walk all around the Rock, finding most of the names at ground level on the south and southwest sides. To find the inscriptions scattered on the north and middle top, most visitors immediately ascend on the northwest corner, which is fairly steep. However, the northeast side offers a more gradual ascent to the names on the top.

Over the years many have thought the sleek, rounded shape of Independence Rock was the result of glacial action. Instead, this gigantic rock formation was created by the geological process of exfoliation. This occurred over a span of millions of years of geologic time as the surrounding mountains underwent enormous changes. Over fifty million years ago the Granite Mountains uplifted and subsequently broke into vertical faults. This deposited huge granite boulders along the flanks of the mountains. The broad granite core along the valley sagged downward and became buried by enormous amounts of windblown sand. In time the rounded summits of the Granite Range were stripped away and are now re-exposed. Independence Rock and other summits appear essentially as they did when buried fifteen million years ago.[2] As erosion uncovered the rock surface over millions of years, the pressure of weight on the overlying surface layers lessened, allowing the rock to expand outward. In this process layer after layer of granite broke off, thereby forming a smooth surface.[3] Wind and weather have further abraded it, shaping the contour that the emigrants knew and that we know today. Dr. Ferdinand Hayden, in his expedition of 1871, described the formation as disintegration by exfoliation. "It resembles a haystack with layers of rock lapping over the top and sides of the mass like layers of hay on a stack." Some sides of the rock sloped so gently that Hayden could lead his horse nearly to the top. William H. Jackson took a photo of Hayden, along with his horse, on the summit.[4]

For much of the twentieth century Independence Rock was on private property with limited access. In 1976 the State of Wyoming acquired the property which is now a State Historic Site. The state acquired the south portion of the Rock through a land swap with the Sun Ranch. The Dumbell Ranch donated the north portion to the state with the stipulation that Independence Rock was never to be used for commercial purposes. Visitors are assured they can experience this pristine site without extraneous tourist embellishments, thanks to the foresight of Norman and Gaynell Park of the Dumbell Ranch.

In an address given in 1915, Dr. Grace Raymond Hebard, secretary of the Oregon Trail Commission of Wyoming, said of the Rock: "The spot will always be a place of pilgrimage for some, as it ought to be for many who hold in reverence the spirit of their pioneer forebears. For all of us it has been an abiding interest, not only as a landmark on the route of travel, but as a monument associated with a glorious epoch in our country's development—a reminder of the eventual years when an army of Americans, three hundred thousand strong, marched Westward Ho! to Oregon to make good the title of the United States to the Pacific territory, and to add to the nation's domain the country which was then Oregon and now is Oregon, Washington, and Idaho."[5]

Ten years later Robert S. Ellison, addressing an organization of petroleum geologists at Independence Rock, remarked on its importance: "For over a quarter of a century, there circled around it a huge mass, the great tide of humanity pressing forward to complete the conquest of the Pacific Slope."[6]

This photo shows some inscriptions from the middle top portion of the Rock. Note the very precise lettering of some of the inscriptions. (Author's Photo)

Independence Rock held many meanings to the emigrants who crossed the plains. It was a milestone on the long journey west, a landmark mentioned in every printed guidebook, and a goal to be reached by July fourth or shortly thereafter if one hoped to get over the western mountains before the snows came. It was a place with good water where a party could rest and recuperate for a few days, or a place to hurry by because the season was late. It was a message center for the early fur trappers and traders, and a place where thousands of emigrants left their inscriptions bearing evidence of their passing. For others it was a place of disappointment for they had expected more, or it was a place of never-to-be-forgotten tragedy.

Independence Rock is a place where the past still lives. On an early spring morning two people are alone on the top of the Rock. One person sits inspecting inscriptions, holding a notebook in her hands. The other is a passing tourist from New England with no background in trail history. He walks slowly, studying the names, then remarks in a low, awestruck voice, "It's like walking in the footsteps of ghosts." Independence Rock still holds many meanings, and the spirit of its past survives if one gives it time to share its mysteries. This landmark was the scene of many exuberant, often wild, celebrations, the scene of joyful weddings and of births, of music and firelit dances, yet also a place harboring the deep, painful sorrow of burials. Traces of the memories of all of these events are there to look at, to touch, and to feel deep in the soul.

Even before the white man ever walked the trails of the area, an early Indian legend told of Independence Rock:

> A great many years ago, long before any white man had looked upon the valley of the Upper Platte, the chief of the Pawnees was known as the Crouching Panther. He was one of the bravest warriors that the famous Pawnee nation had ever produced. He was a legend in his time.
>
> In the village there lived a young woman, considered the handsomest maiden in all the region. She was known as the Antelope.
>
> Crouching Panther had for a long time desired Antelope as his wife and arrangements had already been made for a wedding of the two. On the night preceding the ceremony, a party of Sioux made a night assault upon the village. After a terrible fight they carried off a number of prisoners, among whom was Antelope.
>
> The Sioux were assembled in their camp, planning to torture their captives, when the terrible war-whoop of the Pawnees sounded in the their ears. The Pawnees, led by Crouching Panther, were upon them fighting their way to where the prisoners stood. Crouching Panther caught up Antelope, throwing her before him on his saddle, and dashed off with his band of followers.
>
> The Sioux quickly followed the daring Pawnees. The Pawnees had not gone very far when they were overtaken by the Sioux close to the famous rock formation in the valley. A terrible fight took place and most of the Pawnees were killed. Crouching Panther was near the rock, when he found himself alone, death staring him in the face.
>
> He jumped from his animal with Antelope in his arms, and rushed up the rock. He sprang to the edge of the dizzy

height, standing for a moment confronting his enemies. The Panther hurled his hatchet, burying it deep in brain of his closest enemy. Then with a swift motion, uttering a triumphant battle cry, he pressed close to his bosom the beautiful form of Antelope and sprang out into the clear air. The two lovers were dashed to pieces on the stony ground below.[7]

The heyday of the trail years was from 1840 to 1869, however, the first trappers and explorers may have arrived at the Rock as early as 1812 with the Robert Stuart party. The exact year the landmark was actually christened Independence Rock has not been clearly established. Some say it was as early as 1823 when Thomas Fitzpatrick and other mountain men celebrated here. A Wyoming Division of Cultural Resources brochure suggests it was after a Fourth of July celebration at the site by the William Sublette party in 1830 that the massive granite site became known as Independence Rock.[8] However, in his 1843 diary, journalist Matthew Field wrote that Sublette christened "Rock Independence" July 4, 1831.[9] Since Sublette was traveling with this same 1843 party, it seems plausible that Field received this information from Sublette himself. In his 1899 book *The History of Wyoming*, C. G. Coutant records an interview with early mountain man Jim Baker. Baker first came to the West in 1838, working for the American Fur Company. He later settled in Wyoming. Late in Baker's life, he told Coutant that perhaps explorer Captain Benjamin de Bonneville had named the Rock. Baker did say that in the early years the rock was known as Rock Independence.[10] Coutant's further efforts to trace the exact origin of the name were unsuccessful. Some of the early diaries make reference to Rock Independence.

By the early 1830s the name of Independence Rock or Rock Independence was commonly used by the mountain men and fur traders. They not only left their names on the Rock, they also used it as a type of frontier post office, painting messages on the surface for others to read. William Marshall

This Rilla Elgin inscription, located on the middle top, is one of the few female names on the Rock. (Author's Photo)

Anderson, traveling with William Sublette's party of fur traders in 1834, wrote:

> There are few places better known or more interesting to the mountaineer than this huge boulder. Here they look for and often obtain information of intense interest to them. On the side of the rock names, dates, and messages, written in buffalo grease and powder, are read and re-read with as much eagerness as if they were letters in detail from long absent friends. Besides being a place of advertisement, or kind of trapper's post office, it possesses a reputation and a fame peculiar to itself. It is a large, egg-shaped mass of granite, entirely separate and apart from all other hills, or ranges of hills. One mile in circumference about six or seven hundred feet high, without a particle of vegetation, and with no change known but the varying sparkles of mica which are seen by day and by the moon by night.[11]

In 1837 the artist Alfred Jacob Miller accompanied Sir William Drummond Stewart and other members of a fur brigade heading for the thirteenth fur rendezvous in the Rocky Mountains. In that year, he made note of these names on Independence Rock: Bonneville, Sublette, Wyeth, Campbell, Sarpy, Pilcher, and also Nelson.[12]

Mary Walker and Sarah Gilbert White Smith were two of the earlier white women who passed by the landmark. In 1838 these two women, with their husbands, were traveling with other missionaries to Oregon's Willamette Valley. At this point they had joined the American Fur Company trade caravan led by Captain Andrew Dripps. Though both described the site itself in their journals, neither made mention of any inscriptions. Mary Walker wrote:

> Friday June 15. Last night encamped on the Sweet water at the foot of Rock Independence, so called because the fir company once celebrated Independence here. This morning there being no dew went—in company with Mr. and Mrs. Gray to the top of the rock. It is I should judge more than 100 ft. high & half a mile wide in circumference, Eliptical in form. The rock is a corse granite in which the quartz predominates. It appears as if it has been scraped hardly by something. I forgot to say that near it we passed a salt pond half a mile one way and a mile the other . . .We forded the Sweet water & noon passed the place where the rock Mt. is cleft to its base & this Sweet water passes [Devil's Gate]. The rock on either hand is perhaps 200 ft. high. Rock Independence forms the entrance some say to Rocky Mts., others say not.[13]

Sarah Gilbert White Smith, who was there at the same time, wrote:

> 14th Thurs. Have been travelling over high prairie today, with the Rocky Mts. full in view & white with snow. We have mounted some hills, crossed some ravines, but most of the way has been level. The soil has no grass, no timber, fuel buffalo manure. Are encamped on the Sweetwater, a branch of the Platte, at the foot of Independence rock, so called because here the Fur Company once celebrated Independence. It is very large, covers several acres of ground & goes to the height of perhaps 120 feet. It looks as if thrown up by some volcanic power. At its foot is a salt

lake. Have passed several today. Have travelled 9 hours. Supposed to go 25 miles.[14]

Two years earlier, the Marcus Whitman party going to Oregon in 1836 reportedly stopped long enough to add the names of Narcissa Whitman and Eliza Spalding to the register on the Rock.[15] Narcissa Whitman made no mention of this in her letters, but these would have been the first white women's names on Independence Rock.

Father Pierre Jean DeSmet is commonly credited with coining the phrase "the Great Record of the Desert." In an 1841 letter to a bishop in Saint Louis, Father DeSmet wrote:

> Still, on the following day, lest it might be said that we passed this lofty monument of the desert with indifference, we cut our names on the south side of the rock, under initials, I. H. S. which we would wish to see engraved on every spot. On account of all these names, and of the dates that accompany them, as well as of the hieroglyphics of Indian warriors, I have surnamed this rock 'The Great Record of the Desert.'[16]

Some versions of this quote record that he wrote "The Great Register of the Desert."

Indeed even as early as 1841 Independence Rock was covered with names. This was long before the tide of emigrants had even begun to reach the area. Rufus Sage, who visited the site in 1841, was somewhat disenchanted. He wrote:

> The surface is covered with the names of travellers, traders, trappers, and emigrants, engraven upon it in almost every practicable part, for the distance of many feet above its base,—but most prominent among them all is the word, "Independence," inscribed by the patriotic band who first christened this lonely monument of nature in honor of Liberty's birthday.
>
> I went to the rock for the purpose of recording my name with the swollen catalogue of others traced upon its sides;

This early photo by William H. Jackson from south top was later used in Jackson's 1930 painting of the same scene. (Casper College Library, Special Collections)

but, having glanced over the strange medley, I became disgusted, and turning away, resolved, "If there remains no other mode of immortalizing myself, I will be content to descend to the grave 'unhonored and unsung.'"[17]

John C. Fremont, on an early exploration in 1842, gave us this description:

Everywhere within six or eight feet of the ground, where the surface is sufficiently smooth, and in some places sixty or eighty feet above, the rock is inscribed with the names of travelers. Many a name famous in the history of this country, and some well-known to science, are to be found among those of traders and travelers for pleasure and curiosity, and of missionaries among the savages. Some of these have been washed away by the rain, but the greater number are still very legible.[18]

The Fremont party, with Kit Carson as their guide, visited Independence Rock on August 1, 1842, and then again on

August 23. It was on this latter date that Fremont recorded that he chiseled a cross on the Rock:

> Here, not unmindful of the custom of the early travelers and explorers in our country, I engraved on the rock of the Far West the symbol of the Christian faith. Among the thickly inscribed names I made on the hard granite the impression of a large cross, deeply engraved, which I covered with a black preparation of India rubber, well calculated to resist the influence of wind and rain. It stands amidst the names of many who have long since found their way to the grave, and for whom the huge rock is a giant gravestone.[19]

James Clyman was a fur trapper who first came to the area in 1823 as part of William Ashley's group, led by Jedidiah Smith. He stayed in the West through 1825, returned to civilization for a number of years, and then joined a party going to Oregon in 1843. He wrote in his journal:

> . . . saw the notable rock Independence with the names of its numerous visitors most of which are nearly obliterated by the weather & ravages of time amongst which I observed the names of two of my old friends, the notable mountaineers Thos. Fitzpatrick & W. L. Sublette as likewise one of our noblest politicians Henry Clay coupled in division with that of Martin Van Buren.[20]

Matthew Field also visited Independence Rock on two occasions in 1843, staying long enough to catalog the names that he and a friend, a Dr. Tilghman, found on the Rock (see Appendix A). He also reported many of the names already obliterated in that early year. This suggests that most of the early inscribers simply used grease mixtures or paint. On July 23 of that year, Field wrote:

> It is a large oval-shaped elevation of naked rock, with a few scattering shrubs peeping here and there from cleft and fissure.

A great number of names are marked upon it with 'powder paint,' powder pounded and heated with grease… Got mellow and slept on the rock. Our mess on guard, and the guard in a mess![21]

A later entry that year describes the paint:

We all started back in company, and found camp located at the base of Rock Independence. On this remarkable rock, in the course of the afternoon, we printed the name of HENRY CLAY in large letters. Our paint was a boiled mixture of powder, buffalo grease and glue, which resists the action of the wind and rain with great tenacity. This was on the 22nd of July, and when we returned to the same place in September [actually August 28], we found the name of MARTIN VAN BUREN, in letters three times as large placed over our inscription, '*by Wm. Gilpin.*'[22]

Field also transcribed carefully some Indian signs that still clung to the Rock at that time. He writes, "Indian signs, fresh upon the rock, the vermillion yet wet, the fire yet warm," and then copied down the symbols. They found other symbols in red paint close by the first.[23] This is evidence that the Indians also used Independence Rock as a message center.

Field makes no mention of seeing John C. Fremont's name, nor the cross, on Independence Rock at this time. Some diarists remarked seeing Fremont's name in later years, but C. G. Coutant, in his *History of Wyoming*, suggested that Fremont's name was inadvertently blasted off by Fourth of July celebrants in 1847. According to Coutant, enthusiastic citizens filled wagon hubs with gunpowder, fastened a fuse to them, then placed them in crevices in the rock. When they blasted off the gunpowder tons of granite came tumbling down and with the debris Fremont's cross was forever buried.[24] However, Harriett Talcott Buckingham, traveling with a party in 1851, wrote that she saw Fremont's name at that time. This entry contradicts Coutant's story. She wrote:

[June] 15. At noon found us underneath Independence Rock. From the distance it has the appearance of an oblong sand hill of no great dimensions, but as you approach nearer we find it a stupendous mass of granite standing isolated between two ranges of mountains (for I suppose they might be so called). The Sweet Water runs at its left, I think it is some 120 feet high. I looked in vain amid that medly of names engraven & written upon its sides for one familiar one. It ought to be called the Sweet Water register—I walked I suppose a mile upon the north side and seeing the names still as numerous as when I first started gave up the search. But I had hoped to see Patricks or b—r sturges. Fremonts name still there. We, that is Sue [and] myself, for Cook & Bibs left our cards upon the highest peak for Mr Williams of Ill & Mr. Black. We spent a pleasant afternoon in rambling over the rocks & in the cool fissures which we found.[25]

William Chandless's diary entry of 1855 leads us to believe that Fremont's cross was still there in that year: "On this rock is the cross, placed there by Colonel Fremont, and since a subject of foul-mouthed abuse against him."[26]

Two other well-known names from Matthew Field's list of inscriptions are those of L.W. Hastings and A. L. Lovejoy. These two men were part of a very large colony of people headed to Oregon in 1842. Elijah White, Indian agent, led this party from the start while mountain man Thomas Fitzpatrick joined as guide after the group left Fort Laramie. Fitzpatrick's previous experience dealing with the Sioux may have prevented a tragedy as the emigrants departed Independence Rock.

Lansford Hastings later published his *Emigrants' Guide to Oregon and California*, the guidebook used by the Donner-Reed party in 1846 on their way to California. In the book, Hastings recounted that while traveling with the Elijah White company in 1842, he and Amos Lovejoy decided at the last moment to leave their names on the Rock. The two men had just finished carving their names when they had an unfortunate encounter with a band of Sioux that could have ended in disaster. He wrote:

> Having provided ourselves with materials for lettering, we tied our horses at the foot of this extraordinary rock, where we also left our guns, and commenced our toilsome assent up the rocky declivity. The company had in the mean time, gone on supposing that we could find no difficulty in overtaking them, whenever we had accomplished our purpose. We had scarcely completed our labors, when we were surprised by the sudden appearance of seven Indians, who had descried us from some remote hill or mountain. They presented themselves to us, in the most hostile attitude, rushing towards us with the greatest vehemence, uttering the most terrific and demoniac yells; and with most frightful gestures...[27]

Another member of the party, Miss E. Allen, provided additional details. She wrote that while Hastings and Lovejoy were inscribing their names, a large party of Sioux came around the north side of the rock and rushed upon the men, stripping them of most of their clothing and detaining them for hours.[28]

Finally the Indians, holding the two men captive, advanced on the wagon party which had moved on down the trail. The travelers had grown anxious concerning the whereabouts of Hastings and Lovejoy. Company leaders White and Fitzpatrick entered into lengthy talks with the Indians who said they would no longer permit their country to be invaded by white men. Fitzpatrick assured the Sioux that the emigrants were farmers traveling through to their homes in Oregon and had no intention of harming the Indians nor of staying in the area. After much discussion and the distribution of gifts to the Sioux, the Indians allowed the wagon party to go on with the order never to invade their country again.[29]

A traveler in this party wrote that when Hastings and Lovejoy rejoined the company, "they ran joyfully to their friends, the tears rolling down their cheeks as they recounted their escape."[30]

One of the earliest births at Independence Rock was recorded in 1844. The Stephens-Townsend-Murphy party had halted here for a week to hunt buffalo and "make meat." En route to California, the party was celebrating the Fourth of July at the Rock when a baby girl was born to the James Miller family. The little girl was the granddaughter of Martin Murphy, one of the leaders of the party. They christened the little girl Ellen Independence Miller, in commemoration of her time and place of birth.[31]

The Brigham Young Pioneer Party reached Independence Rock on Monday, June 21, 1847. After setting up camp about a mile upstream the members of the party spent some time examining the names inscribed and painted on Independence Rock. The inscription of Norton Jacob, 1847, a member of the Pioneer Party, is still visible. Wilford Woodruff, also of this party, wrote that nearly all the names were put on with red, black, and yellow paint; some had washed out and were defaced even then.

During a prayer meeting held on top of the Rock, the Mormons observed a party from Missouri burying a young woman by the name of Rachel Morgan.[32] Daniel and Rachel Morgan, along with three children, were traveling with the Woodsides-Morgan wagon train from Illinois to Oregon in 1847. Rachel gave birth to a baby girl at Independence Rock; however, childbirth did not cause her death. The family believed the new copper pots they were using reacted with the alkaline water of the area, causing food poisoning. This party saw several others of their group die while crossing the plains. The baby, never given a name, did not live long enough to complete the journey. Injured by a fallen wagon gate at Mount Hood, Oregon, the baby also died. Rachel was twenty-five at the time of her death and the family records refer to the baby as Baby Morgan.[33]

In late summer of 1997, a visitor left a wreath attached to a polished walking stick in a grassy area next to the Rock. The wreath read, "In memory of Rachel Morgan." For Morgan

Norton Jacob, a member of the Brigham Young Pioneer Party, inscribed his name on Independence Rock in 1847. His fairly large signature is still visible. (LDS Historical Department Archives, Salt Lake City)

family members the past lives on and Rachel is not forgotten, but contact with a descendant of the family shed no light as to who left the memorial.

Once the emigrants started crossing the plains in ever-increasing numbers, diarist after diarist commented on Independence Rock and Devil's Gate. Many wrote with wonder and awe, others spoke merely of another landmark on their long journey west, and some wrote disparagingly. William Riley Franklin, crossing the plains from Missouri to California in 1850, was one of those impressed with the Rock:

> A march of 25 miles brought us to the noted "Rock Independence" on the Sweet Water river. After advancing 3 miles up this stream and crossing it, we encamped upon its southern margin for the night. This aforesaid rock is well

worth the attention of the traveler who may go thither. . . .
Upon it is cut in uncouth, but legible character, thousands,
yes, I may say, tens of thousands of Oregon and California
emigrants' names, dates, etc., other amateur travelers who
have chanced to pass this way.[34]

The next day in his journal he wrote of Independence Rock
and Devil's Gate, "the places are truly grand and stupendous."[35]
Martha Wood wrote in 1852:

Sat. July 20. Traveled 14 miles. Came to Sweet Water creek
passed Saleratus springs [alkali deposits]. It was a curiosity to
see it. The Saleratus was baked all over the top of the water.
We saved what we wanted of it. We stopt at Independence
Rock near Sweet Water and went on it. It was a great curiosity to see it and a real job to get on and off of it. After view-
ing the rock we heard of some first rate feed back 3 or 4 miles
and we went there to lay over Sunday. . . .

[Mon. July 22.] After traveling 6 or 8 miles from
Independence Rock we came to the Devil's gate. This is a
large rock with a deep passage of water running through it.
Some say the rocks are 400 feet high. It is a complete ledge
of rock on one side of us all the way now. I suppose it is the
commencement of the Rocky Mountains.[36]

Lorena Hays wrote this in her diary on June 24, 1853:

About noon we struck the Sweet water near Independence
rock, below which there was a broken-looking bridge, and
some Crow Indian lodges. Above was a ford, about a half mile,
to which our train drove, where they stopped for dinner. Some
of us left the wagons and walked to Independence rock while
they were passing round. We passed over it, and came to the
wagons above it. In approaching it, its appearance does not
strike the eye as anything wonderful, the granite hills surrounding it being much higher than it is, but as one ascends
and surveys its huge mass, its immensity fills one with wonder.

It stands all alone surrounded by a pretty green level bottom of the river, it passing near the south end of the rock.[37]

Cephas Arms was one of those who wrote of his company's disappointment when they reached Independence Rock on their way to the gold fields of California in 1849:

> Monday, June 25th. . . .Two miles brought us to the Great, renowned Independence Rock. We were much disappointed when it was first pointed out to us, for we expected to see (never having had a description of it except as the Great Independence Rock) a spire, pyramid or shot tower looking object, but on the contrary, it was one large mass extending over perhaps four or five acres & being 150 to 200 feet high. The exterior was broken by many deep crevices, extending in some places half through. Between the crevices, on the outside it was smooth. From this reason it has been chosen since the passing of the first white man, as a registering & publishing post. Thousands of names are upon it, some painted well, others tarred, and many cut in the rock.[38]

Eugenia Zieber was another of those disappointed. Eighteen years old, she was traveling with her family to Oregon in 1851. She wrote:

> Thursday, [July] 17. Came to Sweetwater river today at noon. . . .We passed Independence Rock. I was rather disappointed in this. It is certainly a fine rock, but being surrounded by hills even higher than itself, it did not appear at all to advantage. Though being disappointed in what I thought it would be like, I may not have considered it in as favorable a light as I should have done.[39]

Richard Burton, crossing the plains in 1860, likened the country approaching Independence Rock to Eastern Africa. He wrote that the Indians had named it Timpe Nabor, or the Painted Rock, adding:

Prairie travellers and emigrants expect to be followed by their friends, and leave, in their vermillion, or their white house-paint or their brownish-black tar—a useful article for wagons—a homely but hearty word of love or directions upon any conspicuous object. Even a bull or a buffalo's skull which lying upon the road will attract attention, is made to do duty at this Poste Restante.[40]

Independence Rock must have looked somewhat garish covered in many colors of paint and tar. It probably looked even odder on July 3, 1854, as recorded in the diary of Elizabeth Austin and Anne Marie Goodel. Close personal friends, they were traveling in a party from Ohio, going to Washington Territory:

> July 3rd. We have got to Independence Rock about noon. William and I went around it. Lib and Lucretia and the rest of the girls went over it. There is a wagon and a tent on top of it. I do not see any names that I know.[41]

Numerous parties would have liked to stop at Independence Rock but were unable to because of lack of time. Mary Stuart Bailey was one of those. She and her husband were traveling from Ohio to California in 1852:

> Tues, [July] 6th. Started early. Came to Independence Rock about noon. We had intended to be there on the 4th but were behind our time on account of lying by to recruit. It is a massive rock entirely naked. Very many names inscribed on it. We did not stop being as we were in a hurry to get to the Sweetwater, a lovely stream of fine water which was truly refreshing to our horses. We drove through it & as the grass was not inviting continued to drive. Passed Devil's Gate as a deep cut through which the water runs. It is a great curiosity resembling the hotel of the White Mountains excepting for the road does not run through it but leaves it at the left & is on level ground comparatively.[42]

Another 1852 party with no time to stop at Independence Rock included Cecelia Adams and Parthenia Blank. These women were twin sisters and their families were on their way to Oregon. The following is in their diary:

> [July] 25 Sun. This morning we started at 3 o'clock to feed and get breakfast. Sand very deep and dust very troublesome. Stoped for dinner opposit Independence Rock. It is a great curiosity but we were all so tired that we could not go to the top of it. It is almost entirely covered with names of emigrants. Went on to the Devil's Gate and encamped this is a great curiosity but we have not time to visit it and regret it very much.[43]

At times hordes of grasshoppers descended, eating everything on the plains. This was a great hardship to the companies dependent on grasses for feed. The Fremont party faced this challenge in 1842.[44] It must have been that way again in 1850, when John Birney Hill wrote:

> Just before I got to Independence Rock I saw more grasshoppers than I ever saw before or since. They were trimming a swath six miles wide and leaving nothing but stubble and leafless sage brush. They were in no hurry to get through, for there was no gold for them at the end of their journey. They travel all summer to get something to eat, and we traveled all summer for the love of gold.[45]

The Sweetwater River must have been much higher and broader than it is today. In 1850 William Riley Franklin described it as "a beautiful and meandering mountain stream about 100 yards wide."[46] In 1852 a few diarists reported using a commercial ferry at this site. Jay Green wrote, "After two miles I find Independence Rock—I find a ferry cept by three mountaineers they had a raft upon which they crost wagons." In the same year, Dr. John Hudson Wayman wrote, "After leaving the rock we came to the river again & crossed it on a log

Low water in the Sweetwater River in the fall of 2000 exposes foundation stones of the Sweetwater Bridge. (Author's Photo)

ferry boat and are now encamped on the south side."[47] George Laub, traveling that same year, made reference to the ferry on the Sweetwater River.

Although during most years the emigrants had no trouble fording the Sweetwater, in the early 1850s, Louis Guinard built a bridge across the river about one mile east of Independence Rock (the exact date is uncertain).[48] Guinard charged a sliding fee for crossing the Sweetwater Bridge, depending on the flood of the river. He did a lucrative business. Early in the season, during high water, he charged ten dollars per wagon and teams. When the water was lower, the price was five dollars, and he also had a three-dollar rate for the lowest water levels. Guinard built this bridge about the same time John Richard (Reshaw) built his first bridge across the North Platte River.[49] Guinard used the profits from this bridge to later build another substantial span across the North Platte River at the site of Platte Bridge Station, later known as Fort Caspar.

A trading post, located at this site on the Sweetwater River, also served as a station for the stage line when mail service was established in 1851 between Saint Louis and Salt Lake City. The government contract required that the round-trip journey be made in forty-two days, but after a time, the mail went twice a month. The stage line also carried passengers.[50]

Numerous diarists make reference to the bridge over the Sweetwater in 1853. Lorena Hays made mention of a "broken looking bridge" in her diary; Maria Belshaw wrote, "There we had a fine view of Independence Rock, a Trading Post and a Bridge about 1/2 mile east of the Rock. The emigrants do not cross the bridge—they ford the river about a mile from the Rock west." Orange Gaylord wrote in his journal on June 8, "Drove to Sweetwater and nooned. Poor grass. Crossed the river on the bridge and drove to the upper side of the Devil's Gate and camped." In 1854, Sarah Sutton reported they "paid 50 cents a wagon for crossing a bridge" on June 14 at the Sweetwater River. That same year Philip Condit reported that there was a bridge at the trading post but the river was fordable in low water.

Even now, in the early part of the season, the Sweetwater sometimes overflows its banks. In 1995, from mid-May until mid-June, it was out of its banks because of the heavy snowmelt in the mountains. The river was wide and swift-flowing, its waters touching the base of Independence Rock. A person could not walk on the south side of the Rock without wading. The year 1852 was similar to this. Lucy Rutledge Cooke was traveling with her husband and family to California in that year. In mid-June they camped on the Sweetwater, which she described as having a very rapid current.

> In the morning we drove the horse waggon to Independance Rock & staid there some 2 or 3 hours examining names which are inscribed in every available place. Lilly & some others climbed the summit but as sis was awake I had to remain below most of our folks added their names to those already there. Wilm. [her husband] did not he said it looked

too much like hard work to clamber on the rough rock bare
footed for the sake of putting his name there some of the
names are cut in the rock others done with tar white, red &
black lead & some few with paint. . . . I only went on one
side of the rock as there was water so that I could not get all
round without riding.[51]

Two stories exist concerning the source of the name Sweetwater for the river. Some believe it was first called "Eau Sucree"
by early French voyageurs since the day a pack mule slipped
when crossing the river. The pack, laden with sugar, spilled into
the water, thus giving the river its name. The other version tells
that traders on one of William Ashley's fur expeditions so
named it because the pleasant-tasting water in the river was in
such contrast with the other brackish streams in the vicinity.[52]

At the turn of the twenty-first century the inscriptions
remaining on Independence Rock are as varied as the people
who passed there a century and a half ago. One tries to visual-
ize how the Rock must have looked then, covered with thousands of names in a variety of paint colors. One can walk over
Independence Rock and see many names bunched together in
specific areas. Then all at once, in an area barren of names, one
or two solitary inscriptions appear. One wonders, "Were these
solitary names once surrounded by painted names?" or "Did
these people purposely go off to a secluded spot to leave their
mark?" Diary records lead us to believe people left their inscriptions so others coming along behind would know they had
reached this spot safely. Yet others must have had the urge simply to be part of the multitude of names on the Rock. In 1849
Colonel James Tate wrote in his diary, "I cut my name with a
chisel, where it will stand for the ages." His name has withstood
the weathering of ages and is still visible in two different places,
on the south side of Independence Rock.

The emigrant experience still resonates along the trails, perhaps especially at Independence Rock. As one reads the diaries

and visits the sites, the long-ago voices speak once again. As Dr. Grace Raymond Hebard reminded her audience in 1915, "One cannot grasp or have an adequate conception of this Rock out there on the desert, with names carved on it and no sign of life, until one has been there, walked around it, felt of it and traced with his fingers the names that were carved there more than three score years ago and then climbed to the top of it and obtained a sweep of the country along the line of the old Oregon Trail."[53]

Notes on Chapter One

1. Hill, John Birney, "Gold: A Story of the Plains in 1850," *Annals of Wyoming*, Vol. 9, p. 37.

2. Junge, Mark, Ned Frost, *Prospectus on Independence Rock*, pp. 8-9.

3. "Welcome to Independence Rock," Wyoming Division of Cultural Resources brochure.

4. Ellison, Robert S., "Independence Rock and the Oregon Trail," *Midwest Review*, Vol. 8, #2, p. 1.

5. Mokler, A. J., *History of Natrona County*, p. 456.

6. Ellison, Robert S., "Independence Rock and the Oregon Trail," op.cit., p. 1.

7. Inman, Colonel Henry, *The Great Salt Lake Trail*, p. 238.

8. "Welcome to Independence Rock," op. cit.

9. Field, Matthew, *Prairie and Mountain Sketches*, p. 117.

10. Coutant, C. G., *The History of Wyoming*, p. 694.

11. Anderson, William Marshall, *The Rocky Mountain Journals of William Marshall Anderson*, edited by Dale L. Morgan & Eleanor Harris, Huntington Library, San Marino, CA, 1967, pp. 119-121.

12. DeVoto, Bernard, *Across the Wide Missouri*, p. 320.

13. Drury, Clifford, *First White Women Over the Rockies*, Vol. II, p. 93.

14. Drury, Clifford, op. cit., Vol III, p. 87.

15. DeVoto, Bernard, op. cit., p. 255.

16. Inman, Colonel Henry, p. 238.

17. Sage, Rufus, *Rocky Mountain Life*, p. 164.

18. Fremont, Brevet Capt. J. C., *The Exploring Expedition to the Rocky Mountains in the Year 1842*, pp. 50-57.

19. Ibid., p. 72.

20. Clyman, James, *Journal of a Mountain Man*, p. 195.

21. Field, Matthew, op. cit., p. 117.

22. Ibid., p. 117

23. Ibid., p. 176

24. Mokler, op. cit., p. 454.

25. Holmes, Kenneth L., *Covered Wagon Women*, Vol. III, p. 29.

26. Munkres, Robert, "Independence Rock and Devil's Gate," *Annals of Wyoming*, Vol. 40, p. 33.

27. Hastings, Lansford, *Emigrants' Guide to Oregon and California*, pp. 11-12.

28. Ellison, Robert S., "Independence Rock and the Oregon Trail," op. cit., p. 6.

29. Coutant, C. G., op. cit., p. 215.

30. Munkres, Robert, op. cit., p. 31.

31. Stewart, George, *The California Trail*, p. 59.

32. Jensen, Andrew, *Day by Day With the Utah Pioneers*, p. 78.

33. Personal correspondence with Lynn Morgan Sullivan, descendant.

34. Franklin, William Riley, "Journal of William Riley Franklin to California from Missouri in 1850," *Annals of Wyoming*, Vol. 46, #1, p. 60.

35. Ibid., p. 61.

36. Holmes, Kenneth L., op. cit., Vol. V, p. 231.

37. Watson, Jeanne, *To the Land of Gold and Wickedness*, pp. 175-176.

38. Potter, David, *Trail to California*, p. 117.

39. Holmes, Kenneth L., op. cit., Vol. III, p. 199.

40. Burton, Richard, *The City of the Saints*, p. 165.

41. Holmes, Kenneth L., op. cit., Vol. VII, p. 108.

42. Myres, Sandra L., *Ho For California!*, p. 69.

43. Holmes, Kenneth, op. cit., Vol. V, p. 276.

44. Fremont, Brevet Captain John C., op. cit.

45. Hill, John Birney, op. cit., p. 39.

46. Franklin, William Riley, op. cit., p. 60.

47. Wayman, Dr. John Hudson, *A Doctor on the California Trail: The Diary of*

John Hudson Wayman, 1852, p. 51.

48. McDermott, Jack, "Guinard's Bridge and Its Place in History."

    A version of the history of this bridge over the Sweetwater River can be found in the article, "Historic Document Tells Early Day Drama of the West," in *Annals of Wyoming*, Vol. 15, #3, July 1943. This document was related by Amanda Archambault, widow of Alfred Archambault, fifty years after the occurrence of the events. She maintains that Archambault built the bridge over the Sweetwater one mile east of Independence Rock. Archambault did have a trading post on the Sweetwater, but some sources believe it might have been at Devil's Gate. Historical research does not support the assertion that Archambault built the bridge. It was more likely Louis Guinard instead. Other details in the Archambault document seem confusing and possibly hard to believe, for instance statements that the Powder River was one mile from the Sweetwater trading post, that in the spring Archambault collected great sums in gold paid by emigrants using the bridge, or that the traders would give the little girl so many gold nuggets in her apron that the cloth would tear. The actual working of gold anywhere in the Sweetwater vicinity did not take place until a few years later. It is best to read this document with caution, for the recollection is made by an elderly woman fifty years after the events and perhaps made colorful to impress friends and family. Several of her assertions seem a distortion of fact.

    Ruth Beebe in her book *Reminiscing Along the Sweetwater*, p.18, says Archambault built the bridge, however she is basing her information on the above mentioned *Annals of Wyoming* article.

49. Coutant, C. G., op. cit., p. 365.

50. Wilkins, Edness Kimball, "Sweetwater Station," *Annals of Wyoming*, Vol. 43, p. 288.

51. Holmes, Kenneth L., op. cit., Vol. IV, pp. 246-247.

52. Jackson, William H., *Picture Maker of the West*, p. 89.

53. Mokler, A. J., op. cit., p. 458.

THE EMIGRANTS AT
DEVIL'S GATE

IF INDEPENDENCE ROCK was worthy of comment to many diarists, many more were similarly impressed with the sight of Devil's Gate. They had not seen anything like this before and it was therefore a place of remarkable wonder to them. Devil's Gate was the next notable landmark along the trail, about five miles west of Independence Rock. The trail skirted the actual cleft in the mountains, for the opening is narrow and the Sweetwater River rushes and tumbles over huge boulders. The trail went through a natural pass just south of Devil's Gate, known as Rattlesnake Pass.

One of the earliest descriptions of Devil's Gate was written by William Marshall Anderson on August 14, 1834:

> This evening we are again in sight of the sweetwater canyon
> . . . This small, peaceful, and now almost waterless stream,
> after running a long and noiseless course from West to East,
> turns a right angle to the north and rushes with its pigmy
> power, against an earthless, shrubless mountain of rock, two
> hundred feet in height, and by the aid of God, tears asunder
> the mighty opponent, and passes it on to its mother Platte.[1]

Father Pierre Jean DeSmet said this of Devil's Gate when he was there on July 6, 1841:

> Travelers have named this spot Devil's Gate. In my opinion
> they should have rather called it Heaven's Avenue, for if it

45

resembles hell on account of the frightful disorder which frowns around it, it is still a mere passage, and it should rather be compared to the way of heaven on account of the scene to which it leads . . . Above these moving and noisy scenes the eye discerns masses of shadow, here relieved by a glance of day, there deepening in their gloom by the foliage of a cedar or pine, till finally, as the sight travels through the long vista of lofty galleries, it is greeted by a distant perspective of such mild beauty, that a sentiment of placid happiness steals upon the mind.[2]

On August 2, 1842, John C. Fremont depicted it this way:

Five miles above Rock Independence we came to a place called the Devil's Gate, where the Sweet Water cuts through the point of a granite ridge. The length of the passage is about three hundred yards and the width thirty five yards. The walls of rock are vertical, and about four hundred feet in height; and the stream in the gate is almost entirely choked up by masses which have fallen from above. In the wall, on the right bank, is a dike of trap rock, cutting through a fine-grained gray granite.[3]

Just as there is an Indian legend about Independence Rock, so there is an Indian legend about the formation of Devil's Gate:

Long ago there lived an evil spirit in the form of a huge beast with large tusks that once ravaged the Sweetwater Valley. This beast caused great damage and struck terror in the hearts of the people. Through a prophet, the Great Spirit told the Indians to slay the beast. Although they had thought this an impossible task, they followed the Great Spirit's instructions. Using tricks, the Indians cornered the beast against a wall of rocky crags where there was no escape. Then from concealed locations, the Indians fired quiver after quiver of arrows into the animal. The maddened animal, in its agony, used its immense tusks to rip a huge gap in the mountains through which it escaped. The evil spirit disappeared forever and white man later called this place Devil's Gate.[4]

A more detailed version of this legend can be found in the diary of Matthew Field, who recorded it as related by a mixed-blood Indian to the Sir William Drummond Stewart party at the time of their 1843 visit to Devil's Gate.[5]

Field also wrote of an attempt by several men in his party to go through the canyon passage:

> July, 1843. Hell Gate. About 20 of us started to effect a passage through this gate, and 3 of us achieved our aim. Tilghman, Manary, & myself 500 yards through, 400 feet high perpendicular, 6 yards across water surface, and a deafening rush of water over sharp rocks. Met Storer, who had come in at the other end. Drank to each other across the foaming stream. Bathed and formed statues of our persons in a grotto which we called "The niche in the wall." Left our names here, inscribed on a buffalo's skull.[6]

Matthew Field was from New Orleans and at the time of this trip he was assistant editor of the *Picayune* newspaper. He also wrote feature articles for the paper. He was thirty years old, married, and did not feel he could afford the trip when first invited. When Sir William Drummund Stewart offered to pay his expenses, Field became a member of Sir William's last western trip. Since Field was writing articles for his newspaper, his diary contains numerous descriptive details. He also had a fine sense of humor and this is expressed in his diary entries. Field was making this trip for a second reason he kept to himself: he believed he had tuberculosis, and he hoped the journey would improve his health. In reality he had ulcers. This trip, supplied by Stewart with all manner of food delicacies and fine liquors, along with a diet of wild game, must not have aggravated this condition, for Field had few problems on the lengthy journey.[7]

Unlike Sir William's earlier excursions to the Rocky Mountains, this one was purely for fun and adventure. Sir William had been to the West in the 1830s with the fur traders, but this time he spared no luxury. In addition to all types of tinned meats, hams, preserved fruits, cheeses, and other specialties, Sir William even got a permit to transport liquor into the Rocky Mountains. Among the supplies were many kinds of fine alcoholic beverages.[8] This party had ample time for leisure and sport and spent long days visiting favorite places in the mountains. They felt no urgency to rush as the emigrants did. During the summer of 1843 they made two visits to both Independence Rock and Devil's Gate. On the second visit Matthew Field was less successful at getting through the canyon:

> Monday, August 28. Nooned at Hell Gate. After dinner attempted a passage of Hell Gate, on a bet with Dr. Tilghman, and after an hour's labor was compelled to return on account of the fright of my mule, but the old hunters who came in far enough to look on acknowledged the effort was a gallant one.[9]

John Banks, traveling in 1849 with the Buckeye Rovers, a party from Ohio, was another one of those very moved by Devil's Gate. The Rock must not have impressed him much, for all he wrote was, "We are encamped close to Independence Rock. I have been on it and drank water in a cleft."[10] However, he was more eloquent about the sight of Devil's Gate.

> June 29. Crossed the river without trouble. This day we found some of our cattle unable to travel. The mountains are rightly named; they are a mass of rocks. Occasionally in a chasm a cedar or pine finds soil enough to live. Philosophers say there is no such thing as innate beauty, preconceived ideas regulate all this. Be this as it may, who can gaze on the Sweetwater's passage through the mountains (called Devil's Gate) without feelings of the livest emotions? It is grand, it is sublime! Fifty feet of a chasm having perpendicular walls

Aerial view of Devil's Gate from the east side. Emigrants went through the pass in the extreme upper left of the photo. (Author's Photo)

Devil's Gate, looking east from west side. This sketch was done by Charles Pruess during Fremont's 1842 expedition. (Casper College Library, Special Collections)

three hundred feet high yawning over the gulf below. He must be brainless that can see this unmoved. Here memory will dwell.[11]

William Fowler Pritchard, going across to California in 1850, wrote a brief description of Independence Rock but went into some detail of their experience at Devil's Gate. On July 14 he wrote this after leaving Independence Rock:

> Five and a half miles brought us to the gap where the road passes through the mountain. About three quarters mile to the west there is a chasm or dalles in the mountain called the Devil's Gate. The Sweetwater breaks through this canyon which is from four hundred to five hundred feet high. On the south side the rocks project over the stream but on the north it slopes back a little. The whole mountain is a mass of

Devil's Gate today, view from the west side. (Author's Photo)

gray granite rock, destitute of vegetation save an occasional scrubby cedar or pine. From where the river enters to where it emerges through like a torrent, dashing among the huge walls of rock which have fallen from above and they are worn quite smooth. Three of us went through the canyon. By stripping ourselves and crossing the torrent from rock to rock we managed to get through. I never beheld such a grand, terrific, and terrible sight in my life. Although the day was very warm, in the canyon it was quite cold and [it] had a splendid echo. . . . We found gooseberries in Devil's Gate.[12]

John Birney Hill wrote in 1850:

Five and a half miles farther up Sweetwater you come to Devil's Gate, which is a channel cut through a ridge of rock, about one hundred feet wide, and four hundred feet high, and the walls are so nearly straight up and down that they hang over a little. This ridge of rock was lifted up by volcanic force, and left a fissure in the rock, or else the river cut a channel in the rock while it was soft. I was not there when this gate was made or I could tell you more about it. I do not believe that the devil had anything to do with this natural water gate, and why it was named after him I do not know, for there is nothing that looks bad or evil about it.[13]

The high plains are notorious for sudden violent storms and these were a particular hardship to the emigrants caught out in the open country. In 1852 Francis Sawyer was traveling with her husband, going to California. She wrote of a violent storm that struck while they were at Devil's Gate:

> June 22—We forded Sweetwater river this morning, and passed near the Devil's Gate. This is a pass where the river has washed a channel through the mountains. While we were nooning to-day there came up the hardest hail storm that it had ever been my lot to witness. The stones came down thick and fast, and they were as large as walnuts—none smaller than bullets. The wind blew so hard and furiously that all the animals within our hearing stampeded. All hands had a hard time getting them together again. Some escaped entirely, but we had the good fortune to recover all of ours. Some of our men got bruised heads and hands by the heavy hailstones striking them. I was badly frightened and thought the wind would surely blow us away.[14]

Several diaries of the 1850s report the number of emigrant inscriptions found in the Devil's Gate area. Helen Carpenter wrote in 1857:

> Our nooning place was near Independence Rock which is situated on the left bank of the Sweetwater. This is quite a noted place. The rock is granite and is 300 yards long and from 75 to 100 feet high and in shape an irregular oval. It has a very weather beaten appearance with small water washed furrows.

Saw several names high up on the sides and placed mine there writing it with tar. Five miles from here came to the Devil's Gate. This is a narrow gap or fissure, only a few feet wide from top to bottom of a high hill, through it runs the Sweetwater. Running parallel with this is a narrow valley shut in by high rocks upon which are many names of travelers.

Later in this entry she remarks that the trading post at Devil's Gate was "fixed up the best of any seen yet."[15]

A few inscriptions can still be found among the rocks on both sides of the road through the emigrant pass at Devil's Gate. The grave of emigrant Martin Fulkerson is also located in this pass. The details surrounding Fulkerson's death and burial are given on the marker erected by the Wyoming chapter of the Oregon-California Trails Association. More inscriptions can be found inside Devil's Gate itself and a few tar names are still readable in protected overhangs in the canyon. One can climb among the boulders, reach the highest point above the canyon, and find that others left their marks there. There is no trail and the climb is rough, but once on the highest edge one feels the power of this historic canyon and can almost hear sounds of long-ago wagon travel. Looking down into the depths to glimpse the river or gazing out over the broad sweep of the Sweetwater Valley, with Split Rock in the distance, one sees the scenery that greeted Indians, mountain men, and westward travelers alike.

In the words of John Banks of 1849, "Here memory will dwell."

NOTES ON CHAPTER TWO

1. Anderson, William Marshall, *Narratives of a Ride to the Rocky Mountains in 1834*, op. cit., p. 183.

2. Mokler, A. J., "Devil's Gate, A Prominent Wyoming Landmark," *Wyoming Pioneer*, July–August, 1941, p. 171.

3. Fremont, Brevet Capt. J. C., *The Exploring Expedition to the Rocky Mountains in the Year 1842*, op. cit., p. 56.

4. *Wyoming: A Guide to Historic Sites*, p. 167.

5. Field, Matthew, *Prairie and Mountain Sketches*, op. cit., pp.112-124.

6. Field, Matthew, op. cit., pp. 117-118.

7. Porter, Mae Reed, *Scotsman in Buckskin*, pp. 213-214.

8. Ibid., p. 220.

9. Field, Matthew, op. cit., p. 174.

10. Scamehorn, Howard L., *The Buckeye Rovers in the Gold Rush*, pp. 27-28.

11. Ibid., p. 28.

12. Pritchard, William Fowler, Journal of William Fowler Pritchard, Indiana to California 1850, p. 28.

13. Hill, John Birney, *Gold: A Story of the Plains in 1850*, op. cit., pp. 37-38.

14. Holmes, Kenneth, *Covered Wagon Women*, Vol. IV, pp. 98-99.

15. Myres, Sandra L., *Ho for California!*, op. cit., p. 131.

THE MILITARY ON THE
SWEETWATER

A NUMBER OF SOLDIERS stationed near the area in the mid-1860s left their inscriptions on Independence Rock. The military presence near the trail continued for some years.

Not only was there still emigrant traffic through the area in the 1860s, there was also military travel between Fort Laramie and South Pass. This was necessary because of the Pacific Telegraph lines running along the route of the emigrant trails. The stage lines and later the telegraph lines required closely spaced stations for their operations. Many of the abandoned stage stations became the sites of small military posts. The Sweetwater Bridge Station, also called Sweetwater Station, stood just one mile east of Independence Rock. It is natural that some of the men stationed at this post would follow the example of hundreds before them and leave their inscriptions on the Rock. These men had ample time to inscribe their names. They lived under trying conditions and in many ways suffered some of the same hardships and privations as the emigrants trying to make their way to Oregon and California. Instead of just passing through this remote area, though, these men had to endure tedious months of heat and cold. Oftentimes there were long stretches of time with just the barest necessities to make life tolerable.

Tension between the United States government and Indian tribes had escalated throughout the 1850s. Confrontations became more frequent as increasing numbers of white settlers came through the tribal lands. Because of threats of trouble along the long-used road to Oregon, California, and Utah, stagecoach travel and much of the emigrant travel was diverted south. The newer Overland Trail route in southern Wyoming posed less threat to the travelers. However, since the telegraph lines still followed the old route, the government sent troops to protect these lines from destruction by the Indians. The Indians were known to cut down the telegraph poles or the miles of wire along the lines. The troops also provided some measure of protection for those emigrants still using the old route west.

In the 1860s, most of the regular army units were withdrawn from the West because of the Civil War. Replacing them were volunteer units recruited by the states and territories. The Second Battalion, Sixth Ohio Volunteer Cavalry, organized in 1862, had as its commander Lieutenant Colonel William O. Collins of Hillsboro, Ohio. Collins was fifty-two years old and had no prior military experience, but he was a tough and practical manager with a background in law and politics.[1] During the fall of 1861, Collins had recruited close to four hundred men and organized them into the Seventh Ohio Volunteer Cavalry. That winter the War Department temporarily suspended the recruitment of these new regiments and ordered them reorganized. The newly designated battalion became the Sixth Ohio Volunteer Cavalry and in early February they were sent first to Saint Louis, then to Fort Leavenworth, and then overland to Fort Laramie, where they arrived on May 30, 1862.[2]

After a brief stay at Fort Laramie, Colonel Collins left the fort on June 4 and headed west with a large detachment of the Ohio cavalry, following the emigrant trail road towards South Pass. Jim Bridger acted as guide for the troops. Unacquainted with the country, the military relied heavily on mountain men for information and guidance. The column reached South Pass on June 29. Accompanying Colonel Collins on this trip west was his seventeen-year-old son Caspar. Besides sending his

Casper Collins sketch of Sweetwater Station. Independence Rock in right background. (Denver Public Museum.)

family letters regularly, Caspar Collins also sent home a number of sketches depicting the surrounding countryside. He also made precise sketches of the military posts that he visited along the telegraph line. Still of historic value today, the original sketches are housed in the Colorado State University Library Archives in Fort Collins, Colorado. Letters from both father and son giving particulars of the trip west from Saint Louis, and the later campaign west from Fort Laramie to South Pass, can be found in Agnes Wright Spring's book, *Caspar Collins.*

The area that is now central Wyoming was a totally new experience for the Ohio troops. In just a few short months they had traveled from the wooded, verdant Midwest to the unexplored wilderness of the high, arid plains. The average elevation is five thousand feet and it is a region of blistering short summers and long, bitter cold, snowy winters. They traveled through sandy valleys covered in sagebrush and rolling country flanked by towering mountains.[3] For these young men fresh from the farms of Ohio, this unfriendly-looking country was to be their home for the next three years. The strangeness of the countryside coupled with the ever-present threat of attack by Indians must have given many of these men reason to question why they had volunteered.

After this preliminary scouting trip, Lieutenant Colonel Collins deployed his men at different stations along the 140-mile stage route between Platte Bridge (now the city of Casper) and South Pass. These home stations, established in what remained of the stagecoach and pony express stations, were based at forty-mile intervals and known as the Upper Posts.[4] Sweetwater Station, one mile east of Independence Rock, was one of these, serving as the command post for the other minor installations above Platte Bridge Station. These posts were isolated and manned by few men. Whereas the other posts of Upper Crossings (South Pass), Saint Mary's (Rocky Ridge), and Three Crossings might be manned by fewer than ten men, Sweetwater Station's company usually numbered about two

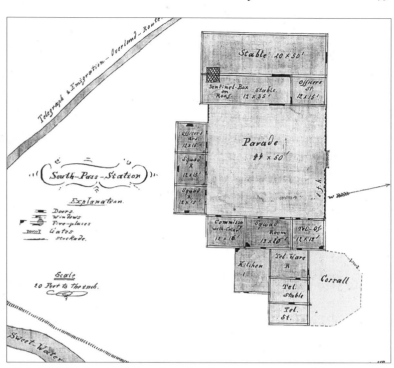

This sketch by Caspar Collins shows South Pass Station, one of the upper posts. These scale drawings of the posts were done on linen in ink and watercolor. (Morgan Library, Colorado State University)

dozen men. It was fortunate in that its location on the Sweetwater River guaranteed an ample supply of water; it was also closest to the Platte Bridge Station so there was frequent travel of soldiers between these two posts. This alleviated some of the tedium of the long winter months. The Ohio men, used to the comforts of home, led lives of long and dangerous isolation at these remote posts, punctuated by numerous confrontations with the Indians.

The first winter for the Ohio Volunteers was a severe one. They were unacquainted with the chilling winds, the excessively bitter cold, and the deep snows of the high plains. Colonel Collins and part of his detachment spent the winter at Fort Laramie. For several nights the thermometer froze. Even a cup of whiskey, which the incredulous Ohioans had left outside, froze. Yet despite the bitter weather, the troops engaged in several skirmishes that winter. In late February a severe blizzard struck a detachment caught in the open. This blizzard left two men dead from exposure, and all the others suffered frostbite before a relief party reached them.[5] For details on this particular engagement refer to the letters in Spring's book on Caspar Collins.

As warmer weather approached, Indian war parties struck sites along the Oregon Trail. On April 3, 1863, twenty-six men at Sweetwater Station drove off an attack; one soldier was badly wounded and died three days later.[6] This man was Private Ira Grossman, who had enlisted at Winchester, Ohio, on November 20, 1861. At the time of his enlistment he was twenty-one years of age; like most of the Ohio recruits, he was a farmer. Private Grossman accompanied the Sixth Cavalry west and then served as nurse at the Sweetwater Station hospital starting on June 5, 1862. He had not even been in the West a year when he died. Private Grossman's service record is shown on the accompanying copy of the Company Muster Rolls.

In the late spring of 1863 Colonel Collins returned to Ohio with a delegation of soldiers to recruit more troops, bringing his son with him. By July 31, four new companies had mustered in. The War Department recognized the continuing need for Collins' unit in the West, and it was at this time that the Sixth Ohio Volunteer Cavalry reorganized into the Eleventh Ohio Volunteer Cavalry.[7] The recruiting flyer printed by the government painted a rosy, adventurous time for the prospective recruits and encouraged "live" young men to apply. Recruits had no hint as to the severe weather conditions, the isolation of the posts, and the threat of Indian attack. Even so, the West might have seemed more appealing to recruits than serving in the Union Army. In March of 1863 the government passed a federal conscription law, so the men who had not already enlisted knew they had no choice. Several young men of the Quaker religion, facing military duty of some kind,

According to Ira Grossman's Company Muster Rolls, he died of a gunshot wound incurred at Sweetwater Bridge. (Edness K. Wilkins State Park, Casper)

joined the western volunteer units, preferring them to the regular battle units.[8] One of these was Hervey Johnson, a twenty-four-year-old farmer. Born in Leesburgh, Ohio, Johnson left a legacy of very informative letters written from the various posts where he was stationed.

Caspar Collins was now eighteen, and on June 30, 1863, he too enlisted in the Eleventh Ohio Volunteer Cavalry. He was commissioned as Second Lieutenant, a member of Company G. He returned to the West, and in 1864, at age nineteen, assumed command of the four upper posts on the Pacific Telegraph line: Sweetwater Bridge Station, Three Crossings, Saint Mary's (Rocky Ridge), and Upper Crossings.[9] Private Hervey Johnson marched to the West with the newly formed Eleventh Ohio Volunteer Cavalry and for a while was posted at Deer Creek Station, at present-day Glenrock, Wyoming. Then

FRONTIER CAVALRY SERVICE!

LIEUT. COL. WM. O. COLLINS is authorized by the War Department to recruit an additional Battalion of Cavalry to add to his present command now in the Rocky Mountain Indian Service, Head-Quarters at Ft. Laramie, in the newly-formed Territory of Idahoe. This service is full of novelty and adventure, and offers a rare chance to *live* young men who would like to see the center of the Rocky Mountain country, which is now assuming great importance, from the discovery of new gold mines, the expected commencement of the Pacific Railroad, etc., etc.

The First Independent Battalion Ohio Volunteer Cavalry (formerly the First Battalion Sixth Ohio Cavalry), with which the new battalion will be connected, has been more than a year in the Mountains, and the constant health of the men, as well as the testimony of all who know the country, shows it to be the most healthy portion of North America. The remarkable purity of the atmosphere renders it especially beneficial to those having a tendency to pulmonary complaints, and the effect upon all, is to invigorate the constitution and prolong life.

The best of arms and equipments are promised, and will be ready when needed.

The subscriber has been authorized to raise a Company for this Battalion, in the Counties of

though recruits offering themselves from any part of the country will be received.

His recruiting Head-Quarters will be at

and he invites active and enterprising young men, who prefer choosing their own service to being drafted, to enlist with him. Recruits will be entitled to the usual bounty of $100, and one month's pay in advance.

As this is the most pleasant season for crossing the Plains, it is desirable to fill the Company at once and be ready to move. Any full Company can start immediately, without waiting for the completion of the Battalion.

MAY 30, 1863.

Recruitment placard used in Ohio by Lieutenant Colonel William O. Collins in 1863. (Wyoming State Archives)

in November of 1864 he was sent to Sweetwater Station where he served under Lieutenant Caspar Collins.[10]

Neither of these men left a lasting inscription on Independence Rock—though several men stationed there at the same time did so—but both sent descriptive letters home of life at this frontier post. Coming from somewhat different backgrounds, they related varying perspectives at times. Together they offer a detailed portrait of military life at Sweetwater Station.

LIFE AT SWEETWATER STATION

Sweetwater Station was similar to the other smaller stations along the Pacific Telegraph Line, with twenty to twenty-six men stationed there at a time. The officers had horses, but many of the men had none. The isolation, combined with the day-to-day boredom, took its toll on the men, who were responsible for repairing the old buildings, building new additions, and fortifying the post. To obtain wood, they had to travel several miles to the mountains, then hike up and drag the wood down over rough mountain country to the waiting wagon. This was especially hard in winter. With very limited food rations, they went months without fresh meat, but in the summer months the soldiers had plenty of wild game to supplement their government supply of food. Caspar Collins enjoyed hunting, and several of his letters tell about the abundance of the wild game.

When Lieutenant Collins first assumed command of the post at Sweetwater Station he wrote the following in a letter to his uncle, dated December 13, 1864. This letter was written from Fort Laramie:

> I am now stationed on Sweetwater River, a tributary of the Platte. I have four block stations under my charge. The first is Sweetwater Bridge, the bridge by which the emigrants cross the river on their way to California and Oregon; the second is Three Crossings of the Sweetwater; the third, Rocky Ridge; and the fourth is South Pass. I make my headquarters at the first. I was summoned down here on a court-martial and came down in five days, two hundred and twenty miles, by myself most of the way, but I had places to sleep at night.
>
> The weather was awful, but I was well protected and had a horse that would travel eight miles an hour for twelve hours,

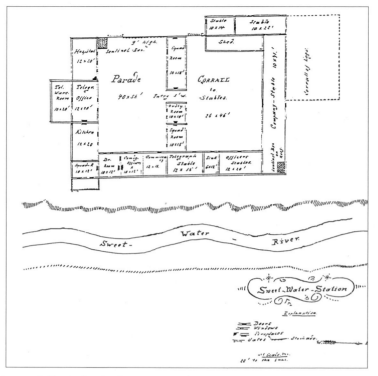

Caspar Collins's sketch of Sweetwater Station. These original sketches, done on linen in ink and watercolor, showed everything to scale. (Morgan Library, Colorado State University)

and I came right through. I rode from Le Bontes Creek to Horse Shoe Station, twenty-five miles in two hours and ten minutes, the thermometer 10 degrees below zero all the time. You bet I hurried.[11]

In this same letter Collins describes Sweetwater Station in more detail:

From my station to the upper one it is one hundred and four miles, and I have to ride it and back about every two weeks, so it keeps me pretty busy. We have plenty of game up there by riding about 20 or 25 miles for it. There are buffalo, elk, mountain sheep, black-tailed deer and antelope.

There is plenty of antelope close by the station, (Sweetwater Bridge) but they have lived so much on sage brush that they taste of it.

This is the form of my headquarters station—Sweetwater Bridge:

1. Block House, 2. Hospital, 3. Telegraph office, 4. Men's cook and dining room, 5. Mine and the doctor's and telegraph operator's mess room, 6. Surgeon's quarters, 7. My own, 8. Commissary and store room with cellar and ice house beneath, 9. Parade ground, 10. Gateway for teams and horses, 11. Small gateway in large gate, for foot passengers, 12. Men's quarters, 13. Passageway, covered, 14. Se'g't's room, 15. Laundry quarters, 16. Telegraph, stable and warehouse, 17. Granary, 18. Gateway to corral, 19. Mule stables, 20. Company stables, 21. Block house, 22. Mine and the Doctor's stable, 23. Corral or stable yard. It is surrounded by a palisade 15 feet high.

The post was built by Co. D and intended as quarters for forty men. But I have only twenty there now. It is situated on a hill about 50 yards from the Sweetwater River and overlooking the bridge.[12]

In winter the food available was of limited amount and had little variety. Hervey Johnson had this to say about the food in a letter dated February 1, 1865:

The boys have been at work the last week getting wood from the mountains. I was out only one day, it is awful work, the snow is three feet deep out there, and the timber all being down is sometimes hard to find . . . Sam Engle is in the cookhouse grinding coffee. I don't know what he is getting for breakfast. We had bread and coffee and pickles for supper last night, night before last we had coffee and "kraut" a dutch mess. Sometimes we have molasses with our bread and coffee, bacon or "sowbelly" as the boys call it is getting scarce here. We have had no beef from the Quartermaster

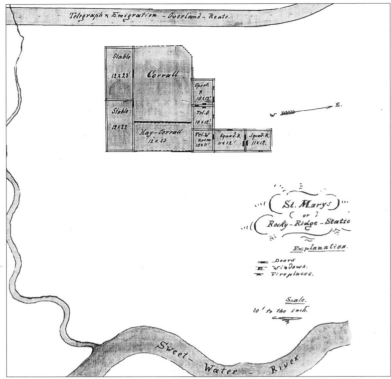

Caspar Collins sketched this scale drawing of Saint Mary's Station, one of the upper posts under his command. (Morgan Library, Colorado State University)

for three months, we have been trying for several weeks to get some here but have failed everytime.[13]

In a letter dated February 19, 1865, Hervey Johnson had more to write about the food:

It is getting on towards dinner time now, I wish I could be at home a few days to get some pie, or sweet potatoes, or apples. We occasionally have dried fruit out here and sometimes pie. We have an article called "dessicated potatoes," it looks like corn meal, we mix it up with water and make little cakes and fry them. They taste like irish potatoes mashed up and fried. Another article of food we have is "mixed vegetables", this is a conglomerated mass of every thing. It looks before cooked like a huge plug of tobacco. There is corn, beans, cabbage, carrots, beets, turneps, "punkins", onions, beet tops, grass & etc found in it. These articles are all chopped fine and mixed together and pressed into cakes. I dont wish you could be here and eat some of it, some of the boys like it, but I dont "go much" on it.[14]

In the same letter he described some of their work:

We have been engaged this past week in building and repairing. We commenced a week ago to day, and have put up a stable for twenty horses with stalls and mangers, we had no framing tools, so we had to dig and set in posts, the ground was almost as solid as a rock so we had to hew out the holes with an old ax. Our only tools were two old axes, two good axes, two dull hatchets, two hand saws, one gravel pick, and an old chisel. No augers about it. With these we put up our stable in about four days, besides the stable we have put up defences at different places on top of the buildings.[15]

In April of 1865 the letters give a glimpse of the long winter's effects on the men, who had lived not only with tedium and isolation, but also with the threat of Indian troubles. Confrontations with the Indians started as early as February in 1865. New military forces were being sent out because of the increased activity along both the telegraph lines and the stage lines now running along the Overland Trail. Corporal Hervey Johnson wrote:

One company of the 11th Kansas left Platte Bridge this morning for this place, another co. of the same reg't. will start up in a few days. There is about twelve hundred men now between here and Fort Laramie at different posts along the road. I do hope we will be ordered to the Fort or be remounted before long, this thing of belonging to the cavalry and having no horses is getting old with me. I am getting tired of it, if there is any scouting to do I want to have a horse and go.[16]

At about the same time, Caspar Collins wrote this letter to his aunt dated April 18, 1865. He had spent three winters in the West when he wrote this:

> I have been shut up this winter in one of the most desolate regions on the American continent. It think this is the natural penitentiary of the United States. I have four posts under my jurisdiction, about forty miles apart, on an average. The only way I had of hearing from abroad was the telegraph, and the news on it, owing to detentions and press of business, have been very slim. . . .
>
> I can not think of anything interesting in the midst of this desert. That is one reason I have been so remiss in writing. Besides, the mail has been very irregular owing to the Indian hostilities. I think, however, that will be over with owing to the large number of troops on the way out. My main employments at present are sleeping, eating, and hunting geese, ducks, and snipe. . . . The Sweetwater River can't boast of any fish but suckers of the boniest description, which the boys sometimes catch and try to eat and are coughing the bones out of their throats the week following.[17]

The detachments of the Eleventh Ohio Volunteer Cavalry stationed in the West since 1862 were now sent back East in 1865 to be mustered out. This left the scattered posts shorthanded. Since the Civil War was coming to a close, some of the men who had seen fighting were now sent to the West. One of the units sent out to help with the increased Indian activity was the Eleventh Kansas Volunteer Cavalry. In early February of 1865 several companies of the Eleventh Kansas stationed at Fort Riley received orders to report to Fort Kearny, Nebraska. These men were not fresh recruits, having just recently seen battle duty. They had had less than a thirty-day furlough before they received their new orders. The distance from Fort Riley to Fort

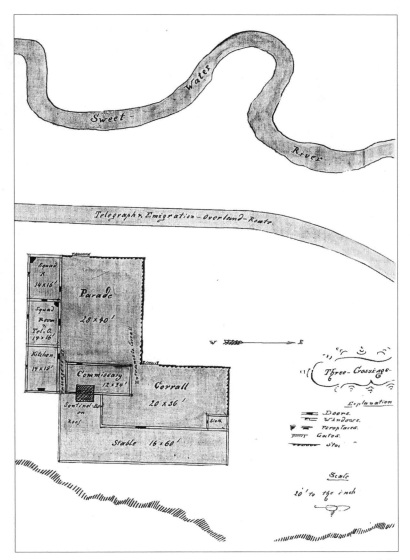

Caspar Collins drew to scale this sketch of Three Crossings Station, one of the Upper Posts. Drawing done on linen in ink and watercolor. (Morgan Library, Colorado State University.)

Kearny was two hundred miles, and the soldiers marched it in twelve days under horrendous conditions. "Heavy storms of snow and sleet rendered the roads hardly discernible; the bitter cold March winds, sweeping over the prairie, penetrated to the very marrow of the shivering poorly clad soldiers, many of whom were on foot and unable to keep up with the command, in the face of the driving storms; the bridges over the swollen streams were swept away, but the order was to report at Fort Kearney, and in obedience thereto, the regiment reported at that post on the fourth of March, and passed inspection the following day."[18] On March 7 the men were ordered to report to Fort Laramie. This march, aggravated by the scarcity of fuel, was a repeat of the terrible march across Kansas and eastern Nebraska. Many of these men were then posted at the various stations along the communication lines.

When the Kansas troops arrived at Platte Bridge Station after their march from Fort Laramie, their situation looked bleak. "But twenty days ration of corn could be drawn at Laramie, and this, we soon found was to be the total supply for the summer. The grass had not yet started, even that of the previous year's growth, scant and also dried and almost worthless was often covered with snow. The horses soon became weak and unserviceable and many of them died. There was shameful lack in every department, not only for the necessities of a campaign, but for troops in camp or garrison. Neither quartermaster, commissary, or Ordnance supplies could be had in anything like needed quantities for even a single regiment and of ammunition suitable for the carbine carried by the 11th, not a cartridge was to be had short of Fort Leavenworth, one thousand miles distant."[19]

Private John H. Crumb, whose inscription is still visible on Independence Rock, was one of these Kansas men. Private Crumb saw service both at Platte Bridge Station and at Sweetwater Station in the spring and summer of 1865. He was born May 14, 1844, in New York, and moved with his family to

Kansas in 1857. When the Civil War broke out, he enlisted in Company I, Eleventh Kansas Cavalry, and saw action in numerous battles before the Eleventh Kansas marched to the western territory. Posted to duty at Platte Bridge Station by late May of 1865, Crumb witnessed the July 26 fight with the Sioux north of the station where Lieutenant Caspar Collins lost his life. He was also one of the first at the scene after the burial of the men killed in the attack on the Sergeant Amos Custard supply train,[20] which occurred at the same time as the Sioux attack near Platte Bridge Station. Traveling from Sweetwater Station, the supply train was west of Platte Bridge Station at the time of the attack. In 1865, supplies were short and garrisons were under threat of attack at any time with very few arms at their disposal. Platte Bridge Station's 110 men at the time included both noncommissioned staff and the band of the Eleventh Kansas. Only eighty of these men had carbines for arms, with but twenty rounds of cartridges per man. Of the remaining thirty men, about half had revolvers and the others had no arms.[21] After the battle which resulted in the death of young Lieutenant Collins, Platte Bridge Station was renamed Fort Caspar in his honor. Fort Collins, in Colorado, had already been named after his father.

Corporal Hervey Johnson was still at Sweetwater Station when the battle occurred. In September of 1865 he transferred to Fort Laramie, where he remained until he mustered out in the summer of 1866. Private John Crumb mustered out in 1865. He came back to the area in 1927 and, accompanied by Robert S. Ellison, revisited the sites of the two battles. He then left a manuscript with Mr. Ellison which described the fights of July 26 and 27 from his viewpoint as both participant and witness.[22] This manuscript is in the Ellison files in the Historical Archives in Cheyenne, Wyoming.

The need for scattered posts along the old route to Oregon waned as new telegraph lines were installed across the southern part of the territory. In September of 1867, the army abandoned

Some remaining foundation stones and rust debris from Sweetwater Station.
(Author's Photo)

all posts west of Fort Fetterman, including Sweetwater Station.[23]
Many men at these far-flung posts then transferred to other forts
along the southern trail. One veteran of the Eleventh Kansas
Volunteer Cavalry said in retrospect: "No history will record the
heroic struggles of the men at the recruiting stations on the
prairies when they resolved to leave their ill-provided families for
the hazards of three years of distant service. No exposure on
picket, no toil on march, no danger in battle ever tried their
manhood like the first struggle of enlistment." It is said these
were not the men to murmur or rebel, even at the extreme hardships of a soldier's life; but, as they thoughtfully and intelligently
offered their services at first, so they intelligently, quietly, and
soberly continued them, even to the end.[24]

Some traces of Sweetwater Station still remain. Remnants
of some foundation stones along with occasional station debris
are still visible. A few of the foundation stones of the emigrant
bridge over the Sweetwater River can be found during low
water. The State of Wyoming conducted an archeological survey at this site in 1986. This parcel of land is now owned by
the Church of Jesus Christ of Latter-Day Saints.

SOLDIERS' INSCRIPTIONS

The list of soldiers who left inscriptions during the 1860s on Independence Rock is given below. Some of these names are of soldiers we know were stationed here (these are marked †). Those names without a mark may or may not have an inscription on the Rock. The actual inscription does not give us enough information to know if it belongs to a soldier or to an emigrant. Refer to the alphabetical list of inscriptions in Part Two for more information on each name.

Private Christopher Adams, Company G, Eleventh Kansas Volunteer Cavalry

Private George Baker, Company C, Eleventh Kansas Volunteer Cavalry

J. Bower, Troy Ohio

Lieutenant James Brown, Company G, Eleventh Ohio Volunteer Cavalry †

Private William Brown, Company H, Eleventh Kansas Volunteer Cavalry

Private John H. Crumb, Company I, Eleventh Kansas Volunteer Cavalry †

P. Cudihy, Company F, Fourth USA Cavalry †

J. J. D., Company H. †

Private Daniel Dodge, Company H, Eleventh Kansas Volunteer Cavalry

Lieutenant William Y. Drew, Eleventh Kansas Volunteer Cavalry

Sergeant Jonathan D. Edge, Company A, Eleventh Ohio Volunteer Cavalry †

Private Jacob Evans, Company H, Eleventh Kansas Volunteer Cavalry

Private John B. French, Company D, Eleventh Kansas Volunteer Cavalry

Private H. S. Hart, Company B, Eleventh Kansas Volunteer Cavalry †

Sergeant Jack J. Hollingsworth, Company A, Eleventh Ohio Volunteer Cavalry †

Sergeant G. W. Hoover, Company A, Eleventh Ohio Volunteer Cavalry †

Captain Henry L. Koehne, Eleventh Ohio Volunteer Cavalry (name inscribed twice) †

Private Benjamin F. Lloyd, Company A, Eleventh Ohio Volunteer Cavalry †

Private James Mason, Company F, Eleventh Kansas Volunteer Cavalry

D. P. (or F.) McFall, Eleventh Ohio Volunteer Cavalry

Daniel P. McLain, Company A, Sixth Ohio Volunteer Cavalry (name inscribed twice) †

Private Hiram Miller, Company A, Eleventh Kansas Volunteer Cavalry

Private John H. Mills, Company E, Eleventh Kansas Volunteer Cavalry

Private William Nelson, Company D, Eleventh Kansas Volunteer Cavalry

John T. Nigh, Company A, Eleventh Ohio Volunteer Cavalry †

Private Charles A. Paine, Company A, Eleventh Ohio Volunteer Cavalry †

C. A. Pom

Private John Porter, Company I, Eleventh Kansas Volunteer Cavalry †

(Private?) William Power, Eleventh Ohio Volunteer Cavalry †

Ed Rugger, telegraph operator †

Captain Francis Shipley, Sixth Ohio Volunteer Cavalry (name twice?) †

Private Fletcher Smith, Company A, Eleventh Ohio Volunteer Cavalry †

Private Henry Smith, Company A, Eleventh Kansas Volunteer Cavalry

Private John Stierle, Company A, Eleventh Kansas Volunteer Cavalry †

Private John B. Taylor, Company B, Eleventh Kansas Volunteer Cavalry

William Thatcher, Company F, Fourth Cavalry, USA †

Private Andrew C. Todd, Company I, Eleventh Kansas Volunteer Cavalry

Niceis Tormey, Company F, Fourth Cavalry, USA †

Sergeant William A. Yager, Company A, Sixth Ohio Volunteer Cavalry (name on Rock three times) †

_____

Notes on Chapter Three

1. Murray, Robert, *Military Posts of Wyoming*, p. 16.

2. Robrock, David P., *The Eleventh Ohio Volunteer Cavalry*, p. 25.

3. Ibid., p. 25.

4. Ibid., p. 26.

5. Ibid., p. 28.

6. Ibid., p. 28.

7. Murray, Robert, op. cit., p. 18.

8. Unrau, William, editor, *Tending the Talking Wire*, p. 9.

9. Spring, Agnes Wright, *Caspar Collins*, p. 50.

10. Unrau, William, op. cit., p. 212.

11. Spring, Agnes Wright, op. cit., p. 158.

12. Ibid., pp. 158-159.

13. Unrau, William, op. cit., p. 212.

14. Ibid., p. 219.

15. Ibid., p. 21.

16. Ibid., p. 239.

17. Spring, Agnes Wright, op. cit., pp. 171-172.

18. Cutler, William C., *History of the State of Kansas*, p. 75

19. "Regimental History of the 11th Kansas Volunteer Cavalry," Kansas State Historical Society Web site.

20. Cutler, William C., op. cit.

21. Ibid.

22. Crumb, John H., typewritten manuscript.

23. Murray, Robert, op. cit., p. 45.

24. Cutler, William C., op. cit.

S ALERATUS,
EMIGRANTS' BAKING POWDER

WHEN APPROACHING Independence Rock from the east, emigrants passed through an area of surprising interest to them. Invariably diarists made some comment about the "saleratus beds" or lakes. On June 7, 1834, William Marshall Anderson wrote:

> I saw today, the earth covered for a half mile, with a white robe, resembling at a distance lime, when closely viewed, is very similar to burnt alumn. This is on an average, three inches in depth. Its taste to me is a compound of salt, some kind of alkali and salt petre, of which last it seems to be to be principally composed. It is call[ed] by the mountaineers glober salts. It has a purgative effect of great suddenness.[1]

Jesse Quinn Thornton, crossing the plains to Oregon in 1846, wrote:

> We saw a large pond of water, so strongly impregnated with the carbonate or bi-carbonate of potash, that the water would no longer hold it in solution. . . Along the edges of the pond it was found in broad and perfectly white sheets, from one to two inches thick . . . That which was taken up from the bottom of the pond looked precisely like fine salt, taken from a bucket of water into which so much has been thrown that it would hold no more in solution. These ponds were numerous in the subsequent portions of our journey.

> The emigrants collected this salt, and used it, under the name of saleratus for the purpose of making bread light and spongy. Most persons liked the bread so made. I did not. . .[2]

In the 1800s baking soda was known by the name "saleratus." The word is derived from the Latin *salaeratus* meaning aerated salt. Made up of potassium or sodium bicarbonate, it resembles a chalklike substance. Saleratus became available commercially in 1840 and was sold in paper envelopes. This was a boon to cooks, for it allowed them to bake without yeast. In order to make their cakes and breads rise, the emigrants carefully packed saleratus among their supplies. This leavening worked best in dough that could be cooked quickly over a high heat, which made it ideal for campfire cooking. If the supply of saleratus became depleted on their journey, the emigrants looked forward to obtaining it from the natural soda deposits found near the Sweetwater River. In 1845 Joel Palmer wrote that "the water, in many of these springs, is sufficiently strong, to raise bread, equally as well as saleratus or yeast."[3]

Henry Page, crossing to California in 1849, wrote the following description of traveling across the barren country after leaving the North Platte. Page sent frequent letters home to his wife in Illinois:

> We had poor quarters at night for our slves & cattle & early next morning started over another long stretch of 18 miles for the Sweetwater River—which we reached safely—Three or four of the oxen, which were drove loose, on those days, have since died—None of the other cattle were affected with the water—Through this place, above mentioned, is for fifty or sixty miles up the Sweetwater the only water that was good was the River water—The cattle were strictly guarded & watered only in the River—The water is saturated with Alkali, and in these Alkali lakes, now partially dry, we could & did pick up Salaeratus, which covered the bottom of the lakes for 3/4 or one inch—All the standing water & many

Note the trail swales through the center and foreground of this aerial view of one of the saleratus lakes, taken at a wet time of year. (Author's Photo)

of the springs were thus effected—These lakes look like a bed of silver, and with a strong alkali stench arising therefrom, made all that barren region appear desolate.[4]

Depending on the time of year and the amount of rainfall during a season, the emigrants found the saleratus in varying depths. Some wrote of scooping it up by the bucketful, while other years it was found in thin layers less than an inch deep. In 1850 Lucena Parsons wrote:

August 23. Started early & are near to the Saleratus ponds. The ground is covered with a thin coat like frost for miles around on both sides of the river. We went to several ponds & found the late rains had injured the saleratus, having covered it with water. The men had to go in & cut it up with spades in some of the ponds. These lumps look like ice & when it is dry on the banks it looks like snow banks. In a dry time it can be obtained very easy & very nice it is, one half the strength of common saleratus.[5]

The same differences are found today in the amount and depth of saleratus that shows on the banks of these ponds. Today people refer to this substance as alkali, and it is a common sight in many areas of the West. In dry years, or after a dry summer, it covers acres of land. The edges around the saleratus ponds are very white, and the substance can be scooped up quite easily. During wet years the alkali shows but little, even in late August. Many diarists wrote of scooping up the saleratus to use in their cooking, yet while traveling through this area, after leaving the Platte River, they warned of the dangers of letting the cattle drink the alkali water. Lucia Loraine Williams wrote in 1851:

> Gathered several pounds of Salerates, very nice, from a lake that dried up. We have to take particular care that our cattle do not drink at any of the alkali springs and lakes. Carcasses of cattle are plenty along here.[6]

Some parties did write of members getting sick a few days after baking with the saleratus. In 1849 Betsy Bailey made this journal entry, "The valleys were all covered with a white crust and looked like salaratus. Some of the company used it to raise their bread. After we got in the right direction people began to get sick."[7] The Brigham Young Pioneer Party in 1847 suffered sickness soon after passing this area. Andrew Jensen wrote in his June 29 entry in *Day by Day With the Utah Pioneers:*

> Many of the brethren had been stricken with sickness within the past three days and a number more were attacked this evening. They generally began with headache, succeeded by violent fever, and some of them were delirious for awhile. Some of the people believed that this sickness was caused by using mineral saleratus for making bread.[8]

This sickness could also have been what the emigrants referred to as "mountain fever" during the years of trail traffic. Several members of the Pioneer Party, including Brigham

Young, were sick with these same symptoms during the rest of their journey to the Salt Lake Valley. Their journals called it mountain fever. The members of the Pioneer Party must have decided that the saleratus was not to blame, for many of them gathered more on their return to Winter Quarters in September 1847. Thomas Bullock wrote:

> Tuesday 14 September . . . .T. B., J. Egbert & several others walked ahead to fill our bags with Saleratus at the Lake. The Lake had dried up & left a solid Ice of Saleratus from 1/2 to 3 inches thick which we cut out with hatchets, axes & knives. I gathered about 50 pounds & was satisfied. Many Carts might have been filled with it, if we had needed it.[9]

A few diarists wrote of having symptoms of illness before they even reached the saleratus lakes. In 1847 Edwin Bryant, shortly after leaving the North Platte River wrote:

> I was seized, during the night, with a violent and exhausting sickness. The soil and water of the country through which we are now travelling, are strongly impregnated with salt, alkali, and sulphur; rendering the use of the water, in large quantities, deleterious to health, if not dangerous. I was scarcely able to mount my mule when we commenced the day's march.[10]

The emigrants looked on these saleratus lakes as a curiosity, or, for practical purposes, a source of natural baking soda. Several years after the busiest trail traffic, these deposits in the area of Independence Rock attracted the interest of scientists and capitalists considering it for commercial development. In the early 1880s, L. Du Pont traveled to the Sweetwater country and purchased the saleratus lakes area from local owners. At the same time he obtained patents in order to mine the soda. According to a United States Geological Survey report of 1886:

> There are four claims under United States patents in the name of L. Du Pont by five eastern companies. The first claim covers 20,000 acres, of which five acres contain carbonate

and sulphate of soda, averaging six feet deep. The second claim is about one mile west of the first; the soda is in solution. The third claim is one-fourth mile farther west and includes sixteen acres of soda solution, the depth of which has not been reached. It has been sounded forty feet without touching bottom. The fourth and fifth claims are four miles west and are on the same lake of solid soda. The depth fifty feet from shore is four feet of solid soda. Two hundred fifty feet from shore showed fourteen feet of solid soda without touching bottom.[11]

In the early 1890s an Eastern syndicate invested a great deal of money in the project, and hopes were high for a bright future for the area. A soda processing plant was erected and one hundred thousand pounds of machinery sent out from Chicago. A new town, called Johnstown, was established, with living accommodations for the workers. A railroad was planned between the soda lake area and Casper. Mine shafts were sunk, timbered, and tons of soda were taken out. Strings of freight teams hauled the materials to Casper until the proposed railroad could be built. However, the railroad never materialized, and the costs for processing and hauling the soda soon became prohibitive. By 1893 operations were suspended, and the property abandoned.[12]

In 1997 some research was informally conducted by the author and a chemist to test the saleratus for its leavening properties and chemical composition. Samples were scooped up from around the lakes, dried, and put through a fine sifter to remove debris. Other samples were gathered in a semi-liquid solution and allowed to dry into a powder. First the author used the saleratus in baking to see if it does indeed cause bread to rise. A simple Indian fry bread recipe consisting of flour, water, salt, and leavening was chosen, for it is probably similar to the bread the emigrants cooked over an open fire. A first test sample was cooked using the saleratus as leavening. The resultant

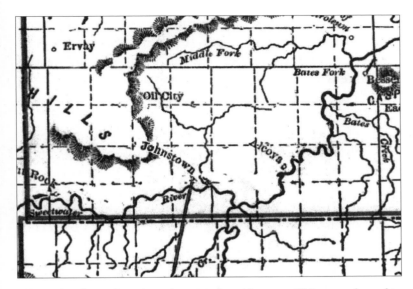

This railroad map from the early 1890s shows the town of Johnstown located in newly-formed Natrona County. The town provided housing for workers at the nearby soda processing plant. Processing and transportation of the soda proved too expensive and operations were closed by 1893. (Hileman Collection)

pan-fried bread did rise some. The test was repeated using the same recipe but with commercial baking soda in place of the saleratus. This bread rose to about twice the volume of the sample. The test was then again repeated but using flour, salt, and water only, with no leavening; this bread came out very flat. So Independence Rock saleratus does have some leavening power, though less than that of baking soda. There was no greenish cast observed in the cooked bread such as some of the emigrants reported. In its raw state the saleratus is very salty with a definite bicarbonate of soda taste.

The chemist then did lab tests to determine the chemical properties of the saleratus. Samples were gathered from three locales in the saleratus areas for comparison analysis. The first test done was an x-ray diffraction of the three samples. The x-ray diffraction method measures the angles and distances between the atoms in a sample, and compares that information to a database to determine what elements are actually present. This analysis shows that the saleratus is sodium bicarbonate ($NaHCO_3$) and sodium sulfate ($NaSO_4$). The second stage of the lab tests was to determine the amount of bicarbonate present in each sample. The three samples showed a distinct variation in their percentages of bicarbonate differing by almost a factor of three.[13] Perhaps the emigrants' success in using the saleratus in baking varied according to where they gathered their supplies. This could also be the reason for varying quantities of saleratus in emigrant recipes. In the lab tests saleratus was also dissolved in water and this solution showed a distinct greenish tinge. Further tests on the green substance have not been conducted at this point.[14]

Care must be exercised if attempting to gather saleratus samples. When the surface of the ground around the lake beds is dry and crusty, gathering the material is simple. However, if the ground is moist and the saleratus is grayish in color, which it is when damp, care must be exercised when walking out onto the soft edges of the lakes. These areas can be treacherous, and a person may have some difficulty getting out of the muck. As Corporal Hervey Johnson, a member of the Eleventh Ohio Volunteer Cavalry stationed at Sweetwater Station, described in a letter dated November 25, 1864:

> I walked out this morning to the lake which lays about a quarter of a mile from our quarters. It is called the Alkali Lake, there are several of them in this country, they are all small, this one is about as large as our farm. Several wolves were playing on the ice. None of these lakes have any outlet neither have any streams running into them. They are just sinks in the earth some of them have no water in them the bottom being covered with alkali which makes it look like snow. Many of them have nothing in them but soft mud in which many an ox and buffalo have perished in attempting

Levida Hileman gathers chunks of dried saleratus east of Independence Rock in the Fall of 2000. This is the same lake as in the photo on page 79—same month, different year. The hot, dry summer has totally dried the lake up in this photo. (Brock Hileman Photo)

to cross them. We can see their skeletons laying about in the mud. I came near getting into one myself one night. I was out hunting the horses, and not being able to find them, was returning home. It was pretty dark, but I could see that I was coming near one of these ponds. I could tell by the alkali over it. I had got tired of riding and was leading my pony, and when I got to the edge of the lake I thought I would go across it, it looked dry and solid in the bottom. I stepped off the bank but instead of stopping when my foot touched the ground I found that the bottom was not there, and I didn't stay to see how far down the bottom was, but I certainly would have done so had I not got out of there as soon as I did. If I had been on the pony I would have went in certain. One of our boys did get into one of them . . . one morning he went out to bring up the cattle and the first thing he knew he was up to his waist in mud, and he would have staid there too if it had not been for a tuft of grass that was in his reach, and on which he laid hold and drew himself out. He was a pretty looking sight when he got here.[15]

In 1999, a person collecting saleratus samples for lab testing had a similar scare. He had been warned about the possible quicksand properties of the damp lake banks in that wet summer. He related his experience:

> We stopped near one of the saleratus lakes. . . I gathered up some white material from the ground surface. It seemed to be a very thin layer on top of the dirt; probably less than 1/4 inch thick. I scraped off the white layer and took some of that. I also got a water sample out of one of the ponds. . . that is treacherous ground. I stepped out onto the "beach," rather carefully, but still just about sank out of sight. I had a small piece of wood which I had been using to scrape up the dry material. This was used like a snowshoe, to distribute my weight. Didn't make much difference; I still sank right in. I was finally able to get a water sample by attaching my bottle to a tent pole, and reaching way out. The pole was about 15' long, but the water depth at that distance was still only about two inches. I did finally get some into the bottle.[16]

The mystery remains as to who first thought of using the saleratus as a natural leavening. Did the Indian tribes use it in their cooking? Did the mountain men experiment with it? William Marshall Anderson writes of tasting the material in 1834, so perhaps the early mountain men cooked with it. Guidebooks mentioned it, and early emigrants wrote of it in their journals and letters. By the time the great masses of emigrants came through, it was commonly used.

Notes on Chapter Four

1. Anderson, William Marshall, *The Rocky Mountain Journals of William Marshall Anderson*, p. 118.

2. Munkres, Robert, "Independence Rock and Devil's Gate," *Annals of Wyoming*, Vol. 40, #1, p. 34.

3. Williams, Jacqueline, *Wagon Wheel Kitchens*, pp. 9, 10.

4. Page, Elizabeth, *Wagons West*, p. 158.

5. Holmes, Kenneth, *Covered Wagon Women*, Vol. 2, p. 262.

6. Ibid., Vol. 3, p. 137.

7. Ibid., Vol. 1, p. 36.

8. Jensen, Andrew, *Day by Day with the Utah Pioneers*, p. 86.

9. Bullock, Thomas, *The Pioneer Camp of the Saints*, p. 284.

10. Bryant, Edwin, *What I Saw in California*, p. 122.

11. Mokler, A. J., *History of Natrona County*, p. 103.

12. Ibid., p. 105.

13. Jensen, Doug, correspondence with author, August 3, 1999.

14. Ibid.

15. Unrau, William, editor, *Tending the Talking Wire*, pp. 195, 196.

16. Jensen, Doug, correspondence with author, August 3, 1999.

HISTORY, MYSTERY, MYTH

WHILE MUCH WAS written in diaries and letters about Independence Rock, even more stories were handed down orally, so that today we have difficulty separating fact from fallacy or even fabrication. This was true even when the emigrants crossed the plains. Much trail lore was disseminated from one wagon train to another and repeated in letters written home. All anyone had to do was speak with authority, and some people would unquestioningly pass the stories on to others.

JOHN C. FREMONT AND HIS CROSS

Erroneous stories about Captain John C. Fremont abounded even in 1852. This could be attributed to the fact that he was well known, for many who were interested in the West read his published reports. Eliza Ann McAuley wrote the following in her journal on June 24, 1852:

> Traveled twenty one miles and camped at Independence Rock. This name was given it by Fremont who arrived here on the fourth of July, on his first exploring expedition. His party climbed to the top of the rock and partook of a fine dinner, which the ladies of St. Louis had prepared for them for this occasion.[1]

On their arrival at Devil's Gate the next day she wrote, "This was also named by Fremont's party." One wonders how this information was started. Even years later it is easy to read this and accept it as truth if one does not know the history of the trails. The Fremont party was at Independence Rock and Devil's Gate on two occasions in 1842, but neither of those visits was on July Fourth nor was he responsible for naming either place. Moreover, on Fremont's first visit to Independence Rock on August 1, 1842, he makes no mention of scaling the Rock—although the party probably did, since this was a scientific exploration. Fremont's expedition took various measurements and notes all along the route. A more certain distortion was the "fine dinner prepared by the ladies of Saint Louis." In fact, the party was on extremely short rations. Long before arriving at the Rock, the members had abandoned their wagons and cached much of their equipment along the river in the area of present-day Casper. They transferred what supplies they could to pack horses and were down to ten days' rations for the party. They were so low on food that they were even looking at the possibility of eating their horses and mules. The exploring party faced these dire circumstances because they had relied on killing buffalo for meat. However, in 1842, a great drought combined with a plague of grasshoppers denuded the plains to such an extent that the buffalo were not to be found. Even the Indians were destitute of meat.[2] In such circumstances, "a fine dinner" is difficult to imagine, and the "ladies of Saint Louis" were not there.

The mystery survives about how and when Captain John C. Fremont's cross disappeared from Independence Rock. We know from diary accounts, including Fremont's own, that in 1842 he inscribed the Rock with a large cross coated with an India rubber solution. C. G. Coutant, an early Wyoming historian, concluded the name was blasted off during a celebration in 1847, based on the recollections of H. B. Kelly who settled in Wyoming several years after crossing on the trail. Kelly was at Independence Rock on July 4, 1847, and recalled a large celebration with a thousand or more in attendance.[3] However,

Harriett Talcott Buckingham recorded she saw Fremont's name in 1851, and William Chandless reported seeing the cross in 1855. The story about the cross being blasted off by exuberant revelers during a Fourth of July celebration is certainly a possibility. Some emigrants very freely used whisky and gunpowder, and the celebrations frequently went beyond what the participants intended.

But where is the evidence? None exists in the few remains of rubble around the Rock. And was it 1847 or some other year? When Fremont later stood as a presidential candidate, could someone who hated him have blasted the symbol from the Rock? We may never know the answer, but Fremont's cross may indeed have been a factor in his unsuccessful bid for the presidency of the United States. In 1856 Fremont was the Republican party's candidate, and the Know-Nothing Party bitterly opposed the nomination. Taking advantage of the strong religious rancor of that time, the Know-Nothings charged that he was a member of the Roman Catholic Church. Since the report of Fremont's expeditions had been published by Congress, the whole country knew he had inscribed a large cross on the Rock. His opponents charged that this was a thing no Protestant explorer would ever do.[4] Fremont lost the election, and whether his cross on Independence Rock was really a factor in that loss remains a mystery.

PROFESSIONAL MORMON INSCRIBERS

Is it really true that the Mormons stationed men at Independence Rock to put inscriptions on the Rock for the emigrants, charging up to five dollars for the service? This dubious story has been repeated as fact over the years. It is even mentioned on an interpretive sign in the kiosk at Independence Rock. Pinpointing a reliable source for the statement has proved impossible. In his book *Historic Sites Along the Oregon Trail*, Aubrey Haines tells that "the enterprising Mormons sometimes had a man or two at the Rock who would undertake to inscribe a name and date for varying prices up to five dollars, depending on location."[5] He credits the source of his information as Irene Paden's book *The Wake of the Prairie Schooner*. However, although Paden refers to the story twice, she unfortunately does not document her source.[6]

∞ ∞

I began to wonder why I had never come across any remark in any historic diary, letter, or report referring to Mormons inscribing names for a fee. I started digging deeper. At first I wasn't really questioning the practice, I just wanted to find documentation of it. I asked two eminent Mormon historians, but both claimed they had never seen any reference to this nor had even heard of this being done. I asked an archivist in Salt Lake City if he would check through Church records for references to professional inscribers being assigned at Independence Rock. After careful checking he could find no record of the practice.[7] So I am still searching for documentation, and I remain skeptical. Five dollars is quite an exorbitant fee. Five dollars was a common sum paid to ferry across the North Platte River. A number of emigrants even balked at paying three dollars to cross the Sweetwater River. With so many names painted on Independence Rock and the materials to do so readily available, it seems questionable that an emigrant would pay someone to inscribe a name. Most of them still had two-thirds of their journey ahead of them, and money was necessary for additional river crossings, for supplies, and for expenses at their destination. Where did the story originate? Someone may yet find a source that documents the practice, but until then it should perhaps be considered a fallacy.

W. H. Jackson's Painting

One of William Henry Jackson's well-known paintings depicts a scene on top of Independence Rock, showing Jackson himself, hammer and chisel in hand, putting his initials on the Rock. This painting is dated 1932, decades after his visit to the

Rock with the Dr. Ferdinand Hayden's U.S. Geological Survey party in 1871. This image has been reproduced in trail books, sometimes with the caption, "William Henry Jackson putting his name on Independence Rock." But although Jackson worked from photographs taken on the Hayden expedition, he also exercised artistic license. A visitor to the spot depicted in the photographs will see that Jackson could not possibly have put his initials at the spot shown in the painting, for the rock face is quite sheer with no ledge to stand on. The painting shows him standing on a rather wide ledge that doesn't exist. Since Jackson was at Independence Rock on several occasions, he may have put his initials at some other well-hidden spot, but the scene depicted in his painting is an impossibility. Perhaps he merely added the ledge and the emigrant putting a name on the Rock to give a focal point to the painting. He took similar liberties in his famous painting, depicting Independence Rock with the highest point, or north end, close to the Sweetwater River, reversing the compass points.

Jackson again visited the Rock on August 25, 1925. Though he was over eighty, he successfully climbed to the top one more time.[8]

Vehicles Atop Independence Rock

Something about Independence Rock impels the adventurous to try something different. Even as early as 1853, Virginia W. Ivins, who was in a group camped at the Rock on July 1, wrote that she saw "a number of men . . . hard at work hoisting a deserted wagon to the top, intending to roll it off to celebrate Independence day, so near at hand."[9] A party in 1854 saw both a wagon and a tent on top of Independence Rock.[10] In a speech at the Rock in 1925, Robert S. Ellison repeated a local story that alleged John Fremont, in a carriage, was pulled to the top by ardent admirers on July 4. A fitting oration by Fremont followed this carriage ride. Six loving couples then surrendered their *independence* in assuming marital obligations. It was after this that the Rock was named Independence.[11] The story is erroneous, of course, but emigrants had to have seen various wagons, buggies, carts, or other possessions pulled to the top, for their diaries tell of very ingenious Fourth of July celebrations.

The coming of the automobile brought a new challenge to the stout-hearted. Around 1930 two daring souls attempted to drive a car up one of the steeper parts of Independence Rock. From a Casper newspaper report written sometime in the 1930s:

> "Independence Rock," "The Register of the Desert," probably the most interesting landmark on the Old Oregon Trail, has been scaled by an automobile for the first time in history.
>
> Last Friday morning Lee Doud and Martin Sather drove a Whippet Six roadster out to this famous rock with the avowed intention of scaling this seemingly unsurmountable block of granite. So steep are the sides of the rock that Doud and Sather used rubber boots to climb over that part the Whippet would be sent over. The north side just inside the fence was decided on, as it offered the best approach and the smoothest surface. [The present chain link fence on the north end of Independence rock was installed after 1930.] Mr. Doud eased his Whippet up to the base and then "opened her up." Slowly but surely the trim little roadster mounted the steep ascent while Mr. Sather snapped pictures of the progress. Because of the extreme roughness of the rock it was necessary to do considerable maneuvering before the top was reached.
>
> The Whippet was put on top at exactly the same spot where on July 4, 1920, the Casper Masons held memorial services to commemorate the convening of Wyoming's first lodge of Masons at the same place on July 4, 1862.
>
> After taking a few more pictures, the car was headed down off one of the steepest places and the large four-wheel brakes held the Whippet at the intrepid driver's command.[12]

This 1932 painting by W. H. Jackson shows a man inscribing the initials WHJ. It is the same scene as in Jackson's 1871 photograph. (American Heritage Center, University of Wyoming.)

This photograph of the south top of Independence Rock shows the same scene as Jackson's 1871 photo and his 1932 painting. (Author's Photo)

This was not the last time a motorized vehicle was driven to the top. The Ancient Free and Accepted Masons hold special celebrations on Independence Rock once every ten years to commemorate the first Masonic gathering on Independence Rock on July 4, 1862. At least once in recent years they obtained special permission for a deputy sheriff's vehicle to drive the disabled members to the top to include them in the Masonic closed meeting. Other years they have used ropes to help the less able ascend to the top. The Masons carry up folding chairs, tables, and other necessary equipment for their ceremony, setting them in the spot of the original 1862 meeting.[13] The first Masonic meeting of this millennium at Independence Rock was held July 4, 2000. A large gathering camped on the east side of the Rock for the two-day celebration.

In 1993, a celebration was tentatively planned to commemorate the sesquicentennial of the Oregon Trail. At this time some planners explored the idea of putting a cannon on top of the Independence Rock and shooting off a blank charge. The sheer difficulty of doing such a thing, along with the dangers of the cannon rolling down out of control, very rapidly aborted this idea.[14] Occasionally young people on mountain bikes attempt to ride to the top, but most start at the steeper northwest side so few get very far. From a distance the ascent looks easier than it really is.

A Dam in Devil's Gate

Even as early as 1849 John Birney Hill saw the possibility of Devil's Gate as the site of a dam:

> This is a gate that has not been shut for a million years, as far as I know, but I think that Uncle Sam will close it in time, and hold the water for irrigating his land, and that will be putting it to good use.[15]

Few people realize that, barely fifty years later, the government actually took steps towards damming Devil's Gate.[16] In the summer of 1897 Captain Hiram M. Chittenden of the United States Engineers made a scouting expedition in the West, the purpose of which was to visit proposed sites for dams and irrigation on public lands. At this time Chittenden was not only working for the United States Engineers, he was also Secretary of the Missouri River Commission. On this trip he visited two sites in the Sweetwater Valley vicinity; one was Devil's Gate.[17] About Devil's Gate he wrote, "as a single proposition for the storage of water, it is almost unequaled anywhere in the West, and the dam is no less remarkable than the gorge itself."[18] The next day Chittenden visited a second site located on the North Platte River, then known as Platte Canyon. The scenery of this canyon impressed Chittenden; he remarked that it would have done credit to Yellowstone Park. Following this scouting trip, survey crews were organized and dispatched to the field. Chittenden reported:

With the approach of Spring I organized my survey party with the aid of Assistant Engineer F. B. Maltby, and in due time we set out to look over the field. We fixed upon two principal sites and several of less importance for which we thought surveys out [ought] to be made. . . .The principal site in Wyoming was at Devil's Gate on the Sweet Water river. With the greater funds of later years the Reclamation Service developed what they called the Pathfinder's site several miles below on the North Platte river. As this collected also the water of the Sweet Water, it was of course a very much better site.[19]

The dam was then built on the North Platte River and called Pathfinder Dam.

Still visible on the rock faces inside Devil's Gate itself are a few inscribed initials and names followed by the letters "USD SUR." The reason for these inscriptions was a puzzle to the group doing the survey work until research answered the question. These inscribers were obviously part of Chittenden's crew sent to survey Devil's Gate at about the turn of the century. These inscriptions are placed such that, if the dam had been built in Devil's Gate, they would have been destroyed forever.

From a trail historian's viewpoint, it is fortunate the dam was never built. An extensive area of existing trail segments and sites, including the historic Martin's Cove, site of the Mormon handcart rescue, would now be under water. When Hiram Chittenden visited Independence Rock on the 1897 scouting trip he wrote: "I walked around it and climbed to the top. I saw many old names but none as ancient as I hoped."[20] Since Chittenden's interest was collecting historic data related to the fur trade, the guess is that the ancient names he was looking for were those left by men of the early fur trade era.

Graves on West Side of Independence Rock

"There were those who looked back with heavy hearts and remembered where they had left the wild winds to chant their funeral requiem over a lonely and deserted grave." William A. Riner uttered those words in an address to a Masonic gathering at Independence Rock in 1920. He was speaking of the emigrants who faced the sad task of leaving loved ones in lonely graves along the trailside. He further remarked, "Their unknown and unmarked last resting places have passed into oblivion, though they line the way."[21] Many diarists tallied the graves they passed on their way west, and it is true that most of these graves have long since passed into oblivion. Nonetheless, there are still three small graves enclosed in a wrought-iron fence on the Rock's west side. Many visitors believe that these graves are those of emigrants who died at Independence Rock. Although death was a common occurrence among wagon trains passing though the area, these graves do not date from the busy emigrant trail years. A small notation in the rest center display relates the details of these graves.[22]

In a letter written to W. V. Morrison and dated July 14, 1946, Mrs. Tom (Ella) Sun reported these are the graves of three children who died of diphtheria, probably during the winter of 1897. One grave contains the remains of Ross Merrill, the three-year-old son of Charley Merrill, a stagecoach driver who lived in the Independence Rock area. His stage run was between Independence Rock and Casper. This information is corroborated in an April 1970 article in the *Casper Herald Tribune,* in which a Mrs. Clayton Danks of Thermopolis identified two graves as those of Ross Merrill and Eva Hunnington. According to Mrs. Danks, young Eva died of scarlet fever a year or so after Ross Merrill.[23] The third grave is believed to be that of a three-year-old child of the McCorkle family, who lived at the old Soda Works at the nearby Soda Lakes.[24] The McCorkles belonged to the community just east of Independence Rock established in the 1890s by investors trying to commercially mine the saleratus.

The large "S" on the wrought-iron gate possibly was put there by the Tom Sun family, since this small cemetery was

An unidentified grave at Devil's Gate on the west side. (Author's Photo)

located on property owned by the Sun Ranch. Old-timers report that originally headstones marked the graves; if so, they have now disappeared. Occasionally someone remembers these three children by putting flowers on their graves. Along the trail, two to three miles east of Independence Rock, several probable unmarked graves can still be found.[25] Numerous other emigrant graves are located on the site of the old Sun Ranch.[26]

A Day with an Emigrant Train, 1850

If some of the things we think we know about Independence Rock are untrue or exaggerated, the same may be said about the actual experiences of wagon train travel. History often dwells on the hardships and privations endured; yet for many emigrants the overall day-to-day journey was frequently uneventful, sometimes monotonous, and in fact contained no more stress than they faced in their lives at home. Wagon trains often took advantage of the good water and grass near Independence Rock to lay over a day or two to rest and to catch up on camp chores. One of the better depictions of an emigrant train's "typical day" comes to us from William Fowler Pritchard's diary.

Pritchard and his party camped five miles east of Independence Rock in 1850. He recorded a scene filled with visual images. Multiply this scene by numerous other wagon parties camped in the vicinity, along with the trains passing by, for a general idea of the activity going at Independence Rock during a typical day in the mid-1800s.

Pritchard recorded a light frost during the night preceding this entry:

13 July---Remained in camp all day. Some went hunting. We had to repair several of the wheels. They were very loose so we had to fix them as before. An unoccupied spectator who could have beheld our camp today would think it a singular spectacle. The hunters returning with their game; of the women some were washing, some ironing, some baking, others sewing, etc. At one of the tents the fiddle and flute were sending forth their melody among the solitudes of the Sweetwater. At one tent I heard singing, some reading novels and another her Bible. While all this was going on, that nothing may be wanting to complete the scene, a Negro woman was singing hymns. Others playing cards, so you see we have a miniature world among ourselves. A mixture of good and evil, which shows that the likeness is a true one. Performed a great tailoring job; the knees of a pair of pants becoming thin. I cut off the legs and turned the back to the front. As we expect cold weather soon I [would] like to be ready for it. Fixed twenty-five wheels. Very warm today. [27]

NOTES ON CHAPTER FIVE

1. Eliza Ann McAuley diary.

2. Fremont, Brevet Captain John C., *The Exploring Expedition to the Rocky Mountains in the Year 1842*, pp. 53-54.

3. Coutant, C. G., *The History of Wyoming*, p. 336.

4. Mokler, Alfred J., *History of Natrona County*, op. cit., p. 454.

5. Haines, Aubrey, *Historic Sites Along the Oregon Trail*, p. 204.

6. Paden, Irene, *The Wake of the Prairie Schooner*, pp. 120, 209.

7. Conversations with historians Will Bagley and Dr. Stanley Kimball, and archivist Gary Gillespie.

8. Ellison, Robert S., "Independence Rock and the Oregon Trail," *Annals of Wyoming*, Vol. VIII, #2, p. 6.

9. Munkres, Robert, "Independence Rock and Devil's Gate," *Annals of Wyoming*, Vol. 40, p. 33.

10. Holmes, Kenneth, *Covered Wagon Women*, Vol. VII, p. 49.

11. Ellison, Robert S., "Independence Rock and the Oregon Trail," op. cit., p. 3.

12. Mokler, Alfred J., Casper College Library Special Collections, newspaper files, Scrapbook A, p. 90.

13. Information from Charles Germain, a Masonic planner, participant.

14. Hileman, Levida, records, personal recollections.

15. Hill, John Birney, op. cit., p. 38.

16. Mokler, A. J., "Devil's Gate, A Prominent Wyoming Landmark," *Wyoming Pioneer*, July–August, 1941, p. 168.

17. Chittenden, Hiram M., *H. M. Chittenden, A Western Epic*, Bruce L. Roy, editor, p. 46.

18. Mokler, A. J., "Devil's Gate, A Prominent Wyoming Landmark," op. cit., p. 168.

19. Chittenden, Hiram M., op. cit., p. 69.

20. Ibid., p. 47.

21. Mokler, A. J., *History of Freemasonry in Wyoming*, Vol. 1, p. 245.

22. Information furnished by the Wyoming Department of Transportation.

23. Newspaper clipping in files at Edness Wilkins State Park, Evansville, Wyoming.

24. Letter in files of Wyoming Division of Cultural Resources, Cheyenne, Wyoming.

25. Hileman, Levida records, field notes.

26. Information from Bernard Sun, early 1990s.

27. Pritchard, William Fowler, Journal of William Fowler Pritchard, Indiana to California 1850, pp. 27-28.

PART TWO

THE
INSCRIPTIONS
AT INDEPENDENCE ROCK
& DEVIL'S GATE

THE
SURVEY OF NAMES

In THE FALL of 1994, a small group of volunteers gathered
from Wyoming's Natrona County Historical Society and
the Wyoming chapter of the Oregon-California Trails Association. Our aim was to conduct a thorough inventory of the
Independence Rock inscriptions dating before the twentieth
century. Most of the volunteers were members of both groups,
and all possessed a real dedication to the task.

We also had a core of research to build on, though we knew
it was incomplete. Robert Spurrier Ellison's 1930 book *Independence Rock* includes a list of over seven hundred inscribed names
that were visible on the Rock in the late 1920s, and includes
general locations. (See Appendix B for an Ellison biography.)
For years this book was considered the definitive authority on
the inscriptions, and later efforts to re-survey the names were
sporadic and inconclusive. However, little is known about the
time span, personnel, or methods of Ellison's survey.[1] Nor did
Ellison list every name he and his assistants found on the Rock.
Some handwritten notes in the Robert S. Ellison files at Wyoming's State Archives in Cheyenne attest to this. These field
notes were recorded in 1927 by Daniel W. Greenburg, who later
wrote the book's foreword, along with another person, possibly
Ellison himself. Perhaps Ellison chose not to include names if
their locations were unidentified. In any case, the Rock clearly
needed to be examined again.

Panel shows names over names. Some very faint painted names can be seen under the inscribed names. (Author's Photo)

We started this project in mid-September, which shows how little we knew about the task ahead of us. We thought we'd be lucky if we found fifty unrecorded names. The group numbered ten to twelve people on each weekly excursion. Since the Ellison book was the starting point for our survey, we used the location system that he had devised. We split into groups of three, each assigned to a different area on the Rock: northeast top, middle top, or south. The reason for dividing into groups of three, when possible, was to help resolve differing opinions regarding the actual letters or dates in the inscriptions.

We soon realized we had a massive project on our hands, for the Ellison records were quite incomplete. Frequently we found a name recorded by Ellison, yet three or four feet away was a similarly dated name which was missing from Ellison's list. By the time October comes to Wyoming, weather conditions are very changeable and winds are brisk and cool. However, the group continued to go out once a week, often wearing wool hats, gloves, and warm jackets. At times the winds were so strong on the top of the Rock that we'd confine our work to the ground and sheltered areas. We also spent time surveying names in Devil's Gate. This usually involved wading in the Sweetwater River, so could be done only in the fall when the water was low. By mid-November it was simply too cold to continue the survey, so we halted for the season.

Since I was the one with all the Ellison names on a database, I kept all the records. I spent most of the next months entering everything on to the database and checking it for errors. After two months of surveying we had over two hundred new inscriptions that weren't in the Ellison book. Our cutoff date for names was the turn of the twentieth century; we felt any inscription one hundred years old was of historic significance. This cutoff date is several years after the trails' heyday years of 1840–1869; however, many emigrants still used the trail as they came west to homestead. The vast majority of the inscriptions recorded by us, however, date from the trails' busiest years.

I became absorbed with the inscriptions over the winter months and could hardly wait for the weather to permit me to get out to Independence Rock. I started again in February although this was really too early in the season; one day snow started falling while a friend and I were working. By the time spring came, most of the volunteers were involved in other projects, but I continued the survey, mostly on my own. By the end of 1995, I had over seventeen hundred inscriptions in my database. This included the seven hundred given in the Ellison book and about a hundred found at Devil's Gate. In the summers of 1996 and 1998 a dear friend, Leneigh Schrinar, spent many hours with me on Independence Rock. I continued to look for new names each year, crisscrossing the Rock many times. Even after all my searching, in the summer of 1999 I discovered several inscriptions that I hadn't seen before, including three listed in Ellison's book.

Over the five years of the survey I have walked, crawled, scooted along, and inched my way over all of the accessible areas of the Rock. I have been on Independence Rock during every month of the year and at every time of day. The varying light angles affect the visibility of an inscription. In early summer some of the inscriptions just seem to glow. At times, even when I know a name's location, it may not show up at all or may be very difficult to see, due to the variations of sunlight. During my solo work, if I came upon an inscription I was not sure of, I always sought a second opinion before I recorded it in the database.

We kept track of the inscriptions listed by Ellison that are still visible, listing each as "found" or "not found." If we found an error in the way Ellison had recorded a name, we also indicated this in our data. This difference between Ellison's reading and ours could have been due to the way an inscription was viewed, or simply to transcription or typesetting errors. In our data the name is recorded the way Ellison had it along with our correction, for example: "Hiram Meek," Ellison's spelling, and "Hiram Meck," our correction. Such errors can make a big difference to descendants looking for records of an ancestor. We are aware that errors may and probably will be found in our own inventory, but we worked very diligently to minimize them.

Besides surveying visually, we used various methods of photography to bring out faint inscriptions, often indicating this in the data. I used regular color film and black-and-white technical pan film. I also tried unsuccessfully to bring out names with infrared film. I have taken many slide photos and studied them intently. Some work has been done with digital camera and computer enhancement of photographic images. We used a video camera to record the names in the cave, some on the top of the Rock, and some inside Devil's Gate. The video work was done by Kevin Anderson of Casper College Library, whose Special Collections now house the videotapes.

During visual surveying we have often bent down and actually traced faint letters with our fingers in order to read them. So many of the names are very weathered and faint; many others are covered by lichen so they are unreadable. New methods of photography may be able to bring out these faint names, but this could be expensive and time-consuming. When I started I did not record partial names or stray dates, but in 1997 I realized it could be a very long time before anyone took on this massive job of re-surveying Independence Rock again. I knew I had to record everything still visible at the turn of this century, so I retraced my steps and took a full inventory. This information can be used as a starting point for anyone who may want to try new methods of bringing out inscriptions.

The lichen continues to be a problem. It is obvious inscriptions are under the lichen, but there is no way to read them. I have often heard that lichen takes hundreds of years to grow upon a rock, but many 1930 names are lichen-covered. I even found a name dated 1966 which was almost totally lichen-covered. This negates the "hundreds of years" theory. I also frequently saw names that were light shadows surrounded by lichen growth, the letters standing out as distinct bare spaces. One day in Devil's Gate I observed a name showing in this manner, and yet the last few letters still visible in tar. I knew paint or other foreign elements could leave lasting damage even on granite, so I concluded a name left in paint or tar could mar the rock in such a way that lichen would not grow over it. A Bureau of Land Management archaeologist concurred that this was a good explanation. We now call such names "negative relief" inscriptions. They are indicated in our data, for instance in the W. S. Ebey inscription. More than one diarist has recorded that he put his name on the Rock with paint, and the inscription that does remain is often in negative relief.

Our data also includes references to people or parties who may have traveled together. We base this information on the way the names are left on the Rock. Frequently names on the

Rock are boxed together with a common date. Sometimes an arrow is drawn from one name to another. In one instance two names are close together; both are pecked instead of inscribed, suggesting they belong together. We also gleaned similar information from descendants or from diaries.

Visitors may be disturbed by the presence of twentieth-century names on the Rock. Since several celebrations commemorating the trail years have been held at Independence Rock, dating back as early as 1920, it is no surprise that some participants left inscriptions. This is especially true of the early twentieth-century Masonic celebrations; many of their inscriptions are right among the old names.

Sometimes it is difficult to know twentieth-century from nineteenth-century names. A large portion of the nineteenth-century names is on the north top, and this is where most visitors first climb up. Unfortunately this is also where one will see modern-day names from the last three decades inscribed among and sometimes over the old inscriptions. Even as recently as the summer of 1999 a couple wrote their names and the year right over some very old inscriptions, despite the signs that inform visitors that this is a historic site and that it should be respected as such.

For many years the Rock was on private land and visitors were not encouraged. As a state historic site it is now readily accessible. Independence Rock is not close to any town, and patrolling efforts to reduce vandalism and graffiti are very difficult to maintain. However, most visitors exercise respect. Nineteen ninety-seven was a busy season at Independence Rock due to the sesquicentennial celebration of the Mormon Trail. At times busloads of people could be seen all over the Rock and yet less than half a dozen new inscriptions or graffiti were in evidence after the season. (One person that summer left initials on the Rock with the date of 1797.) It is gratifying to note that nineteenth-century names still far outnumber the twentieth-century ones.

I am frequently asked how we distinguish a valid trail-related name from a twentieth-century name. Sometimes this is very difficult; therefore we have relied on the opinions of more than one person when in doubt. Of course sometimes it is certainly a judgment call, and we have probably made some errors in judgment. One cannot rely on the simple appearance alone. At times I have felt an inscription looked too new to be trail-related, only to find the name in the Ellison book, dating it at least to the mid-1920s. When a date is not visible, we relied on other indicators. Early inscriptions more likely had letters and numerals printed backwards, for example. This is frequently true of the letters *s, r, n, j,* and sometimes *f.* The numeral *4* is frequently backwards. A very elaborate style of printing or writing is another good indicator of nineteenth-century inscriptions. Many of the emigrants traveling on the trail were well educated; this is evidenced in many of the inscriptions and in their diaries. Some inscriptions are so beautifully precise, they invite one to trace them with the fingertips. Some inscriptions are in very elegant script and some in a combination of printing and script, but the majority are printed. The style of printing with tails on the letters is a good indication that the name is from early times. Sometimes the printing is so precise, in outline or block lettering, that one would believe the inscriber was using a present-day stencil. The best example of this type of stenciling is the inscription of P. G. Sessions, an early Mormon. These types of inscriptions are not the norm, for most were just cut in plain lettering. Some inscriptions are clearly printed, but with an *X* after or under the name, denoting that someone else probably put the name on for a person who could not write.

Some emigrants even took the time to leave a brief biographical sketch along with their names, such as their age, home, or year of birth. Many military men included their company and outfit. James Hunt must have had some spare time while at Independence Rock for he left his record in extremely large

This inscribed church and chalice on rock shows evidence of early missionary traffic in the area. (Author's Photo)

letters. His inscription is still very legible, telling the world not only his name but also his age (18), and that he was of Company D and a member of the Powder River Expedition, S.L.C.U.T. He dated it June, 74. Obviously he was a recruit from Salt Lake City, so U. T. would stand for Utah Territory. The actual Powder River Expedition was not in this immediate area so he may have been passing through on his way to his assignment.

Many people showed their creativity while inscribing their names. Some etched boxes around their names, sometimes decorating them with designs such as triangular shapes. One enterprising person's name appears inside a chiseled, scrolled box on a single pedestal. One inscription has an outline of a dog; another has a gun drawn by the name. One inscription is enclosed in a shield, with a chalice and a church drawn by the

E.M. McIlroy's inscription artistically follow the contours of color in the Rock.
(Author's Photo)

name, similar to symbols found in old Spanish glyphs in the Southwest.[2] Some areas on the Rock are of a smooth pinkish-colored granite and several emigrants inscribed their names following the contours of the color. A good example of this is the E. M. McIlroy inscription on the middle top.

All of this is astonishing in view of the fact that the granite is very hard to carve. These people must have spent several hours putting their inscriptions on Independence Rock. Very little is written about this in diaries. Some people wrote that they left their names, but did not say what tools they used or how difficult it was. There are a few diary references to using a "coal chisel," a cold-forged chisel which is very hard and strong.[3] One descendant reported that his ancestor used the tip of a horseshoe, according to his diary. Due to the hardness of the surface and the lack of time, most people simply painted their names on the Rock. Diary after diary reports that the Rock was covered with names but most of them were painted on in different colors or with tar. Even if the emigrants had no paint with them, they might have learned from local tribes or other travelers how to obtain paints from natural materials. Some diaries tell of mixing bear or buffalo grease with gun powder. Over the years only a few painted names have survived in protected areas such as the so-called cave. The remains of a few red and blue painted names are still faintly visible even in exposed areas, and at a few places on Independence Rock and at Devil's Gate remnants of tar names still survive.

When this inventory was complete, in 1999, the data comprised 2,056 entries. About two hundred of these inscriptions are initials only, partial names, or partial dates, which furnishes little data for descendants or researchers. The earliest date still visible is 1831; two Campbell names close together both indicate that year. About seventy percent of the names in the Ellison book were still visible, although the earliest date listed in Ellison (M. K. Hugh, 1824) was not found in our survey. Possible information related to destinations, families, or wagon parties was found for about twenty-five percent of the inscriptions.

One hundred five of the total inscriptions are located either at Rattlesnake Pass or in Devil's Gate. Five inscriptions were found on the large rock formation directly south of Independence Rock across the Sweetwater River. This is known as Sentinel Rock or at times has been called Traverse Rock. Deep trail swales are found on the other side of the river showing evidence of heavy emigrant traffic. We expected to find more inscriptions on Sentinel Rock but they are not there.

One inscription not included in the data is that of Robert S. Ellison with the date of 1930.

Tar and paint names can be found in the cave. These names remain fresh look-ing as though put on recently. (Author's Photo)

TABLE ONE: OVERLAND EMIGRATION TO OREGON, CALIFORNIA, AND UTAH

Table One gives the estimated total of emigrants who traveled the trail going either to Oregon, California, or Utah. A comparison with Table Two shows that in almost all cases, the years with the most dated inscriptions match the years of high trail traffic. Conversely 1851, a year of low trail traffic, shows few inscriptions.

1847	6,650	1854	21,167
1848	4,100	1855	6,684
1849	26,950	1856	11,400
1850	52,500	1857	6,800
1851	6,200	1858	7,650
1852	70,000	1859	20,431
1853	41,700	1860	12,130

Source: *Reading, Writing, and Riding Along the Oregon California Trails* by William E. Hill, Oregon California Trails Association, 1993, pg. 14.

Table Two: Summary of Dated Inscriptions

While most inscriptions are undated, those that do include dates offer a very approximate measure of emigrant traffic on the trails. This data was assembled from our survey work up to Fall 1999 and from Ellison's survey. Not all of these dates are necessarily still visible.

1847	6	1858	14
1848	4	1859	86
1849	58	1860	9
1850	106	1861	22
1851	18	1862	61*
1852	121	1863	19
1853	38	1864	47
1854	24	1865	8
1855	12	1866	14
1856	8	1867	2
1857	8	1868	5

*The year 1862 shows a considerable jump in the number of inscriptions as compared to 1861 and 1863. Emigrants were still going over the trail, but at least fifteen of these 1862 inscriptions are probably those of soldiers stationed in the area. These men were not traveling through or going further west, so would not be considered part of the regular emigrant travel.

Notes on Chapter Six

1. We have two clues in Ellison's book as to the people involved in the survey. In his foreword Daniel Greenburg mentioned those who assisted Ellison, including Mr. Thomas Cooper, Mr. G. R. Hagens, Mr. C. C. Hoffhine, Mr. C. B. Stafford, Mr. James A. Shoemaker, Daniel Greenburg, and many others. On page 25, Ellison states some members of the Casper Chamber of Commerce and the Natrona County Historical Society helped compile lists. Of course, at least some of the people mentioned by Daniel may be the same individuals included in Ellison's statement.

2. Bollinger, Gene, "When You Don't Pay Attention," *The Institute News Magazine*, Sept. 1997, p. 12.

3. A "coal chisel" or cold chisel is a cold-forged chisel, a tool made from tempered steel. The tempering hardens it, making it capable of cutting metal when the metal is cold. This was a very hard chisel which would work well on the surface of the granite of Independence Rock and Devil's Gate. Source: Carl Closs, Metals instructor, Natrona County (Wyoming) School District, retired.

KEY TO THE
INSCRIPTIONS

THE APPROXIMATE LOCATION of the names on Independence Rock is shown by the following symbols. Bear in mind that there may be some overlapping of the different locations for it is difficult to be precise. If the key does not indicate "top or t" then the inscriptions can be found by walking around the base of Independence Rock. The accompanying aerial view of Independence rock with some of the locations marked will help orient the visitor.

Some of the above designations were used by Ellison on the inscriptions in his book but not necessarily by the recent survey crew in our new entries. We have also included locations not used by Ellison. Studies were done comparing the list of inscriptions at these two sites to lists of names recorded at other trail sites. If a name is possibly found at some other site along the trails, this information is recorded in the data.

A portion of Devil's Gate itself is on private land. Respect the rights of property owners and obtain rancher permission before going onto private property.

INDEPENDENCE ROCK:

n	north
ne	northeast
nw	northwest
w	west
e	east
s	south
se	southeast
sw	southwest
saddle	middle low part (on top) easily ascended from the east side
nt	north top
net	northeast top
nwt	northwest top
mt	middle top
met ·	middle east top
mwt	middle west top
st	south top
set	southeast top
swt	southwest top
cave	south south east, mid way up
behind fence	behind the chain link fence on the north end of the Rock

DEVIL'S GATE AND SENTINEL ROCK:

R Pass n	Rattlesnake Pass north
R Pass s	Rattlesnake Pass south
R Pass w	Rattlesnake Pass west
D Gate	inside the Devil's Gate canyon
D Gate top	on the high part above the canyon not quite to the summit
D Gate summit	on the very highest point above the canyon on the south side of the river
Sentinel Rock	the large rock outcrop directly south across the Sweetwater River from Independence Rock

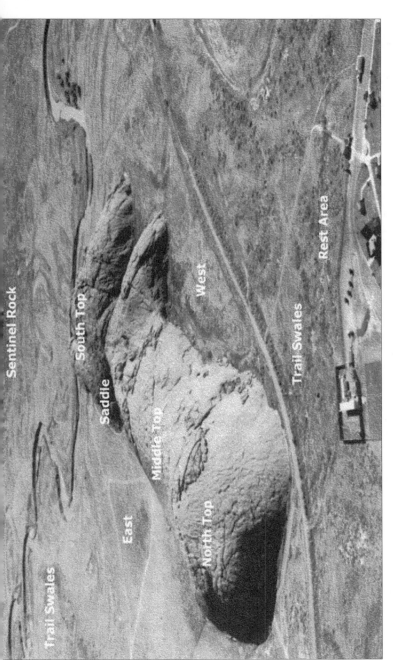

This aerial photo shows the general locations of inscriptions. Many inscriptions can be found on the north and middle top. Numerous inscriptions are along the base on the south end where the very early trail went. (Author's Photo)

THE INSCRIPTIONS AT
I NDEPENDENCE ROCK
AND DEVIL'S GATE

THE INSCRIPTION ITSELF is printed in bold. The rest of the data entry gives more details about the inscription.

This list includes the over seven hundred names recorded in the 1920s survey conducted by Robert S. Ellison. If the inscription Ellison recorded is still visible, it is indicated with the notation "*Ellison,* found"—meaning that our surveyors found the name. If recent surveying could not locate an inscription recorded in Ellison's list, the notation reads "*Ellison,* nf" indicating the inscription is no longer visible or could not be found.

Cemetery information comes from field notes taken by the author and her husband. Inscriptions are alphabetical and are not listed in the text index at the back of the book.

NAME	LOCATION	DATE
A -?-urey, J. Backwards J.	s	
A—?oh, R.M.	s	**May, 1850**
A. A. (*Ellison,* nf)	mt	
A. F. (*Ellison,* found)	swt	**52**
A., R. M. The word **Ohio** is also with these initials.	s	

A, W.T.   nt   **52**
(*Ellison*, nf)

Abraham, J.   sw

Achey, N.   sw   **June, 61 (?)**

Acker, Adam   R. Pass n   **June the 12, 1852**
J.L. Stewart, Geo. Freeman, Alfred Row, and Acker are all on the same
boulder, with the same date. Freeman, Row, Stewart all listed among
arrivals at Shasta, California, in early August 1852. *Rasmussen, pg. 149.*

Adams, C.   net
(*Ellison*, nf) In 1852 Cecelia Adams was one of the individuals with this
initial and last name who traveled the trail to Oregon. She was traveling
with her family group. This group included her father, Joseph McMillan,
her husband, Dr. William Adams, and her twin sister Parthenia, along
with Parthenia's husband Stephen Blank. This family left Kanesville and
crossed the Missouri River on June 4, 1852. *Webber, pg. 9, 18.*

The McMillan–Adams family group was in a company of eight wagons, sixteen men, ten women, and children. They traveled on the north
side of the Platte River until Fort Laramie. They arrived at the Dalles
October 24, 1852. Cecelia and her sister Parthenia Blank left a joint diary
of their crossing, *The Oregon Trail Diary of Twin Sisters, Cecelia Adams
and Parthenia Blank. Platte River Narratives, pg. 336.*

Or another possibility is the inscription could be that of Christopher
Adams who was a private in Company G., the Eleventh Kansas Volunteer
Cavalry. Several of these military men left their inscriptions on
Independence Rock while stationed at Sweetwater Bridge Station, one mile
east of the Rock. *Index to Kansas Volunteer Regiment Enlistments, 1861-1863.*

Another C. A. Adams was with the Barry Union Pioneer Company of
Pike County, Illinois, headed for California in 1849. *Rasmussen, pg. 48*

Adams, D. J.   w

Adams, D. V.   sw
V and A connected. On corner between ground and top.

Adams, E. (or L.?)   nt
Seen with use of black and white technical pan film.

Could be Elias Adams, Mormon who traveled to Salt Lake Valley in
1849. *LDS Crossing the Plains Index.* This Elias Adams recorded his experiences on the trip across the plains in the private printing, *Ancestors and*

Descendants of Elias Adams, the Pioneer, edited by Frank Adams. Mintz, The Trail, pg. 9.

Or it could possibly be Ellen Thompson Adams who traveled to California with her physician husband in1863. They left Omaha May 8, 1863 traveled through Salt Lake City and arrived in California on September 5, 1863. In her diary she wrote that the soldiers at Platte Bridge, Independence Rock, Three Crossings, and elsewhere were sociable. She also wrote about visiting emigrant camps and once bringing a violin to entertain them. *Platte River Narratives, pg. 557.*

ADN PHC (initials)	nwt	**Jl, 19, 50**

Ague, A. T.	nt

Ahlan, John G.	nt	**July 4, 1859**
(*Ellison*, found)		

Aiken (r?)	se

An Aitken family was a member of a party going to Oregon in 1852. *Webber, Comprehensive Index to Oregon Trail Diaries.*

James Akin, eighteen years old, could possibly have been a member of the Aitken family traveling to Oregon in 1852. He kept a daily record of the trip from Iowa to The Dalles, in Oregon. This party traveled by ox team and seven people from this party died on the trip before they reached Oregon. One little girl of this party, five-year-old Elva Ingram, is buried in eastern Wyoming on the north side of the Platte River. *Mintz, The Trail, pg. 9.*

A Henry Aiken of Clatsop County, a Francis Aiken of Clackamas County, and a Richard Aiken of Marion County are all listed in the *Oregon Territorial Census of 1850.*

Aimine, J.	D Gate

Very difficult to read.

Aitkin, R.C.	mt	**July 2, 60**
(*Ellison*, nf)		

Akyer, J.H.	cave
(*Ellison*, nf)	

Albers	smt

With Blorrbs. Very faint. Hidden in overhang.

A Paul Albers, originally from Germany, is listed in the *1890 Census Register* of Butte County California. He was fifty-five at the time of his registration in 1884 and his occupation was a money lender. *Butte County California 1890 Great Register, pg. 2.*

Albert, W.   sw

Albert, Wm   sw
(*Ellison*, found). We believe this last name is Albett.

Albett, Wm.   s
See Ellison's Wm Albert.

Alexander, A.   mt
(*Ellison*, found). Very faint.
An Aaron Alexander was a member of a wagon train traveling to Oregon in 1852. *Webber, Comprehensive Index to Oregon Trail Diaries.*
Another possibility is Alex Alexander of Washington County who is listed in the *1850 Oregon Territorial Census.*

Alexander, B.   mt   **8, 64**

Allbers, L. K.   mt

Aller, W. M.   cave (under)

Allred, J. A.   s
Very close to Taylor, Crosby, and other probable Mormon names.
A James Allred was a member of Company B of the Mormon Battalion in 1846. When Colonel Philip St. George Cooke assumed command of the battalion in Santa Fe, he decided to send the women, children, and the sick soldiers back to the Pueblo area under Captain James Brown. James Allred was a member of this Brown Sick Detachment, arriving in Pueblo November 17, 1846. In 1847, this group made their way to Fort Laramie and followed the Brigham Young Pioneer Party into Salt Lake Valley, arriving a few days after the Pioneer Party. *Utah Crossroads Newsletter.*
Also, in 1851 a James Allred crossed the plains to the Salt Lake Valley as a member of Captain Barton Kelsey's Company. This James Allred was born in 1784 in North Carolina. He was baptized into the Mormon Church in 1832 in Missouri and served as a bodyguard to the Prophet Joseph Smith. *LDS Biographical Encyclopedia, Vol. 3, pg. 583.*
Or this could possibly be Julia Ann Allred who crossed the plains from Nauvoo to the Salt Lake Valley. *Information from a descendant, 1997.*

Allred, R. W.   s   **Sept 10, 49**
This is Reuben W. Allred of the First Hundred in Heber Kimball's Company in 1848. He then crossed again in 1849 as captain of a wagon

train. The inscription reads **R.W. Allred A. Taylor & Co.** Allred descendants in 1995 referred to this Allred as William. Martha Morgan was a member of the group under Captain Allred and left a diary covering this trip.

Reuben W. Allred was a clerk and marshal in Reddick N. Allred's Fifty, the first Fifty of this company. Rueben and Reddick were cousins. Allen Taylor was captain of the whole company. Refer to the notes under the Allen Taylor inscription for more information on this company. *Correspondence dated June 19, 2000 from Melvin Bashore, LDS Historical Department.*

Also Reuben W. Allred was a member of Company A of the 1846 Mormon Battalion. Along with James Allred he was a member of the Brown Sick Detachment sent back to Pueblo from Santa Fe in October 1846. In the spring of 1847 this group traveled north to Fort Laramie and followed the Brigham Young Pioneer Party into the Salt Lake Valley, arriving a few days after the Pioneer Party. These men were frequently sent back east to guide other Mormon parties across the plains. *Utah Crossroads Newsletter.*

Amey, John   nt   **1848**

Amey, Robt L.   nt   **1878**
This date could possibly be 1848. See the John Amey inscription on north top in 1848.

Anderson, A. L.   D Gate

Anderson, Axel   D Gate   **Aug. 91 NEB**
Fro'D inscribed by name, possibly traveled with N. A. Anderson.

Anderson, N. A.   **91 NEB**
Fro'D after name. See Axel Anderson.

Anderson, W.D.   nt   **July 4, 1861**
(*Ellison*, found.)

Andrew, C. W.   mt   **7, 20**
Two big **X X** after name.

Andrews, R. F.   mt   **June 24, 859**
The **8** inscribed above the **24**. The **J** in June is backward.

Ankrim, W.J.   nt   **1852**
(*Ellison*, nf) A W. J. Ankrim was a traveler going to California in 1849.

He was captain of a large wagon train from Pennsylvania. It was the largest to set out in 1849 but it soon divided into smaller groups. *Bernard Reid diary, pg. 188.* Since many gold seekers later returned home, he could possibly have gone across the trail again in 1852 going back east.

Another possibility is William J. Ankrim who was captain of the Pittsburgh and California Enterprise Company going to California from St. Joseph in 1849. *Rasmussen, pg. 17.*

Antee, D.   nt   **June 18, 1860**
Possibly with G. Holson, J. W. Ellis.

Apasrott   s
Name almost gone.

Arick, R.E.   nt   **9, 52**
(*Ellison*, found) Possibly with C. H. Fish.

Arnsrong, T. H.   mt   **July 12, 1852**
(*Ellison*, found) Ellison recorded this as Arnsrong, but we believe it is T.H. Armstrong. The T and R are linked together in the name Armstrong.

Armstrong, E.T.   nmt
(*Ellison*, found)

Armstrong, J.   s   **J 29, 60**
This could be the same as Ellison's J Armstrong however Ellison had no month and day. A J. Armstrong, 1859, from Macomb, Ill inscription at Register Cliff. *Scottsbluff Survey List.*

Armstrong, J.   s   **60**
(*Ellison*, maybe found.) See above.

Armstrong, T. H.   mt   **July 12, 1852**
This is a second inscription. The **T** and **R** are not linked in this one.

D. W. Greenburg who did a survey of Independence Rock on August 22, 1926 had T. H. Armstrong and J. M. Davis as probably together. Their inscriptions are close together and they were there on the same date. *Ellison Files, WY State Archives.*

Armstrong, T.H.   mt   **July 12, 1852**
(*Ellison*, found) Ellison has Armsrong. T and R linked in name. Inscription in two places.

Arner, T.L   swt
(*Ellison*, nf)

Arthur, R. C.   mt   Jy 2, 1860
Box around name.

Aryle ??   s

Ash, F.D.   w   53
(*Ellison*, found)

Asherburke, M.   mt   59
(*Ellison*, found)

Asn—pam—, U.H.   s

Asue, A. T.   n
Tails on letters. Believe name all there.

Attix (Attia?), C. S.   mt

Attron, J. C.   sw   J—, 59
Ellison has Cattron but J C together and then a space before Attron.

Atwood   e
A M. E. Atwood, 1865 inscription found at Register Cliff. *Scottsbluff Survey List.*
   Or this could be Samuel Frink Atwood born in Connecticut in 1825. He traveled to Utah along with his father's family in 1850. They were in Wilford Woodruff's Company. In 1857 he traveled back to Deer Creek on the Platte River in Wyoming in connection with the YX Company. *LDS Biographical Encyclopedia, Vol. III, pg. 301.*
   Or this could be J. F. Atwood of Washington County who is listed in the *1850 Oregon Territorial Census.*

Aubry, E. A.   cave   58
(*Ellison*, found)

Aud—?, P.   w

Auer (?)—, D. L.   R. Pass s
Behind tree, on boulder. Very faint.

Austin, C.   mt
(*Ellison*, nf)

Austin, R. C.   (unknown)   **July 7, 1860**
This inscription was recorded by D. W. Greenburg on August 22, 1926.
He did not record locations. *Ellison Files, WY State Archives.* We have
not found this inscription in recent surveying.

Autesen, F G (or C)   nw   **1882**

Ayer, E.   mt
(*Ellison*, found) Could be Edward Everett Ayer who went to California
in 1860. He left Council Bluffs April 30 and arrived in San Francisco on
October 1. He left a diary which describes him putting his name on
Independence Rock "with a coal chisel." *Platte River Narratives, pg. 519.*

Ayer, Milo J.   net   **1849 Mass.**
(*Ellison*, found) Milo Ayer was a member of the Boston & Newton
Joint Stock Association. This party left Boston April 16, 1849, and
arrived in California in September 1849. *Rasmussen, pg 204.* The diary
The Boston Newton Company Venture, by Jesse Gould Hannon, describes
the trip of this group. Although Milo Ayer left a very distinctive inscription on Independence Rock, Hannon writes just a couple of sentences
about camping near Independence Rock in his diary.
    Milo J. Ayer was born in Vermont and was twenty nine when he left
for California. He was a strict temperance man and refrained from
smoking, drinking, gambling, and swearing. He was skilled as a carpenter and millwright. He left his wife, Phoebe, and a son and daughter at home when he traveled to the gold fields. *Hannon, pg. 37.* After
their arrival in California, the Boston Newton Company wound up
mining in the Mokelumne Hill area and the mining venture paid off
for Ayer. In 1850, he bought mining property in the Downieville area
and developed several mines on this property. His wife and children
joined him in California in 1851. In 1866 the family moved to Vallejo
and Milo is credited with building the first stamp mill in the California
gold fields. He died in California in 1900. *Hannon, pg. 208.*

B—?, L.   sw

B—???, J.   net

B—n ?, L. C.   n

B., E.   s   **47 (maybe July)**
    In tar.

B., E. J. nt

B., E. P. nt

B., H. w

B., J. mt Aug. 11, 58
(*Ellison*, found.) Written **Mrs. J. B.** also **C C & L.**

B., J. ne
Together with M. B. and Jim. On ground.

B., J. S. sw corner

B., J .M. mt
(*Ellison*, found)

B., M. ne
Together with J. B. and Jim. On ground.

B., W.T. net 59
(*Ellison*, found) Boxed with J. W. G.

Ba—p-?, Ch. H. D Gate June 26
Very weathered.

Ba—m?, T. e

Babcock, S. D. sw 18??
On corner halfway up.

Babcox, O. R. Pass n June 2 (?), 1852
M. Neal, A.B.P. Wood, Babcox, and J.D. Barnard all together. Could possibly be Babcok with the **k** tilted.

Bace, C. H. mt July, 16, 52
(*Ellison*, nf)

Bacon, Jas. E. e 7-19-47
Possibly not a nineteenth century inscription, but the Jas. seems to be a nineteenth century contraction.

Bailey, A. W. s June 24, 1851
(*Ellison*, found)

Bailey, A. W.   s

Two A. W. Bailey inscriptions. No date on this one. An A. W. Bailey of
Marion Co, Missouri was in the McPike & Strother 1850 wagon train
on the way to California No way of knowing if this is the same. He
could possibly have crossed in 1850 and gone back east in 1851.
Rasmussen, pg. 112

Bailey, M.   mt   **1853**
(*Ellison.* found)

Bak (er?), G.   R. Pass n   —y 6,—8-?

Baker, A. G.   se   **June 4, 1850**
Close to ground. Digital photo shows a name under this inscription,
but difficult to read.

Baker, G.   w   **— 22**
K and e connected in name. G. Baker believed also at Devil's Gate.

Could be George Holbrook Baker who crossed in 1853. "*Crossing the
Plains, Views Drawn from Nature in 1853,*" diary, Mattes Library.

Or a George Baker was a private in Company C of the Eleventh
Kansas Volunteer Cavalry. Several of these military men left their names
on Independence Rock while stationed at Sweetwater Bridge Station in
the 1860s. *Index to Kansas Volunteer Regimens Enlistments, 1861-1863.*

A George McNamee Baker and wife, Rebecca, were among those
arriving in Oregon in 1847. They were in a party called the Osklaoosa
Company. Captain Wylie Chapman led this party of approximately
forty members. *Flora, Emigrants in 1847.*

Or a George H. Baker who traveled from New York to California in
1849. *Records of a California Journey.*

Yet another George Baker was a member of the Prairie Rover
Company arriving at Kanesville May 29, 1850 en route to California.
Rasmussen, p 122.

Or a George M. Baker of Marion County is listed in the *1850
Oregon Territorial Census.* He lived there with his wife and children. *US
Gen Web Archives.*

Baker, T. P   D Gate   **1864**

Baker, T. P   R. Pass s

This inscription is on a large rock by the trail side which for years was
thought to mark the grave of T. P. Baker. Research by Randy Brown of

Wyoming shows the grave to be that of Martin Fulkerson who died while crossing in 1847 bound for Oregon. Baker came later and put his name on the rock used as a headstone for Martin Fulkerson. There is another T. P. Baker inscription with a date of 1864.

Balantyne, A. net **52**
(*Ellison*, found)

Balcomb, A. mt **July 4, 62 Minn.**
(*Ellison*, found)

Ball, C. H. mt
Two C. H. Ball inscriptions within six feet of each other. This one alone, and if a date, unreadable.

Ball, C. H. mt **Je 16, 52**
Boxed in with P. Miller, B. F. Norton, S. C. Caery, G. Lemon.
A Charles Ball, originally from New York, is listed in the *Butte County California 1890 Census*. He was sixty-five at the time of his registering in April 1884 and his occupation was a watchmaker. *Butte County, California, 1890 Great Register, p. 10.*

Ban -?s, (S)? or B R. Pass n
Very weathered. Maybe Banks.

Banberry, M. s boulder

Barb, J. C. unknown
This name is included in a June 5, 1927 survey done by an unidentified person. No locations are given in this list. Although this list is found in the R. S. Ellison files, the name is not included in his book. *Ellison Files, WY State Archives.* This name has not shown up in our recent surveying.

Barclay, W. R. nt **June 22, 59**
(*Ellison*, found)

Bark—?, G w

Barker, B. M. D Gate **July 19, 54**

Barnard, Halow mt

Barnard, J. D.   R. Pass n   **June 2 -(?), 1852**
M. Neal, A.B.P. Wood, O. Babcox, and Barnard are all together.

Barnard, J. E.   unknown   **June 30, 1850**
This name is included in a list compiled by D. W. Greenburg on August 22, 1926. Locations were not recorded. *Ellison Files, WY State Archives.* We have not found the name in recent surveying.

Barnard, J. G.   mt   **June 19, 50**
(*Ellison*, found) Maybe in a Pekin, Illinois party.
A John Granville Barnard, from Indiana, is listed in the *1890 California Census.* His occupation was as a teamster.

Barnard, J. S.   mt
(*Ellison*, found) A J. Barnard is listed as one of the emigrants who arrived in Placerville the first week of September 1852. *Rasmussen, p. 164*

Barnes, Harlin   mt

Barnes, Harlow   mt   **Jul 3 1850**
Probably with J. Rigg.

Barnes, R.   mt   **59**
(*Ellison*, found)

Barnes ??   s

Barney, Harlow   mt   **July 3, 1850**
(*Ellison*, found?) This is probably what we saw as Harlow Barnes.

Barnhart, Wm.   nmt   **69, 74, 77, 82, 84, 87, 89**
By the dates left by this man, he visited Independence Rock more than anyone else still visible on the Rock.

Barry, J. A.   s
(*Ellison*, nf) An unidentified person who did a survey of names on June 5, 1927 has J. A. Barry together with V. A. Vincent, and J. Capper all on May 20, 1850. The handwritten notes are in the Ellison files. *Ellison Files, WY State Archives*
A John Barry is listed among the emigrant arrivals in Oregon in 1850. *The Oregonian, Dec. 4, 1925.*

Bary—r?, S. M.   s

Basbett, E. J.   s   Ju 28, 1848

Bason (?), L. H.   s
Backwards s.

Bassett, C. J.   s   1849
(*Ellison,* found)

Bassett, G. C.   s   49
(*Ellison,* nf)

Bauer, T.   nwt   June

Baughan, W. (?)   st

Baughman, J. H.   mt   July 4, 1850
(*Ellison,* found) A Mormon descendant in 1995 pronounced this "Bockman."
     A Jacob H. Baughman is listed among those emigrants arriving in Oregon in 1850. *The Oregonian, Dec. 4, 1925.*

Be—?, J. A.   D Gate

Beam, G. W.   net   July 4, 18 ?.
Large, stands out with lichen surrounding the letters—this is called negative relief.
     This is George Beam, who was a cousin of Winfield Scott Ebey, crossing the plains in 1854. He was twenty-two at the time and was from Adair County Missouri going to Washington Territory. Refer to the Ebey entry.
     George W. Beam settled in Island County, Washington Territory for he is listed in that county's 1860 census. This would be Whidbey Island. He lived there with his wife, Elmira and son Arthur. He listed his occupation as a farmer. *US Gen Web Archives.*

Beane, P. A.   s   June 4, 49
(*Ellison,* found)

Beard, S. P.   mt   June 18, 52
(*Ellison,* found) In box with C. F. Wilson.

Beardsley, Earl A.   s
(*Ellison,* found)

Beautty ?, John   s
Very weathered. A William Beatty is listed among those in the emigration to Oregon in 1850. Since this name is a little unusual, there could be a connection to someone of the same family. *The Oregonian, Dec. 4, 1925*

Bebe, A.W.   s

Beck, A. T.   mt
(*Ellison*, found) A Beck family crossed the plains to the Salt Lake Valley in 1850. *LDS Biographical Encyclopedia, Vol. II, p 594.*

Beck, John   mt   July 4, 62
(*Ellison*, found) We saw **Iowa**.

Beck, S.   net
(*Ellison*, found) An S. Beck is listed among the arrivals at Placerville, California in September 1852. *Rasmussen, p. 167.*

Beebe, A. W.   s   June 24, 51
(*Ellison*, found) Date had weathered off by 1996.
An unidentified Beebe family is listed as leaving Arkansas with the Brewer family bound for Oregon in 1851. *Linn County Oregon Records.*

Beels, W. J.   mt
(*Ellison*, nf)

Beers, W. J.   mt
(*Ellison*, found) We saw the date J 6 in 1995.

Belieu, ? J.   w   62
(*Ellison*, nf) A Belieu traveled to Oregon in 1850. Since this is an unusual name, it is possible this Belieu could be related to the earlier Belieu's. *The Oregonian, Dec. 4, 1925.*

Bell, George W.   s   June 6, 50
(*Ellison*, found) The inscription is **Geo. W. Bell**. A G. W. Bell, from Pennsylvania is listed as one of the emigrants who arrived in Placerville the first week of September 1850. *Rasmussen, pg. 98.*

Bell, R.   st
A Robert Bell is listed in a small party arriving in Kanesville, May 4, 1852, departing for California on May 18. *Rasmussen, p. 138.*

Belmap, J. H. nt 55
(*Ellison*, nf)

Bemiss, H. P. nmt July 4, 1850
(*Ellison*, found) This is probably Hallet Porter Bemiss of Sandusky, Erie County, Ohio. *Brown, Emigrant Inscriptions.*

Benecke, F. nt

Bennett, H. K. net
(*Ellison*, found)

Benson, H. nt Jul 2 61 ILLS
(*Ellison*, found) Backwards J in Jul. ILLS (Illinois) seen in 1995.

Benson, Tom mt June 18, 1861 Bel, ILL
(*Ellison*, found)

Berry, P. C. (unknown)
This name was in a handwritten list of names recorded June 5, 1927 by an unspecified person. We have not found it in our recent surveying. *Ellison Files, WY State Archives.*

Bert, H or A ?? R. Pass n
In tar.

Berth, R. O. n 74
Lisa inscribed above this.

Berwick, J. R. st June 26, 61

Beswick, J. W. et June 25, '64

Beswin, J. M. s July 4, 56

Bid, J. net 87

Bidsworth, J. nmt 57
(*Ellison*, found)

Bigelow, T. sw
(*Ellison*, found)

Bingham, G. s 46
(*Ellison*, found)

Bingley, N.   s

Binning, R. L.   s   **33**
The **33** is in area of worn tar names. Old style **3**'s, but possibly twentieth century.

Birch   e corner

Birden, D.   D Gate

Bishop, B.   n   maybe **JY 60???**
A Bishop (no initial, no date) recorded at Emigrant Springs, WY. *BLM 1989 Survey of Emigrant Springs.*

Bishop, C. W.   s   **June 29, 51**
Midway up. A C. W. Bishop, Mormon, traveled from England to the Great Salt Lake Valley. *Information from Mormon descendant in 1997.*

Bishop, G. W.   s   **June 20, 56**
(*Ellison*, found)

Bishop, N. B.   net   **61**
A Noah Daniel Bishop, from Ohio, is listed in the *1890 California Great Register.* His age at the time of registration in 1887 was fifty-seven and his occupation was a blacksmith. *Butte County, California, 1890 Great Register, p. 20.*

Bishop, U   sw   **1850**
(*Ellison*, nf)

Bishop, W. B.   net   **64**
A William Brammell Bishop is listed in the *1890 California Great Register.* He was originally from New Hampshire and was forty-three at the time of registration in 1884. His occupation was a carpenter. *Butte County California 1890 Great Register, p. 20.*

Black   cave
Scratched in. Most cave names are tar or paint.

Black, R.   ne
Very faint.

Blair, W.   w   **July 20**
Blair can only be seen under certain light. A J. W. Blair, 1864 inscription can be found at Register Cliff. *Scottsbluff Survey List.*

A William Blair is listed among the emigrant arrivals in Oregon in 1847. He was a member of a party led by Captain Jordan Sawyer. There were thirty-five men in the party accompanied by their wives and children. They crossed the Cascade Mountains via the Barlow Road and arrived at Foster's October 1, 1847. *Flora, Emigrants in 1847.*

Blaylock, M. A.   s

Blondingen, James   mt
(*Ellison*, nf)

Blorbbs R. O.   smt
Could maybe be (Bloress?), Very faint. Hidden in overhang. Negative relief.

Bo, J.   D Gate

Bo, W.   D Gate

Bo—?, R. W.   s boulder

Bogan, J.   s
(*Ellison*, found)

Bon (l-g?) s   nw
Very large letters.

Bon -?-c?, L.   n   **66**

Bond, E.   e
(*Ellison*, found)

Bond, J.   nt
(*Ellison*, found) In 1852, a Jesse W. Bond crossed the plains going to Salt Lake City. He left Council Bluffs May 22 and arrived at Salt Lake Valley July 4. He left a letter describing this trip. *Platte River Narratives, pg 341.*

Another possibility is Jesse Bond from England who was one of the first settlers of Heber, Utah. Born in Gloucestershire in 1832, he emigrated to America, sailing from England in November 1854. He arrived at New Orleans on January 1855 and traveled up to Iowa. He then crossed the plains in Isaac Allred's Company leaving Mormon Grove, Kansas July 28, 1855 and arrived in Salt Lake City in November 1855. *LDS Biographical Encyclopedia, Vol. III, p. 25.*

Bond, L.   s

Boney, H. F.   w

Bonner, S. T.   mt   **1852 xx**
(*Ellison*, found)

Booce ?, A.   w
Near graves. Almost gone.

Boomer, J. B.   D Gate   **July 4, 59**
J. P. Robinson nearby and on same date.

Booth, L.   n   **1864**
(*Ellison*, nf)

Bor???, J.   mt

Borbaux   s   **1850**

Both, F. R.   net

Bowden, G. W.   mt
G. W. Bowden inscription also on nmt.

Bowden, G. W.   nmt   **June 24, 75 ?**
(*Ellison*, found) G. W. Bowden also on mt.

Bowder, Jo   mt

Bowder (Po D?),Jon   nmt   **52**
Together with J. L. Flack.

Bowen, H. H.   mt   **June 24**
(*Ellison*, found)

Bowen, L.   n   **60**
Behind fence.

Bower, J.   cave   **July 11, 1847**
(*Ellison*, found) Blue paint. Very large letters. Wrote **July 11, A. D.,
1847**
     A John Bower, from West Virginia, is buried in the cemetery at
Chico, California. He died in Marysville, California in 1899.

Bower, J. mt **June, 1862 Troy, Ohio**
A J. Bower also in cave, 1847. We believe this 1862 Bower is with Lieutenant J. A. Brown of the Eleventh Ohio Volunteer Cavalry.

Bower, Saml sw

Bower, Samuel s
(*Ellison*, found) We read **Samel**, rather than Samuel.

Bowles, J. M. swt **July 7, 52**
(*Ellison*, found)

Bowman, J. W. mt **July 4, 62**
Maybe with S.E. Ellis, S.C. Ellis, T.T. Ellis and Macsttotts. In 1862, a John Bowman and family crossed the plains going to Salt Lake. However they did not arrive in the Salt Lake Valley until October 19, so this is probably not his inscription. *LDS Crossing the Plains Index.*

Boyden, G. W. mt

Boyer, K. unknown
Probably middle top. Maybe June 11, 1852. This name is found on a list compiled by D. W. Greenburg on August 22, 1926. He did not record locations but he has it with Staley's who are on the middle top. He also believed this Boyer was with a party from Richmond, Indiana. *Ellison Files, WY State Archives.* We have not found the name in recent surveying.

Boyer, M. mt
(*Ellison*, found)

Boyer(Dyer?),V or W. w **Jly 29, 55**
In tar, with another name. Seen best on color slide. A Washington Boyer, from Illinois, is listed in the *1890 California Census.* He was forty four at the time of his registration in 1884. His occupation is listed as a stage driver. *Butte County, California, 1890 Great Register, p. 25.*

Br-gull ?, W. D. D Gate **18—1**

Bradbury, J.M. nt **June 19, 54**
Perry, Illinois.
(*Ellison*, found) W. O. McFarland, M. W. Fletcher, J. Coon, and this J. M. Bradbury all together. Same date, same town. Refer to J. Coon notes for possible destination in California.

An M. Bradbury, no date recorded, can be found at Emigrant Springs, WY. *Kelly 1930 Survey of Emigrant Springs*

Bradway, C. B.   nt   **18?0**

Breaux   se

Brian, J. B.   unknown   **May 9, '50 ILL's**
This name was included in a survey list done June 5, 1927. Locations were not recorded. Although this list is found in the R. S. Ellison files, this name is not in his book. Whoever did the surveying believed J. B. Brian was traveling with D. B. Gillam and A. L. White. *Ellison Files, WY State Archives*. We have not found this name in our recent surveying.

Brines, H.   mt
(*Ellison*, found)

Bris,   s   **1857**
Very weathered.

Brisbee   cave
A John Brisby, born in 1822, is listed among the arrivals in Oregon in 1847. *Flora, Emigrants in 1847.*

Bristol, F.   s   **May 9, 50 ILL.**
(*Ellison*, found) Could be **Brisual** as we read it.

Brnbway, Janie & L E   nt   **1900**

Brook   w   **July (?) 3**
It is possible that there may be an **s** on the end which is not visible. A John P. Brooks traveled to the Willamette Falls area in Oregon in 1843. He became one of the first public school teachers. *Reflections of Oregon Pioneer Families.*

Brooks, J. J.   net   **66**
(*Ellison*, found) Halfway up.

Brooks, M. S   w
Initials **RO** and **MS** before Brooks.

Brooks, R.O.   w
Initials **RO** and **MS** before Brooks.

Brown, A. J.   nw

An Alexander Brown is mentioned in a Donation Land Claim Record in early Oregon. He was born in Pennsylvania and married his wife in Missouri. *Oregon Donation Land Claims Records.*

Brown, A. T.   wmt

(*Ellison,* found) An Alexander Brown, of Company C, Mormon Battalion, was a member of the Brown Sick Detachment. Colonel Philip St. George Cooke sent the women, children, and sick soldiers from Santa Fe back to Pueblo in late October 1846. Captain Brown led this Brown Sick Detachment. In the spring of 1847, this group traveled up to the Platte River and followed the Brigham Young Pioneer Party into the Salt Lake Valley. They arrived a few days after the Pioneer Party. *Utah Crossroads Newsletter.*

Brown, H.   s

(*Ellison,* found) We saw **L. H. Brown** in 1996.

A Henry Brown and wife Malinda are listed among the emigrant arrivals in Oregon in 1847. *Flora, Emigrants in 1847.*

Brown, I. H.   s

With L. H. Brown and D. Richardson, M.D. Probably in P. G. Sessions' 1847 party. This party came after the Brigham Young Pioneer Party and arrived in Salt Lake on September 24. *LDS Crossing the Plains Index.* In the list of company members given in Patty Sessions' diary of this company's crossing a Brown and Sister Brown are listed.

An I. Brown inscription can be found at Register Cliff. *Scottsbluff Survey List.*

Brown, J. A.   mt   **June, 1862 Troy, Ohio**

(*Ellison,* found) This is probably Lieutenant James A. Brown, member of the Eleventh Ohio Volunteer Cavalry. See Lieut. Brown entry.

Brown, Lieut.   met   **Troy, Ohio**

(*Ellison,* found) Probably the same as J. A. Brown, mt. This is Lieutenant James A. Brown, Company G., of the Eleventh Ohio Volunteer Cavalry. Lt. Brown was twenty-two when he enlisted in Ohio on October 22, 1861. He mustered out July 14, 1865. *Roster of Ohio Soldiers, Vol. XI.* Some of the soldiers stationed at the Sweetwater Bridge Station put their names on the Rock more than once.

Brown, S.   nmt   **Sept. 11, 52**

(*Ellison,* found) There is a T. Brown on same date.

In 1852 two different Samuel Browns made the trip to the Salt Lake Valley. One Samuel Brown crossed in the Twenty-first Company under Captain Allen Weeks. *LDS Crossing the Plains Index.*

A Samuel Brown, born in Cincinnati, Ohio in 1832 migrated to Utah in 1852. It could be the same Samuel Brown as above. This Samuel Brown was killed by Indians in 1858 on a road leading from Salt Lake City to California. *LDS Biographical Encyclopedia, Vol. II, pg. 598.*

Also a seven-year-old Samuel Brown crossed with his family going to Salt Lake in 1852. They came from Liverpool England, and crossed in the A. O. Smoot's Company. It's doubtful a seven year old would leave an inscription however. *LDS Crossing the Plains Index.*

Brown, T.　　　　　　nmt　　　　　　**Sept. 11, 52**

(*Ellison,* found) There is an S. Brown on same date.

In 1852, two different T. Browns made the trip to Salt Lake. One was in the Fifteenth Company under Captain Robert Weimer and the other was in the Fourth Company under Captain Joseph Outhouse. *LDS Crossing the Plains Index.*

Brown, W. D.　　　　　　se

A W. Brown from Illinois is listed as having taken the Lander Cutoff on the way to Oregon in 1859. Four wagons and eight people were in the party. *House of Rep. Exec. Document #63, 1859.*

Note: Ellison also has a WD Brown inscription in the cave.

Or this could be Private William Brown who was a member of Company H, Eleventh Kansas Volunteer Cavalry. Several of these military men left their names on Independence Rock while stationed at Sweetwater Bridge Station in the 1860s. Company H was the same company of Sergeant Amos Custard whose supply train party was wiped out by Indians close to Platte Bridge Station

William Brown, early day Mormon whose inscription could be on the Rock. (L.D.S. Family History Center, Casper.)

in 1865. *Index to Kansas Volunteer Regiment Enlistments, 1861-1863*

Or a William Brown crossed to the Salt Lake Valley in 1847, crossing the plains in Ira Eldredge's Company of Fifty, arriving in Salt Lake City September 22, 1847. *LDS Biographical Encyclopedia, Vol. I. p. 467.*

Brown, W. D.   cave

(*Ellison*, found) It is just outside the cave. In a survey done June 5, 1927 by an unidentified person the date 1861 was recorded as being with one of these W. D. Brown inscriptions. *Ellison Files, WY State Archives.* We've not found any evidence of a date. No locations were given in the 1927 survey.

Bruce, C.   s

(*Ellison*, nf)

Brumbaugh, J.   mt

(*Ellison*, nf)

Brumbaugh, Sarah   nmt   **66**

(*Ellison*, found)

Bryan, S.   w

An S. W. Bryan is listed among those from Kalamazoo, Michigan arriving in Kanesville, Iowa by May 16, 1849. *Rasmussen, p. 59.*

Bryn, ?   s   **June 16**

Buck, C. D.   s

A Costello D. Buck was a member of the Badger Company wagon train leaving Kanesville, May 29, 1849 going to California. *Rasmussen, p. 67.* A C. D. Buck inscription can also be found at Names Hill, WY. *Brown, Emigrant Inscriptions.*

Buell, O.E.   s   **July 10, 1857**

(*Ellison*, found) We didn't see the **O**. We believe the date is really **47** with the four printed backwards instead of **57**. Research done after the surveying supports the date of 1847.

An Elias Buell started from Iowa in May 1846 and went as far as Holt County, Missouri, too late to go on to Oregon in that year. He started again in May 1847, and reached Fort Vancouver in November of 1847. The town of Buell, Oregon, west of Salem, was named after him. *Reflections of Oregon's Pioneer Families.*

He was born in 1797 and died in 1871. He made the trip with his wife Sarah. In 1847, they stopped briefly at the Whitman Mission and then learned of the massacre at the mission when they reached The Dalles. On his arrival in Oregon Elias set up a mill. *Flora, Emigrants in 1847.*

An Elias Buell is listed as living in Polk County in the *1850 Oregon Territorial Census.*

Bugue (Buque??)   cave

Bunce, L. D.   nm   **June 9, 1851** (or 54?)

Burch   s   **May 11**
A James Burch migrated to the Great Salt Lake Valley in 1848 and was
one of the early pioneers of Weber County. *LDS Biographical
Encyclopedia, Vol. II, p. 242.*
A large number of members of a Burch family are listed among the
emigrant arrivals in Oregon in 1847. *Flora, Emigrants in 1847.*
A Charles Burch is listed among those arrivals in Oregon in 1851.
Oregon in 1851.

Burchoman, P.   s

Burgert, S.   net   **52**
(*Ellison*, found)

Burget, C.   nt   **59**
(*Ellison*, found) Two Burgets together. A C. Burget from Indiana is list-
ed as having traveled on the Lander Cutoff en route to Oregon in 1859.
There was one wagon and three people in the party. *House of Rep. Exec.
Document #63, 1859.*

Burget, W.   nt   **59**
(*Ellison*, found) We read **1859**. A W. Burget crossed on the Lander
Cutoff en route to Oregon in 1859. *House of Rep Exec. Document #63,
1859.*

Burn, H.   net

Burnell, F. E.   ne   **ILL**
Close to fence.

Burnett, E.   mt   **June 28, 1859**
(*Ellison*, found)

Burnett, L.C.   sw   **67**
(*Ellison*, nf)

Burnham, R.M.   mt   **July, 59**
(*Ellison*, found)

Burpee, L.P   s   **62**
(*Ellison*, nf)

Burr, A.   s

An Andrew Burr from Illinois arrived in Placerville in early August 1851. *Rasmussen, p. 133.*

Burrows, W.   mt   **Sept. 12, 52**

(*Ellison*, found)

Burt, A. H. (?)   s

Very large, very worn.

Burt, H.   net

(*Ellison*, nf)

Bush   D Gate   **July 4, 1881**

U. S. Survey inscribed by name.

Bush, J.J.   nmt

Butterfield, Wm   R. Pass w   **July**

Several members of a Butterfield family from Nauvoo and then Council Bluffs crossed the plains to the Great Salt Lake Valley before 1850. This William could be a member of that family. *LDS Biographical Encyclopedia, Vol. I, p. 582.*

Buttery, A.   D Gate

C & W   nt   **59**

C—?, B. P.   s

Rest of last name gone.

C—?, H. T.   R. Pass s   **J**

In tar. Last name gone.

C—???, A. L.   st

C., B.   w

C., C.   wt   **Jun 8, 63**

Three sets of initials—**C.C.**, **T.W.** and **M.S.**—are all together.

C., D. Y.   mt

Large inscription.

C, E. H.   sw

C., G.   w

C., G.   w
Ellison has these letters as part of the Cudihy inscription. We think it is a separate initial inscription.

C., H. W.   wt   **8 25**
Old style 25. Tailed letters.

C., H. G.   set   **74**
(*Ellison*, nf)

C., J. I.   mt
(*Ellison*, nf)

C., R. E.   net
Written above Correl.

C., S.   swt
(*Ellison*, nf)

Ca—?, J. H.   st

Ca—??, H. M.   net
Very difficult to read.

Cabry, S. C.   mt
In a survey done by D. W. Greenburg on August 22, 1926, he believed S. C. Cabry, C. H. Ball, B. F. Norton, and P. Miller might be traveling together with a common date of June 16, 1852. *Ellison Files, WY State Archives.* Ellison has these people traveling with S. C. Caery. We found S. C. Cabry and S. C. Caery inscriptions.

Cady, S. M.   s
This name is inscribed on top of and covering that of G. W. Gibson. A Samuel Cady left Union, Wisconsin on March 11, 1850 and arrived at St. Joseph May 1, 1850. From there he joined a wagon train going to California. He was with an outfit of five ox teams. In later years he recorded his recollections of the trip across. *Mattes, p. 240*

Caery, S. C.   mt   **Je 16, /52**
Boxed in with P. Miller, C.H. Ball, B.F. Norton, G. Lemon. See other S. C. Carey on middle top. Not boxed with others and spelled differently, but same date.

Cahlan, John   nt   **July, 1859 Sullivan Co. NY.**
Could possibly be 1889? Upside down U in Sullivan.

Caliston, J (?)   mt
A Callison family first came from Scotland to America, living in
Virginia, Kentucky, and Illinois before crossing the plains to Oregon in
1852. John Callison left a diary of this trip prior to dying of cholera on
August 23, 1852. The family continued on to the Willamette Valley.
Mintz, The Trail, pg. 26.

Callett   w
Lovely script writing.

Cameron, E.   w   **NY**
With Loomis.

Campbell, B. J.   w
(*Ellison*, nf)

Campbell, C.   s   **June 50 Wis**
(*Ellison*, found) Ellison has Wed. It reads Wis. not Wed. G. Campbell
has the same date and is in the same area.

Campbell, d.   cave   **Juen**
This is the spelling of the inscription of the month. A David Campbell
is buried in the cemetery at Chico, California. He was born in Pennsylvania on July 9, 1820. He died December 10, 1896. He is buried
beside his wife, Mattie, who was a native of New Hampshire. She died
in 1895. Cemetery records lists the next of kin as Dawson Campbell.
   Of further note: a David Campbell, from Pennsylvania, is listed in
the *1890 California Census*. He was sixty-three at the time of his registration in April 1884, and he listed his occupation as a teamster. *Butte
County, California, 1890 Great Register, p. 37.*
   D. Campbell, age thirty-two, is listed in the *Island County, Washington Territory, 1860 Census*. He listed his occupation as a laborer. *US Gen
Web Archives.*

Campbell, G.   s   **June 3, 50 Wis**
C. Campbell has the same date and is in the same locale.

Campbell, J. A.   nt   **31**
With J. C. Campbell, 1831.

Campbell, J. C.   nt   **1831**
Lichen over name. Sometimes very difficult to find. See J. A. Campbell.

Campbell, M.   st
In tar. A Martin Campbell is buried in the cemetery at Chico,
California. He died June 17, 1887 at age seventy-eight.

Campbell, M (MC)   st
Same script as Coates. This could be Miss M. C. Campbell of Polk
County, Missouri listed in the El Dorado News, August 28, 1852 as
having died while making the trip. *Rasmussen, p. 156.*

Cannon   n
Behind fence. Several members of a Mormon Cannon family crossed the
plains from Nauvoo to the Salt Lake Valley. No initials, no date on this
one, so not much to go on. *LDS Biographical Encyclopedia, Vol. I, pg. 167.*
Sylvester Cannon, born in 1833, is listed as one of those who arrived
in Oregon in 1851. *Oregon in 1851.*

Cannon, W.   sw   **1858**
Corner between ground and top. A second inscription on west side. In
a survey done June 5, 1927 by an unidentified person, the middle ini-
tial L. was recorded. We did not see this initial. *Ellison Files, WY State
Archives.*
A William Dalby Cannon, from New York, is listed in the *1890
California Census.* He was sixty at the time of his registration in 1884.
His occupation was a painter and his place of residence was Ophir.
Butte County, California, 1890 Great Register, p. 39.

Cannon, W.   w   **58**
A second W. Cannon inscription, same year, is on the southwest.

Canovosee, J.   nt
Very difficult to read. Shows up in photos. Maybe 1860.

Cappen, J.   s   **May 29, 1850**
This is what we believe Ellison recorded as Capper.

Capper, J   s   **May 29, 1850**
(*Ellison,* found) We believe this reads Cappen, not Capper, however,
this name shows up in a survey list done June 5, 1927 by an unidenti-
fied person. This list shows a date of May 20, 1850 and shows J. A.
Barry, V. A. Vincent, and J. Capper as probably traveling together.
Ellison Files, WY State Archives.

Carey, C. mt **Ju 23, 66**
Right beside J. Carey. Oxbow **and** connects names.

Carey, J. mt
Right beside C. Carey. Oxbow **and** connects names—a Joseph Doan Carey, from Indiana, is listed in the *1890 California Census*. He was fifty-one at the time when he registered in 1888 and he listed his occupation as a miner. His residence was Lovelocks. *Butte County, California, 1890 Great Register, p. 39*

Carey, S.C mt **J E 16, 52**
(*Ellison*, found)

Carey, J. & C. nt
A second inscription for C. Carey is on mt with a date. See C. Carey.

Carick, W. R. mt **July 9, 18—**

Carlock, W.T. mt **June 21, 1853**
(*Ellison*, found) We see **1859**. The **o** in the name is above the name between **l** and **c**.

Carlon, J. R. D Gate **July, 59**

Carr, D. s **Jul, 51**
(*Ellison*, found)

Carr, S. s **59**
(*Ellison*, found) A Seymour Carr party from Iowa used the Lander Cutoff en route to California in 1859. There was one wagon and three people in the party. *House of Rep. Exec. Document #63, 1859*
   Or this could be Samuel Milton Carr, from New York, who is listed in the *1890 California Census*. His place of residence was Chico and he was forty-seven at the time of his registration for the census in 1884. His occupation was listed as a driver. *Butte County, California, 1890 Great Register, p. 40.*

Carr, S.B. s
(*Ellison*, found)

Carrlson, W. mt **59**
(*Ellison*, found)

Cart, J. mt

Carter   cave

Carter, J. S.   nt

A Johnson Carter living in Benton County and a Joseph Carter of Washington County are listed in the *1850 Oregon Territorial Census.*

A Joseph and Laura Ann Carter crossed to Oregon in 1854. They were married in 1846 and they made the trip with three children, ages six, four, and two. Flora, *Oregon in 1854*

A James Carter is buried in the cemetery at Chico, California. He died March 13, 1894 at age sixty-four. His son is buried beside him.

A J. S. Carter went to California from Missouri. *Information from descendant, 1999.*

Yet another possibility is Jonas Carter, born in 1832 in Ohio, who is buried in the Chico, California Cemetery. He died March 13, 1894.

Casad, J.   swt   **July 20X, 49**
(*Ellison*, found) There is an **X** after 20.

Castle, May   mt

Catherington, W.   nt   **July, 4, 1859**
                                         Coles Co. Illinois
(*Ellison*, found)

Catlett   unknown

This name is included on a survey list of June 5, 1927 done by an unidentified person. Locations were not recorded. *Ellison Files, WY State Archives.* We have not located this name.

Cattron, J.   s   **59**
(*Ellison*, found)

Cedne, J. A.   net

Inscription shows up in photograph using black and white technical pan film.

Chalfant, Mr. M. L.   wt   **6, 96 (95?)**
With Miss Leeper and D.A. McCorkle.

Chamberlain, F. B.   cave   **1849 Age 25.**
(*Ellison*, found) Chamberlain put name on top of Slack. Date **June the 19th** can be seen in digital photo.

Chaneea   s
  Below L. Peak.

Chapin, H. L.   s
  (*Ellison*, found)

Chapman, E. B.   unknown   **June 30, 1850**
  This name is in a list compiled by D. W. Greenburg August 22, 1926. Locations were not given. *Ellison files, WY State Archives.* We have not found the name in recent surveying.

Chapman, F. B.   mt   **June 19, 50**
                                          Pekin, Illinois.
  (*Ellison*, found) Chapman appears twice on the Rock with George Hill. This one has day of month and place of origin.

Chapman, F. B.   mt   **June, 50**
  (*Ellison*, found) F. B. Chapman appears twice with George Hill.

Chase, B.H.   mt
  (*Ellison*, found)

Chase, H.   mt   **A. A. M.**
  Written after name. An H. Chase is listed as arriving in Placerville between August 29–September 4, 1852. *Rasmussen, p. 158.*

Chase, L.   swt
  (*Ellison*, nf)

Chatfield, B.   D Gate   **59**

Cheer (Cherr?), J(O?)   s   **June 17, 52**

Chubbuck, C.E.   nt   **59**
  (*Ellison*, found)

Chubley, W. R.   st   **July, 89**
  With E. M. Grubb.

Churchill, L B.   s   **60**

Churchill, L.B.   s   **June 11, 1850**
  Another L. B. Churchill inscription on the Rock, date ten years later. A J. Churchill, 1850, inscription found at Register Cliff. Could be of the same family. *Scottsbluff Survey List.*

Ciss   w
   Name virtually gone.

CL, S   s   **June 21, 1849**

Cla—???, G.   nt
   Hard to read because of other names.

Clark, E. C. or C. C.   s
   Possibly the same as in Ellison, however no visible sign of any date. A Charles Clark from Hinderson Grove, Illinois was a member of the Jayhawkers Party going to the California goldfields. They arrived in the Salt Lake area late in the summer. They then journied south and made the ill fated decision to cross Death Valley in 1849. *Belden, Goodbye Death Valley.*

Clark, E. C.   s   **June, 50**
   (*Ellison*, nf) See other E. C. Clark notation.

Clark, L. P.   mt   **June 9, 50 LaPorte, Indiana**
   (*Ellison*, found)

Clark, Mr. I. E.   nt   **7 20 69**
   Arrow is drawn to R. H. and J. Dickson.

Clark, P.A.   s   **June 22, 1850**
   (*Ellison*, found) Ellison has a ? for the date. We saw the date clearly in 1994.

Clark, T. or I. B.   se
   A Thomas Clark of Scott County, Illinois, first went to Oregon in 1848 and then went to California to meet his brother in the goldfields. After mining successfully he returned to Illinois via the Isthmus and then brought his family back to Oregon in 1851. They were attacked by Indians near Raft River crossing resulting in the loss of several members of the family. *Oregon in 1851.*

Clarke, H. W.   nt   **64**
   (*Ellison*, nf)

Clegg, J.   s   **June 2, 60**
   (*Ellison*, found) We could see no date in 1994.

Clemon   mt   **J 8, 1852**

Clemons, D P.   mt   **June 27, 1859**
Very worn.

Cline, P. D.   s   **Ju 9**
A Peter D. Cline, living in Clackamas County, is listed in the *1850 Oregon Territorial Census.*

Cline, R. D.   s   **46**
(*Ellison*, nf)

Cloud, B. M.   s   **June 24, 60**

Clouser, W. L.   mt   **7 15, 94 Ind**
Definitely old style.

Coates, B & D   st
Same script as M. Campbell (McCampbell?). In tar.

Coble, J. S.   se   **1849**

Coburn, N. C.   D Gate   **June 5 ???town**

Cogbny, John E.   sw

Col???, J. (?) P.   s
Weathered tar, below cave.

Colb, W. M.   mt

Colcord, W. D.   s   **60**

Coldwell, F. E.   se
Probably with Greenstreet.

Cole, C.W.   sw
(*Ellison*, found) We see **Chas. C. S. Cole.** The inscription is almost gone.

Colgord, W.   s

Collins, A.   nmt   **1850**
(*Ellison*, found) An A. M. Collins, from Indiana, is listed in the *Sawamish County, Oregon Territory, 1857 Census.* He was married, age forty-six, and listed his occupation as farmer at the time of this census. *US Gen Web Archives.*

Collins, W.H. (*Ellison*, found)	mt	**July 4, 1862**
Colt, R .P. (*Ellison*, nf)	sw cave	**69**
Colter, R. P. (*Ellison*, nf)	se	**1849**
Comstock, B. F.	D Gate	**25, 62**

Connor, J.G.   cave
(*Ellison*, nf) A Job Connor and wife Polly Ann are listed among the emigrant arrivals in Oregon in 1847. *Flora, Emigrants in 1847.*

Conterio, J. O.	mt

Cook, C.W. (*Ellison*, found)	mt	**May 24, 65**

Cook, T.   mt   **59**
This name is included in a survey list done by D. W. Greenburg on August 22, 1926. He did not record locations. He also recorded the date 1852. This could be the same as our listing unless T. Cook crossed the plains more than once. Although this list is in the R. S. Ellison files, this name is not in his book. *Ellison files, WY State Archives.*

A Thomas Elwood Cook, originally from Indiana, is listed in the *1890 California Census.* He worked as an engineer in Gridley. At the time of his registration in 1884, he was forty-five years old. *Butte County, California, 1890 Great Register, p. 51.*

Coolidge, Hobart   n   **82**

Coon, J.   nt   **June 19, 54**
Perry Pike Co., ILL
(*Ellison*, found) J. Coon, J. M. Bradbury, M. W. Fletcher, and W. O. McFarland all from same town, same date.

A John Coon is buried in the cemetery at Dayton, California.

A John Coon is listed in the *1890 California Census.* He lived in Inskip and was seventy-four at the time of his registration in 1884. His occupation was farmer. *Butte County, California, 1890 Great Register, p. 52.*

Coon, Wm   s
(*Ellison*, found) We saw **W. M. Coon.** This could be William Coon from Coles County, Illinois. He was born in Ohio September 30, 1819.

He first went to California via St. Joseph in 1850. He was a member of a party of a group of men who went to Hangtown. He later went back to the states over the Isthmus of Panama. His journal records it was there he "ate the monkey". He then took his family to California in 1860. He is buried south of Chico, California in the Dayton Cemetery. He died December 25, 1898. *Information from interview with descendant Larry Richardson of Paradise, CA.*

Of further note: a William Coon, originally from Ohio, is listed in the *1890 California Census.* He lived in Dayton and he was sixty-four at the time of his registration in May 1884. His occupation is listed as farmer. This is probably the same as the information given on Wm. Coon above. *Butte County, California, 1890 Great Register, p. 52.*

Cooy, T.	mt	**59**

Corbin, Ellen	mt	**June 27, 1864**

(*Ellison*, found) The date could possibly be 61. Together with S. Echard.

Corbin, John E.	w

Corbin, John E.	sw corner

Another John E. Corbin on the west side.

Cord	s	**60**

(*Ellison*, nf)

Cord, J. A.	w

Last name very weathered.

Corn, T.C.	cave

(*Ellison*, nf)

Correl, J. E.	net

Corrin, John E.	w

Coun, W. M.	s

Courtney, D.	mt	**Jun 10, 62**

(*Ellison*, found) The initial may be an **O** instead of a **D**.

Couyer, C. S.	s

Couyer, S.	s	**June 8, 49**

Cowen   w
   (*Ellison*, nf)

Cowherd, C. J.   s   , 49
   (*Ellison*, found) **June 27** seen with date in 1994.

Craig, A.   e
   Our surveyors thought this could possibly be Graig, however in a survey done June 5, 1927 by unidentified persons they list A. Craig.
   Although this list is found in the R. S. Ellison files, this name is not in
   his book. *Ellison Files, WY State Archives.*

Cran—as, C. R.   se
   In crevice east of cave.

Crane, J. A.   net

(*Ellison*, found) A James Crane, born in
South Wales in 1830, emigrated to
America in 1856. In 1859 he and his
wife crossed the plains to the Great Salt
Lake Valley. *LDS Biographical Encyclo-
pedia, Vol. I, p. 579.*

James Crane. (L.D.S. Family History Center,
Casper.)

Cranne, G. A.   D Gate

Crannell, A.   nt   **July 2, 1861**
   The date could possibly be 1881?

Crawford, J.   s, near cave
(*Ellison*, found) A J. Crawford, 1871 inscription found at Register Cliff.
Scottsbluff Survey List.

   A John B. Crawford, from Illinois, is listed in the *1890 California
Census.* He lived in Oregon City and listed his occupation as miner. He
was fifty-six at the time of his registration in 1884. *Butte County,
California, 1890 Great Register, p. 56.*

   Another possibility is John Sayles Crawford, from New York, who is
listed in the *1890 California Census.* He lived in Chico and listed his
occupation as miner. He was fifty-two at the time he registered in June
1884. *Butte County, California, 1890 Great Register, p. 56.*

Or this could be Jasper Vincent Crawford, (1839-1915) who is listed as crossing the trail to Oregon in 1851. *Oregon in 1851.*

Crawford, J. F.   w   **87**

Crawford, John   nmt   **June 26, 66**
(*Ellison*, found) The name could possibly be Crainford. 26 written above the June.

A John Crawford, born in Scotland, emigrated to Utah in 1864 crossing on the ship the Hudson. He traveled in Warren Snow's company to Fort Kearny and then transferred to a government train for the rest of the journey. He could possibly have gone east and then back in 1866 as many of the Mormons did. *LDS Biographical Encyclopedia, Vol. I, p. 391.*

John Crawford. (L.D.S. Family History Center, Casper.)

CrawpR???, J.   s

CRE   ne

Creighton, S.C.   s near cave
(*Ellison*, nf)

Crenell (Crenfell)?, J.T. s   **May, 1850**

Cripps, T. N.   s   **1864**
Masonic symbol by name. See note under P. W. Cripps.

Cripps, P. W.   s   **1864**
(*Ellison*, found) We believe it is R. W. Cripps. A Masonic symbol and scales symbol are drawn by the name. T. N. Cripps, 1864, in same area, both with a Masonic symbol so must be of the same family.

Crisp, P. W.   se corner

Crit, S.   s

Critchfield, S.   s   **1860**
(*Ellison*, found) May be traveling with J. Winet.

Crosby, J. W.   s

Jesse Wentworth Crosby. (Courtesy Sylvia Crosby.)

(*Ellison*, found) This is probably Jesse W. Crosby, Mormon, who first crossed to the Great Salt Lake Valley by ox drawn wagons in 1847, went east in 1850 and was later Captain of the Third Company in 1853. With no date on this inscription, there is no way to tell on which trip he left his name. He left a journal but gave no description of inscribing his name.

Jesse Crosby was born in Yarmouth, Nova Scotia and while still young his family moved to New York. He became a Mormon convert in New York when he was eighteen. His son Jesse Crosby, Jr. was born in Utah in 1848. Jesse, Jr. and brother George Crosby were founders of the town of Cowley, Wyoming. Jesse, Jr. had a son named Jesse Crosby. *Annals of Wyoming, Vol. II, #3, July, 1939.*

Many diarists wrote about the saleratus lakes just east of Independence Rock more than about the Rock itself. Jesse Crosby was one of those. He wrote: "August 23rd, 1847. Lay in Camp. 24th, traveled 12 miles at 12 o'clock arrived at Saleratus Lakes—was found dried down to a crust of from one to six inches in thickness, which we broke with axes and gathered all we wanted, tons of white and pure, so far as we know, Saleratus lay here a wonder and an astonishment to the passersby. The earth under this crust appeared to us like potash, equally as strong. There is considerable heat in it. Two miles further we arrived at Independence Rock, a place of moment with travelers, where hundreds of names are painted or engraved; here we enter the pass to the mountains, rocky points appear on every side with a narrow defile. Before arriving at this rock we strike the Sweetwater—a branch of the Platte." *Annals of Wyoming, Vol II, #3, p. 178.*

Jesse Crosby, Jr. (L.D.S. Family History Center, Casper.)

Of interest: in 1864, Jesse Crosby, Jr., at the age of fourteen, drove a four yoke box team from St.George, Utah to the Missouri River and back. This was probably part of one of the Down and Back Companies. *LDS Biographical Encyclopedia, Vol. I, p. 541.*

Crumb, J. H.   mt   **65 Co. I, 11th K. V. C.**
(*Ellison*, found) John H. Crumb was born in Chatauqua County, New York, on May 14, 1844. His family moved to Kansas in 1857 when he was thirteen years old. When the Civil War broke out he enlisted in the Eleventh Kansas Cavalry. He saw fighting in Arkansas and in early 1865 was stationed at Fort Riley, Kansas. The Eleventh Kansas Cavalry was then ordered to march to Fort Laramie to help protect the telegraph lines. His rank was Private in Company I. His company was sent to the Platte Bridge Station and arrived there around June 1. John Crumb was at Platte Bridge Station on July 25–27 and was involved in the Indian fighting that took place when Lieutenant Caspar Collins was killed. In 1927 he again visited Casper and met with Robert S. Ellison, going over the sites of the battle. In correspondence with Mr. Ellison he relates particulars of the fight with the Indians, and, in conclusion, had this to say: "After all, they were no more savage than we. We scalped one of their Chiefs; I couldn't have done it, but just the same it was done, and there is no greater torture to the living Indian than to know that a friend has been scalped, and thus excluded from the Happy Hunting Grounds." *Crumb ms, Ellison Files, WY State Archives.* Sergeant Amos Custard, whose supply train was wiped out by the Indians at the same time, was also of Company I, Eleventh Kansas Volunteer Cavalry. *Index to Kansas Volunteer Regiment Enlistments, 1862-1865.*

Cudhiy, P. G. C.   sw   **Co. F, 4th Cavalry**
(*Ellison*, found) We believe the **G. C.** is a separate inscription. See Wm. Thatcher and Nic H. Tonney for Fourth Cavalry reference.

Cuffy, Wm   mt   **July 20, 59**
A Wm. G. Cuffy inscription recorded at Emigrant Springs, WY. *Kelly 1930 Survey of Emigrant Springs.*

Culberson, G.   s
(*Ellison*, found)

Culberson, H.   s
Two Culbersons side by side within three feet of each other.

Culberson, S.A.   nt

Culberson, S.A.   s

An S. A. Culberson also on nt. We saw two Culbersons within three feet of each other on the south side.

Culberson, W.B.   s

(*Ellison*, found) The initials could possibly be **W. M.** Wm. Culverson of Yamhill County is listed in the *1850 Oregon Territorial Census.*

Culp, Chas. C. W.   unknown

This inscription is included in a list of names compiled by an unidentified person June 5, 1927. Locations were not identified. Although the list was found in the R. S. Ellison files, this name is not included in his book. *Ellison Files, WY State Archives.* We have not found the name in recent surveying.

Cummere   net   82

Cummings, L C   under cave   **July 4, 60**

In tar.

Cundy, D. P.   R. Pass n

Another name is on top of this one.

Cunningham, J or R   st

A J. R. Cunningham inscription is at Register Cliff. *Henderson 1930 Survey of Register Cliff.*

A J. Cunningham family is listed in the *Lewis County, Oregon 1849 Territorial Census.* He, his wife, and five children are listed. *US Gen Web Archives.*

Cur ? chill, P.   R. Pass n

Names are all over each other here.

Curran, H   sw

(*Ellison*, nf) An H. Curran is listed as a member of the Buffalo Exploring and Mining Company going to California. They left St. Joseph on April 12, 1849. This was a New York wagon train. *Rasmussen, p. 7.*

Or a Hugh Curren living in Clackamas County is listed in the *1850 Oregon Territorial Census.*

Curtis, A.J.   nt

(*Ellison*, found) The first initial could be an **S.**

Curtis, S. J.   nt

This inscription could possibly be what Ellison has as A. J. Curtis.

Cushing, E. N.   nt   **64**
(*Ellison*, found)

Cutler, Ed N.R.   nmt   **52**
(*Ellison*, found) Is inscribed as **EDx RxCutler x.**

Cutler, H.   mt   **July 18**
(*Ellison*, found) Ellison has the date as **58**, but in 1995 we read **July 18** only.

Cutler, L.A.   mt
(*Ellison*, found)

D, B U   R. Pass n   **MO**
Could be BUDMO. Could be a twentieth century inscription.

D., A.   mt   **June, 1852**

D., B.   nmt   **June 16, 53**
(*Ellison*, nf)

D., D.   mt

D., G.   mt   **July, 74**
(*Ellison*, nf)

D., I   nmt   **64**
(*Ellison*, nf)

D., J.   mt   **64**

D., J. W.   D Gate   **July 23, 1862 MAINE.**

D., J. J.   mt   **July 13, 74 Co. H**
(*Ellison*, found) Name all encased, lovely printing. This soldier could
possibly have been with James Hunt, also a military man. See James
Hunt entry.

D., L.   w
Together with R. M.

D., P.   nmt   **Jun 16, 53**
Backwards n.

D, S.   s
Tails on letters.

D. XXX, S.   swt
XXX written after the initials.

D—??, A—??   mt   **June, 1852**
Very hard to read for a modern name is inscribed over this.

Dal ???, Vn   D Gate

Dale (Dalf?), A . E.   s   **July 16, 1852 (?)**

Daliston   mt

Dard, J. A.   s

Darst, R W   mt   **July 15, 1894**

Dautesen, F.   nw   **7 9 82**

Davenport, T. S.   mt
(*Ellison*, found) A T. S. Davenport from Illinois is listed among those
arriving in Placerville between July 17-24, 1852. *Rasmussen, p. 145.*
Also a large family of Davenports was mentioned in the migration in
1852. *Holmes, Vol 5*

Daves, J. M.   mt

David, A . A.   st   **June 22 (?), 54**

David, J . M.   mt
A James David left Boscobel, Wisconsin on April 7, 1852 bound for the
gold fields. He traveled with two friends in one wagon and four yoke of
oxen. The party split up near Chimney Rock. He left a diary of the trip
across. *Mattes, Platte River Narratives, p. 351.*

Davi (d)?(s) ???   s
Very hard to read for names are over names here.

Davis, A.   cave   **June 21, 60 (?)**
On ceiling.

Davis, C W.   s   **June 6, 50**
(*Ellison*, found) **XX** under the name. A Charles Davis, from England, is
listed in the *1890 California Census*. He was a hotelkeeper in
Thompson's Flat. He was seventy-three at the time he registered for the
census in 1884. *Butte County, California, 1890 Great Register, p. 62.*

Davis, J. M.   mt
A date of July 12, 1852 was recorded with this inscription by D. W.
Greenburg on August 22, 1926. Greenburg believed J. M. Davis was
probably traveling with T. H. Armstrong. Although Greenburg's list is in
the Ellison files, this name is not included in his book. *Ellison Files, WY
State Archives.* The inscription is visible today although we saw no date.
A J. M. Davis is listed among the arrivals at Placerville in early
August 1852. *Rasmussen, p. 148.*
   Another possibility is Josiah Davis who is buried in the Georgetown,
California Pioneer Cemetery. He was from Missouri. He died January
28, 1851, at the age of fifty-two.
   Or a John Davis is buried in the cemetery at Chico, California. He
died February 11, 1889.
   Or a James Davis was a member of Company D of the Mormon
Battalion. Colonel Philip St. George Cooke sent women, children, and
sick soldiers back to Pueblo from Santa Fe under Captain Brown. This
group was known as the Brown Sick Detachment. After wintering in
Pueblo they made their way up to the Platte River and on into the Salt
Lake Valley in late July, 1847. *Utah Crossroads Newsletter.*
   Or a J. Davis and a Jos. Davis, both twenty-one, are listed in the
Tuality County, Oregon 1849 Territorial Census. US Gen Web Archives.

Deakins, D. (Miss)   nmt   **June 7, 1853**
(*Ellison,* found) Deakins name is in a box with Miss R. M. Edwards.

Dean, W. H.   sw
Directional arrow marked in the rock. This name was included on the
list of names done by an unidentified person on June 5, 1927. Although
this list was located in the Ellison files, the name is not included in the
1930 Ellison book.
   A William Dean, living in Washington County, is listed in the *1850
Oregon Territorial Census.*

Deans (?)   sw corner
Could be Deaus ?

Deardorff, L.G.   above cave   **July, 50**
(*Ellison,* found) We believe the name is **Deatdotff** for it seems to read
that way. It may be the old style printing is Deardorff. We also read the
date **July 12.**
   However, a Christian Deardorff arrived in Oregon in October 1850
and settled in Clackamas County, so our reading could be wrong.
Oregon Donation Land Claim Records.

Deatdotff, L. G.   s above cave   **July 12, 50**
See Ellison's Deardorff.

Deaus, Atwood   e
Possibly Leaus.

Decker, C.   mt   **1861**
X under name. A Cornelius Decker, Mormon, went from New York to
the Great Salt Lake Valley. *Information from a descendant in 1997.*

Decker, W.   D Gate   **1864**

DeGroff, G.W.   nt   **June, 59**
(*Ellison*, found)

Dennis, S.E.   nt   **June 19, 1858**
(*Ellison*, found) Probably with W. Mullins.

Denny, D.T.   st   **1851**
(*Ellison*, found) Very weathered. Lichen covered. A David T. Denny is
listed among those who traveled to Oregon in 1851. *Oregon in 1851.*
    An Arthur A. Denny traveled from Illinois to the Oregon Territory
in 1851 and left a diary of the trip. This Denny party left Illinois in
April and arrived in August. *Mintz, The Trail, pg. 40.* David T. Denny
could possibly be a family member in this party.

Dereath, Miss   st

Dexter, M. A.   s
Another M. A. Dexter inscription with a month also on the south side.

Dexter, M. A.   s   **Jul**

Dibble, J.C.   net
(*Ellison*, found) A Josiah Dibble from Ohio is listed as one of the emigrants bound for California who arrived in Kanesville during the week
of May 6 -13, 1852. *Rasmussen, pg 137.*

Dickson, J.   nt   **7 20, 69**
Written R. H. and J. Dickson. Backwards J.

Dickson, R. H.   nt   **7 20, 69**
Written R. H. and J. Dickson. Arrow to Mr. I. E. Clark

Dinin, Wm.   D Gate

Dipon (Dupon?)   s
In tar. Below cave)

Dobb, John A.   mt
(*Ellison*, found)

Dobbin, L.   cave

Dodd, W.   nt
There was a W. Dodd from Ohio who arrived in Placerville July 12-17, 1852. *Rasmussen, p. 143.*

Dodge, D.   st
A Private Daniel Dodge was a member of Company H, Eleventh Kansas Volunteer Cavalry. Several of these military men left their names on Independence Rock while stationed at Sweetwater Bridge Station in the 1860s. Company H was the same company of Sergeant Amos Custard whose supply train was wiped out by Indians close to Platte Bridge Station in 1865. *Index to Kansas Volunteer Regiment Enlistments, 1861-1865.*

Doe ?—?, H.   st
In red paint among many carved names.

Dogan, J.   s
(*Ellison*, found)

Dolgard, W. D.   s   60
Probably with D.J. O'Connor.

Donahue, S.   D Gate   June 2, 59 (79?)

Donim, Orkin J.   cave
(*Ellison*, found)

Dorl-k—n ?, A.D.   s

Dorlin???, A. K.   s

Dorr, R.   w   July 4, 18(?)7 (?)

Dos ?, John A.   mt
Backwards s.

Doty, J. W.   w   1890
Near the graves.

Doug (c?) e, O.   st

Dowis, J. S.   s
(*Ellison*, found) We believe it is **Downs.**

Downar, ?T.   s   June 3, 52
(*Ellison*, found)

Downing, W.   s   June 8, 1854
A William Downing, from Tennessee, is listed in the *1890 California
Census.* He lived in Biggs and listed his occupation as carpet weaver. He
was fifty-seven at the time he registered for the census in 1884. *Butte
County, California, 1890 Great Register, p. 69.*

Downs, J. S.   s
Could possibly be Ellison's Dowis. We read Downs. Pecked lettering.
See C. Wilson entry.
    A James Downs is listed as one of those who crossed the trail to
Oregon in 1851. *Oregon in 1851.*

Dozer, John A.   mt

Draper, Bishop W.   s

Bishop William Draper. (Courtesy
Joy Thomas, descendant)

(*Ellison,* found) No date given, however
in 1849 a William Draper, Mormon,
Counselor to President Clark, crossed in
the Fourth Company under Captain
George A. Smith on the way to Salt
Lake. This party was caught in a terrible
blizzard at South Pass in early October.
Mattes, Diary and Recollection Survey.
    William Draper was born November
25, 1818, in Easterton Wilts, England.
He bore the title of Bishop for he acted as
Bishop in the frontiers before his arrival
in the Salt Lake Valley. *LDS Biographical
Encyclopedia, Vol. IV, p. 457.*
    William Draper left Council Point,
Iowa on July 5, 1849, and went to Winter Quarters to help organize the
wagon train leaving for the Great Salt Lake Valley. They reached Salt
Lake City October 26, 1849. Of the storm at South Pass, he writes,
"We travelled on slowly, and nothing special occurred, there being lit-
tle sickness and no deaths. But on the second of October near the South

Pass we were caught in a great storm that lasted thirty-six hours, which killed over seventy head of our cattle and horses. That weakened our teams, but after the storm ceased we shoveled our way out and travelled again." *Draper, p. 74.*

Mary Ann, wife of William Draper, recalled more detail of the October storm. "As they neared the top (South Pass) Mary Ann noticed a lowering of temperature and a rising of fitful winds. It suggested storm to her. She began to gather buffalo chips, dry grass, antd such fuel as she could find, which she tossed on her cooking platform in preparation against a possible storm. In the early Morning, Mary Ann was awakened by a muffled voice calling her name. It was George A Smith, Captain of the train asking if she was all right. She answered back that she was, except that she had a smothered feeling. Well she might have, because her wagon and the wagons in the circle were buried in snow and all the men in camp had been up for hours shoveling paths and tunnels from one wagon to another. Seventy five head of weary livestock were huddled together, dead and buried in the snow." The train had sheltered in a hollow which had been a mistake for this permitted the snow to drift and pile upon them. Because of Mary Ann's foresight she was able to supply a warm fire and food for many in the group. *Draper, p. 141. Information furnished by Joy Thomas, descendant.*

Dream, A B.   mt
An A. B. Dream also found on south. This inscription very weathered.

Dream, A. B.   s
A. B. Dream also found on mt.

Drem, A B.   mt   June, 1851 (?)

Drew, W.Y.   net   May.
(*Ellison*, found) This could be Lieutenant William Y. Drew who was a first lieutenant in the Eleventh Kansas Volunteer Cavalry. Several of these military men left their names on Independence Rock while stationed out here in the 1860s. *Index to Kansas Volunteer Regiment Enlistments, 1862-1865.*

Dubuque, D.W.   cave
(*Ellison*, nf)

Dudley, C.E.   mt   June 28, (18?) 59
Masonic symbol by name.

Dudley, C.E.   nmt
(*Ellison*, found)

Duds   nt

Duley, C.E.   nmt
(*Ellison*, found)

Dun (?), E.   s

Duncan, T.   s
A Duncan family of five people from Illinois used the Lander Cutoff en route to California in 1859. *House of Rep. Exec. Document #63, 1859.*

Dune, R.   R. Pass w
R. Dune also on Independence Rock.

Dune, R.   s
R. Dune also in Rattlesnake Pass.

Dunlap, K.   s   June Wis
In 1864 a Kate Dunlap crossed the plains on the way to the Montana gold fields. She left a diary of this journey and recorded the journey traveled by way of the Platte River, South Pass, and Lander's Cutoff. *Mintz, The Trail, pg. 44.*

Dunn   st
A Mary M. Dunn left reminiscences of a trip across the plains to Oregon in 1852. This party traveled by boat to Athens, Missouri from Tennessee and then went overland. One of the Dunns listed could be of this party. *Mintz, The Trail, pg. 44.*

Dunn, J. R. JR (?)   s
Difficult to read. A James Dunn living in Clackamas is listed in the *1850 Oregon Territorial Census.*
A James Dunn, Captain, and his wife Mary are among those listed as crossing to Oregon in 1851. *Oregon in 1851.*
Another possibility is John Freeman Dunn, from Kentucky, who is listed in the *1890 California Census.* He lived in Chico and listed himself as a merchant. He was sixty-six at the time he registered in March 1884. *Butte County, California, 1890 Great Register, p. 72.*

Dunn, R. Bell   st

Dunn, W.   s   **69**
(*Ellison*, found) A William Bedford Dunn, from Virginia, is listed in the *1890 California Census*. He lived in Chico and worked as a farmer. He was fifty-seven at the time of his registration in 1890. *Butte County, California, 1890 Great Register, p. 72.*

Dunstan, J.   s   **July 25, 1850**
A Duston family arrived in Oregon in November 1850 and settled in Washington County. *Oregon Donation Land Claim Records.*

Dyer, Allerd (Ollerd?)   s
Difficult to read in most light, names over names.

Dyer, L.E.   s

Dyer, R. O.   s
Very large, very worn. A Robert Dyer is listed as a member of the Maine & New York Company going to California leaving in April 1849. *Rasmussen, p. 84.*

Dyer, V. or W.   w   **J 55**
Refer to Boyer on w. In tar. Seen best in photo.

E.   D Gate   **J 4, 1852 Millard, ILL.**
Two inscriptions from Millard, ILL. The other is H.L.W.

E—???, D.   st

E—????? X   R. Pass n
In tar. Virtually gone. **X** after name.

E., C.C.L.F.   mt
(*Ellison*, nf)

E., J.   R. Pass w

E., K.   mt
(*Ellison*, nf)

Eakin, R.   net   **1866**
(*Ellison*, found) An Eakin party went from Illinois to Oregon in 1866. *Brown, Emigrant Inscriptions.*

Eaton, J.   mt   **July 6, 1864**
(*Ellison*, found)

Eberbach, Elsa A. D Gate summit

Ebey, W. S. net **July 4, 54 MO**

Winfield Scott Ebey. (Whidbey Island County Museum.)

Large, large letters in negative relief. This is Winfield Scott Ebey, twenty-two years old, who was traveling with his family from Adair County, Missouri to Whidbey Island, Washington Territory. Winfield was born December 21, 1831, son of Jacob and Sarah Ebey. In 1854 Jacob and Mary with their three children, Mary, Elizabeth, and Winfield made the journey to Whidbey Island. *Ebey, Diary, p. 4, 9.*

In his diary, Winfield Scott Ebey left this description of his experience on Independence Rock. "Tues July 4th, 1854...I had quite an adventure this morning, though it was nothing but getting Scared almost to death. Geo. B—(Beam) had discovered a fissure leading up the North end of the rock (which is the highest & steepest part) & from the difficulty of the ascent, few had ever attempted it. He thought it a good chance to put our Names in a conspicuous place. So, getting some paint we managed to climb up some 200 feet, onto a Small ledge of the rock where we could Stand. Here we were to put our names which we did, but then to get down was the thing, a single false Step, or Slip of the foot, & we would be dashed to the bottom in an instant. On looking the danger in the face I became so alarmed that I could not return. Could do nothing but lay down and hold on. We were only some 10 feet from the top of the Rock, but I would not attempt to get up for worlds. As I lay pondering how to get down I saw Mr Headley, & got him to come to me George then got up & H[eadley] lifted me up to him & this way I got up on top when I made tracks for an easy place to descend and that is the last time I have been on Rock Independence. My name is in fair view from the road." *Ebey Diary, p. 103.*

Author's note: Most of the time I was by myself doing the surveying of the inscriptions on the Rock. Long before I ever read the Ebey Diary, for reasons of my own safety, I had decided this was one ledge I would not climb out on when I was on the Rock alone. It is a long steep drop to the ground.

More on this W. S. Ebey: He is listed in the *Island County, Washington Territory, 1860 Census.* He was twenty-eight at the time and listed his occupation as farmer. He apparently was unmarried at the time. His parents and family also lived in the same county. From the census records his holdings seemed quite small compared to the other farmers in the area. *US Gen Web Archives.*

The George Beam and J. Eby inscriptions are close to this Ebey inscription. There is a W. S. Ebey inscription also at Holden Hill, dated July 17, 1854. *Brown, Emigrant Inscriptions.*

Eby, J.   net

Although the spelling is different this J. Eby is probably Jacob Ebey, father of Winfield Scott Ebey listed above. This inscription is just above the W. S. Ebey inscription. Both inscriptions are in negative relief. Jacob Ebey was born October 22, 1793 in Huntingdon County, Pennsylvania. He was the son of George and Magdalena Ebey. Jacob Ebey married Sarah Ann Blue of Virginia. The Jacob Ebey family moved to Ohio and then to Sangamon County, Illinois around 1830 and their last child Winfield Scott Ebey was born there. The family moved to Adair County, Missouri in the mid 1830s. From there the family traveled to Washington Territory in 1854. Jacob Ebey died February 24, 1862. *Ebey Diary, pp. 5-7, 13.*

Echard, S.   mt   **June 27, 1864**

(*Ellison*, found) Date could possibly be **61**. Together with Ellen Corbin.

ECK, S or (W?)   R. Pass w

Can't read date.

Eckorn, P. W.   se

Edge, E. J. D.   mt   **June 11, 62 & 64 Ohio.**

(*Ellison*, found) This man was a soldier in the 6th Ohio Volunteer Cavalry which later became the Eleventh Ohio Volunteer Cavalry. Jonathan D. Edge was a Sergeant in Company A of the Eleventh Ohio Volunteer Cavalry. He was probably stationed at the Sweetwater Bridge Station located one mile east of Independence Rock. He enlisted in Ohio on October 10, 1861 and mustered out with the other Ohio volunteers on April 1, 1865. *Roster of Ohio Soldiers, Vol. XI.*

Edge, J. D.   mt   **64**

Also an inscription reading E. J. D. Edge is on middle top. See above.

Edward   s

Edwards, A.   nt   **July 4, 1853**

In 1853, two different Ann Edwards' crossed the plains going to the Salt Lake Valley. One was in Captain David Wilkins train and the other was in Captain Moses Clawson's Company. *LDS Crossing the Plains Index.*

Edwards, E M.   nt   **June 11, 52**
(*Ellison*, nf) An Elisha Edwards crossed the plains going to the Salt Lake Valley in the Fifteenth Company under Captain Robert Weimer. *LDS Crossing the Plains Index.*

Edwards, F. M.   nmt
This inscription is also included in a list of names compiled by D. W. Greenburg on August 22, 1926. He lists F. M. Edwards, P. W. Edwards, S. S. Slater, and J. K. Waller as probably traveling together. He saw no date but S. S. Slater has an 1849 date. Although this list is in the R. S. Ellison files, this name is not included in his book. *Ellison Files, WY State Archives.*

Edwards, J.   mt   **Sept. 4, 79**
(*Ellison*, nf)

Edwards, J.   nmt   **1853**
Could be James Edwards who crossed in 1853 going to the Salt Lake Valley in Captain Moses Clousson's Company.

Or it could be John Edwards who traveled with the 1853 Captain David Wilkins Company going to the Great Salt Lake Valley. *LDS Crossing the Plains Index.*

Or this could be John Edwards, from Ireland, who is listed in the *1890 California Census.* He lived in Thompson's Flat and was a farmer. He was fifty-one when he registered for the census in 1884. *Butte County, California, 1890 Great Register, p. 75.*

Edwards, L.   nt   **July 3, 1863**
(*Ellison*, found) We read I. **Edwards**.

Edwards, P. W.   unknown
This name is included on a list compiled by D. W. Greenburg on August 22, 1926. He listed P. W. Edwards, F. M Edwards, S. S. Slater, and J. K. Waller as traveling together. Although this list is found in the R. S. Ellison files, this name is not included in his book. *Ellison Files, WY State Archives.* Greenburg did not list locations or see a date on these inscriptions but S. S. Slater has an 1849 date and F. M. Edwards and Slater are found on the north middle top. We have not found the P. W. Edwards inscription in recent surveying, but this panel has inscribed names over painted names and some are difficult to read.

Edwards, R.M. (Miss)   nmt   **June 7, 1853**
(*Ellison*, found) In same box with Miss D. Deakins.

Elgin, Rilla   mt   **July 4, 52**
(*Ellison*, found) A George Elgin, born in 1808, and his wife Ruby Elgin
took their family to Oregon in 1852. There were a number of Elgin
family members in this party. *Flora, Emigrants in 1852.*
     More on this Elgin family. George Wethers Elgin and wife, Levica
Elvira Ruby, began their journey across the plains in the spring of 1852
from Blue Springs in Jackson County, Missouri. They had six children
who accompanied them on their trek. James Henry Elgin, the oldest
son, was eighteen at the time. He wrote: "On the 2nd of July 1852 we
crossed the North Platte and on the 4th of July were at Independence
Rock. It was a cold day with mixed snow and rain. Then we crossed the
Sweetwater and camped for the night above the Devil's Gate, where we
lay over the Sunday. On this Sabbath day we had preaching and two
funerals as well as a hanging...." "*Over the Plains 50 Years Age*" *James
Henry Elgin, dated 1902 for publication in* The Oregonian, *courtesy
Susanna Elgin Lingross, descendant.*

Elli (s?)   R. Pass n

Elk, Anne   mt

Elliott, J. A. B.   D Gate   **84**

Elliott, W. H.   s   **66**
     A William Elliott, originally from Ireland, is listed in the *1890
California Census.* He was a farmer in Gridley. In the March 1884 reg-
istration, he listed his age as forty-eight. *Butte County, California, 1890
Great Register, p. 76.*

Elliott, W. H.   s   **CO**
Boxed with double line in tar, very hard to read. Two W. H. Elliott
inscriptions on the south side, one has a date.
     A Wm. H. Ellliott of Lewis County is listed in the *1850 Oregon
Territorial Census.*

Ellis, J. W.   nt   **June 18, 1860**
     Probably with D. Antee, G. Holson. A John Wesley Ellis, from
Missouri, lived in Lovelocks at the time of the *1890 California Census.*
He was sixty years old when he registered in 1884 and listed his occu-
pation as a miner. *Butte County, California, 1890 Great Register, p. 77.*

Ellis, S. E.   t   **July 4, 62**

Ellis, S. C.   nt   **July 4, 62**
(*Ellison*, found) S. E. Ellis and T. T. Ellis have the same date.

Ellis, S.D.   s
(*Ellison*, found) We believe it is possibly D. D. Ellis.

Ellis, T.T.   nt   **July 4, 62**
(*Ellison*, found) S. E. Ellis, and S. C. Ellis have the same date.

Ellis, Tom   R. Pass n
This inscription could be twentieth century, but there are 1800s Ellises
on Independence Rock.

ELME   s
Eighteen inch high letters.

Ely, J.   nt   **July 14, 1853**
(*Ellison*, found)

Emams, L.   s   **June, 1849**

Enberthy, H.P.   s   **May, 50**
(*Ellison*, nf)

Epley, J.   net   **June 11, 52**
(*Ellison*, found) A John Epley from Stevenson County, Illinois is listed
among the arrivals in Shasta, California in early August 1852. This
party was one of the first to use Noble's Shasta Route. *Rasmussen, p.
149.*

Er—??-in, Harry   n

Ery, J.   s   **June**
(*Ellison*, found) We saw **June 50**. Very close to J. Erye. Probably with
C. W. Davis.

Erye, J.   s   **June 50**
Very close to J. Ery.

Est (?) olbe???   smt   **18??**
Very difficult to read.

Estel, P. D.   s
(*Ellison*, nf)

Estell, T. D.   s   **60**
(*Ellison*, nf)

Evans, E. K.   n

Evans, J .P. or E.   s
(*Ellison*, found) We read an old **P**. A John Evans living in Washington
County is listed in the *1850 Oregon Territorial Census.*

Or this could be Private Jacob Evans who was a member of Company
H, Eleventh Kansas Volunteer Cavalry. Several of these military men
left their names on Independence Rock while stationed at Sweetwater
Bridge Station in the 1860s. *Index to Kansas Volunteer Regiment
Enlistments 1861-1865.*

Or a Jeremiah Evans, born in 1826, crossed the trail, with his wife
Jane, to Oregon in 1851. *Oregon in 1851.*

Or a Jonah Evans, born in 1838 in South Wales, emigrated to the
United States and traveled across the plains to the Great Salt Lake Valley
in 1863. *LDS Biographical Encyclopedia, Vol IV, p. 520.*

Evans, J. W.   s   **June 6?, 1850**
(*Ellison*, nf) A John W. Evans, 1850 inscription surveyed long ago on
Chimney Rock. *Information from Chimney Rock Historical Site.*

This could be John W. Evans, from Arkansas, who crossed the plains
going to California in 1850. He left home in Arkansas on March 24
arriving at Fort Smith March 30. His party of eight men and two mule
drawn wagons went up to Westport and left Westport May 8, 1850. For
the first stage of the trip they traveled on the Santa Fe Road. He was at
Fort Laramie on June 11 and South Pass on June 27. Since the inscribed
date is questionable, this could be his inscription. John Evans left a
journal of his trip, "A Missouri Forty-Niners Trip Across the Plains."
Mattes, p. 251.

Everett, J. A.   D Gate summit   **59**
In same area as A. O. Hill /59.

Evert, A. L.   mt

Eyre, J.   s   **Jun 8, 59**
Towards stile.

F, F.D.   w

F(r?)—, T. J.   R. Pass s

F—??, T.	R. Pass w	
F., F. J. Backwards J.	s	
F., G.	s (midway up)	
F., J. D.	wt	**52**
F., J. H.	D Gate	
F., L.E. (*Ellison*, nf)	s	**1849**
F., T.	s	
F., W. W.	sw	
F., Z. D. Initials appear to be old style.	mt	
F—?, D. P.	s	**July 4,(?) 49 IOOF**

Fanney, J.   unknown

This name is included in a list of names compiled by D. W. Greenburg August 22, 1926. No locations are given. We have not found this name in recent surveying. It is possible this is what Ellison later read as Fanning, but Greenburg had no date listed.

Fanning, J.   nt   **June 11, 52**
(*Ellison*, found)

Farrar, L. (N?)   nt   date unreadable

Farrell, J. T.   nt

A John Farrell, born in 1834 in Scotland, crossed the Atlantic with his wife, sailing from Liverpool in 1857. With nine of their relatives they migrated to Utah in 1862. *LDS Biographical Encyclopedia, Vol. 2, p. 334.*

John Farrell. (L.D.S. Family History Center, Casper.)

Farry, Rosa   mt
(*Ellison*, found)

Feely, J. C.   nt   **1887 NIA FALLS, NY**
Went through two different times. See other J. C. Feely entry.

Feely, J. C.   nt   **1864 Niagra Falls, N. Y**
(*Ellison*, found) Went through two different times for two inscriptions in different years.

Felion, C.   nt

Felton, G.   nt   **June 19, 1858**
(*Ellison*, found) Possibly with Dennis & Mullins.

Fer(n?)g Few?, D M   w

Ferguson, James   cave
(*Ellison*, found) A James Ferguson, from Brownville New York, is listed as one of those who took the Lander Cutoff on the way to California in 1859. There were two wagons and ten people in the party. *House of Rep. Exec. Document #63, 1859.*

Ferrel, A. J.   R. Pass s
Behind tree, on boulder.

Ferris, P.   D Gate

Fezler, W. S.   nmt   **51**
(*Ellison*, found)

Field, H.   swt
(*Ellison*, found) An H.B. Field, living in Washington County, is listed in the *1850 Oregon Territorial Census.*

Fierce, W.   nt   **June 2, 1861**
(*Ellison*, found) Probably what we read as W. Pierce. See our Pierce.

Findley, J. M.   cave   **May 25, 1850**
(*Ellison*, found)

Finn, L.   nt
(*Ellison*, found)

Firestock, W. H.   n

Fish, C. H.   nt   **Sept. 52**
(*Ellison*, found) CH Fish also on sw. Possibly with Arick.

Fish, C. H.   sw
(*Ellison*, found) This person was probably with T.N. Machin, same
printing, and right under Machin. CH Fish also on nt with date.

Fish, H.   w   **1911**

Fish, K.   s

Fisher, J. E.   unknown
This name is included in a survey list done June 5, 1927 by an unidenti-
fied person. Locations were not recorded. Although this list is found in the
R. S. Ellison files, this name was not included in his book. *Ellison Files,
WY State Archives.* We have not found the name in recent surveying.

Fisk, H.   w
Old style lettering. **19**.**11** after name. This is possibly the same as H.
Fish, 1911 at another place on the west side. The last letter of Fisk is
difficult to read. Both inscriptions are in reddish orange places on the
Rock. It definitely looks like a period between the 19 and the 11.
   A Sarah Fisk, Mormon went to Great Salt Lake in 1848. She was a
widow of Mormon Battalion member E. H. Allen. She could have been
married to this Fisk. This dating could be European style with day first,
then month. *Information from descendant, 1997*

Fitch, C.C.   net   **July 12, 60**
(*Ellison*, found)

Flack, J. L.   mt   **Sept. 2, 62**

Flack, J. L.   nmt   **52**
Together with L. Fowler or Bowder.

Flavin   nw
May not be an old name.

Fleet, D. W.   D Gate   **Aug, 1881 VA U S D S**
By name.

Flelsaauer, A. T.   nt   **July 8, 1897**
With D. U. Herbert.

Fleming, C.M. nt **41?**
(*Ellison*, nf)

Fletcher, M. W. net
Also on north top with date.

Fletcher, M. W. nt **June 19, 54. Perry, ILL**
(*Ellison*, found) This inscription also on north east top with no date. M.
W. Fletcher, J. Coon, W. O. McFarland, and J. M. Bradbury all from
same town, same date. Refer to J. Coon notes for possible California
destination.

Flint, J.J. & C. mt **Jun 18, 52**
This could be Mormons who went from England to the Great Salt Lake
Valley. *This information from a descendant, 1997*

Floodwell? s
(*Ellison*, nf)

Fo—?/n, J. n
Backwards n.

Fobals, W. L. E. sw **JUN (E?)**
Something else that is hard to read. A large shield shape is drawn around
the inscriptions and drawings. A small church and a chalice are drawn
inside the shield shape. It's hard to read the inscription with the naked eye.
It shows best by scanning and manipulating the photo on the computer.

Folee cave

Folker e

Folts, C. nt **N Y**
(*Ellison*, found)

Ford, J. L. st **78**

Ford, R. nmt **June 27, 54**
(*Ellison*, found) A Rebecca Ford, age forty-one, is listed in the *Island
County, Washington Territory, 1860 Census*. Her husband was L. M.
Ford, farmer. *US Gen Web Archives.*

Ford, T. L. above cave

Ford, W.H.   swt   **1855**
(*Ellison*, found)

Foreman, W.   sw
A J. W. Forman, 1865 recorded at Emigrant Springs, WY. *Kelly 1930 Survey of Emigrant Springs.* Still visible in 1989 Emigrant Springs BLM survey.

Foreman, W. M.   s boulder   **Mich**
With Taft, I.A. Smith, of Mich. all on same boulder. A William Foreman, born in Ohio in 1826 and reared in Michigan, crossed the plains to California in 1849 when he was twenty-three. He stopped first at Bidwell's Bar and then settled at Berry Creek first operating a sawmill and then a hotel and a merchandise store. He died July 18, 1886. *Mansfield, History of Butte County, p. 452.*

Forgert, S.   nmt   **52**
Probably with J. Kennedy.

Forgey, A. W.   nt
gey written in script, rest printed. A William Forgey and wife Hannah are listed among the emigrant arrivals in Oregon in 1847. *Flora, Emigrants in 1847.*

Forgy, A. W.   nt
(*Ellison*, nf) Could possibly be the A. W. Forgey we saw on nt.

Forney, John   nt   **July, 64**
(*Ellison*, found) Two John Forney inscriptions, different years. This Forney is probably traveling with J. H. Watkins.

Forney, John   nt   **7, 53**

Fort Steele   s
Fort Fred Steele was laid out on June 30, 1868 at the place where the newly built Union Pacific Railroad met the North Platte River in southern Wyoming. This was on the route of the Overland Trail. It was established to help protect both the railroad line and the communities that sprang up along the line. *Wyoming, A Guide to Historic Sites, p. 35.* When the Sweetwater Station military post was abandoned, most of the military were transferred down to Fort Steele.

Fowler, A.   s   **Ju 24, 49**
An Almon Fowler from Illinois is listed as one of the emigrants bound for California who arrived in Kanesville prior to May 1, 1849. *Rasmussen, pg. 105.*

Fowler, L.   nmt   **52**
(*Ellison*, found) A Levin Fowler from Illinois is listed as one of the emigrants bound for California who arrived at Kanesville the week of May 13-20, 1852. *Rasmussen, p. 140*
    Another possibility is that there are two Fowlers listed on Independence Rock. I spoke with Fowler descendants who said their Mormon ancestors went across the trail to the Salt Lake Valley. I have not been able to find any other information.

Fox, F.A.O.S.   mt   **June 29, 52 Cinn, Ohio**
(*Ellison*, found) Boxed with H. Kite in same box.

Fox, G. O.   mt
(*Ellison*, found) The **x** in name has fallen off. A Mormon named G.O. Fox traveled from England to Utah, year unknown. *From Mormon descendant, 1997*
    Or a Jared Fox left Delton, Wisconsin in April 1852, went through Council Bluffs and traveled on the north side of the river on his way to Oregon. He crossed the Missouri River at the upper ferry on May 14. He was forty-seven at the time he took his trip and had left a pregnant wife and five children home alone in Wisconsin. On reaching the Columbia River he traveled the Barlow Road and arrived at Oregon City August 17, 1852. Jared's journey is a little unusual in that it took him just a little over three months to make the trip. He left a diary covering this trip. *Mattes, p. 356.* See note under J. Foy.

Foy, J   se   **52**
This could possibly be the Jared Fox of above.

Frans, T.   unknown
This inscription is found on a handwritten list of names recorded June 5, 1927 by an unidentified person. No location of inscriptions was included in this list. *Ellison Files, WY State Archives.* We have not found this inscription.

Freeman, E.J.   s   **June (?)**
(*Ellison*, found) See date on L. C. Freeman. John Freeman, born in 1808, traveled to Oregon with his family in 1853. Could be a member of that family. *Flora, Emigrants in 1853.*

Freeman, Geo.   R. Pass n   **June the 12, A. D., 1852**
J.L. Stewart, Freeman, Alfred Row, and Adam Acker are all on the same boulder, on the same date. A G. S. Freeman from Stevenson County,

Illinois, is listed among the arrivals in Shasta, California in early August 1852. Alfred Rowe, and James Stewart, same point of origin, are also listed among these arrivals. *Rasmussen, p. 149.*

Freeman, L.C. s **June (?)**
(*Ellison*, found) See E. J. Freeman. They are maybe together.

Freemyer, J.W. nt **July 2, 62**
(*Ellison*, found)

French, J. w
(*Ellison*, nf) A Jacob French, of Augusta, Lee County, Iowa, is listed arriving in Kanesville, May 2, 1849, bound for California. *Rasmussen, p. 45.*

Or this could be Private John B. French who was a member of Company D, Eleventh Kansas Volunteer Cavalry. Several military men left their names on Independence Rock while stationed out here in the 1860s. *Index to Kansas Volunteer Regiment Enlistment, 1861-1863.*

Frisby, J. P. mt
(*Ellison*, found) D. W. Greenburg who did a survey of Independence Rock August 22, 1926 read the date June 1852 with this inscription. *Ellison Files, WY State Archives.*

A J. P. Frisbee is listed among the arrivals in Placerville in the first week of September 1852. *Rasmussen, p. 163.*

Fritts, K. I. mt **Marlow, OK**

Fry, J. s
(*Ellison*, found) A John Fry left Knox County, Ill. April 2, 1851 traveling to Oregon. *Platte River Narratives, pg. 325.*

Further research shows this John Fry was traveling with his wife, Margaret. *Oregon in 1851.*

Frye, J s **June, 50**
(*Ellison*, found) Could possibly be what we read as **J. Erye. June, 50.** See Erye.

G., E. set
(*Ellison*, nf)

G., E. L. swt

G., H. E. mt
(*Ellison*, nf)

G., J. (S?) W.   s
Large letters. In negative relief.

G., J. W.   net   **59**
(*Ellison*, found) Boxed with W. T. B.

G., L .F.   swt
(*Ellison*, nf)

G., P. L.   swt   **56**
Very large letters.

Galla, H. T.   D Gate

Gallery, J—?   nwt
Very weathered.

Gannon, W. L.   sw   **1858?**
(*Ellison*, found)

Gardlow, N. S.   nt
(*Ellison*, nf)

Garey, J.& C.   nt
(*Ellison*, found) Possibly what we read as J. & C. Carey.

Garret (?)   nt
Do not know if first or last name. An Augustus O. Garrett from Peoria,
Illinois was a passenger on the ill fated Pioneer Line of 1849. B. Reid
inscription also on nt, *Reid diary, p. 193.*
   Or a John Garret, living in Clackamas County, is listed in the *1850
Oregon Territorial Census.*

Garrett, B.   mt   **June 6, 1853**
(*Ellison*, found)

Garrison, W.   s   **57**
(*Ellison*, nf)

Gay, F. B.   D Gate

George, A. L.   s   **July 29, 49**
(*Ellison*, found) Ellison recorded the date wrong for he had July 26, 49.
Our reading is correct. This man was traveling with the same party as
Colonel James Tate. They left from Saline County, Missouri in April

1849, and crossed the Missouri River at St. Joseph. They arrived at Sacramento on September 27. Refer to the James Tate entry.

George, J.   mt   **— 18, ?89**

Gibson, G. W.   s
S. M. Cady written over this name. A George Washington Gibson was a member of the Mississippi Saints who wintered in Pueblo in the winter of 1846-47. In the spring of 1847 this group left Pueblo traveling north to the Platte River and followed the Pioneer Party into the Salt Lake Valley arriving a few days after the Pioneer Party. *Utah Crossroads Newsletter.*

Or a George Gibson of Marian County, or a Gideon Gibson of Morrison County, and a George Gibson of Washington County are listed in the *1850 Oregon Territorial Census.*

Gibson, J.   s   **62 ?.**
(*Ellison*, found)

Gibson, J.   unknown   **July 21 ___?**
This inscription is included in a June 5, 1927 survey list done by an unidentified person. Although this list is found in the R. S. Ellison files, the name is not included in his book. *Ellison Files, WY State Archives.* We have not found this inscription in recent surveying.

J. Watt Gibson made three overland trips to California from Missouri. He first crossed in 1849 seeking gold. He returned to Missouri in 1851 and then crossed again going to California in 1852, driving cattle on this journey. He made another cattle driving trip in 1854. He then crossed to Salt Lake City in 1865 and then to Montana in 1866. He left recollections of his journeys. *Mintz, The Trail, pg. 54.*

Gibson, O. S   net   **1853 Wis**
(*Ellison*, found)

Gilbert, W. W.   net   **July 8,1853**
A W. W. Gilbert left Milwaukee, Wisconsin on April 15, 1853. His party then left Council Bluffs May 26. They traveled to California going through Salt Lake City and then traveled via the Humboldt-Carson route to California arriving in Placerville October 14, 1853. He left a diary of his journey in which he states they passed Fort Laramie on June 29 and were at South Pass on July 15 so this fits in with the date on the inscription. In his diary he does record that he left his name on Independence Rock. *Platte River Narratives, p. 411.*

Gill, W.   cave   **60**
(*Ellison*, found) A William Gill sent letters to his wife from the gold fields in California. His mining efforts failed and he returned home in 1852, however he crossed the trail again going to California the next year. It is possible he left this inscription on another journey either east or west. *Mintz, The Trail, pg. 54.*

Gillam, D. B.   s   **May 9, 50 ILL's**
(*Ellison*, found) In a survey done June 5, 1927 by an unidentified person, D. B. Gillam, A. L. White, and J. B. Brian were believed to be together with a common date of May 9, '50. ILL's. Although this list is found in the Ellison files, the other two names are not in his book and we saw no evidence of them. *Ellison Files, WY State Archives.*

Gillan, D. B.   se

Gillis, P.   net   **June 18 (?), 54**
Could possibly be what Ellison has as R. Gillsi.

Gillsi, R.   net   **June 18, 54**
(*Ellison*, found?) Could possibly be what we read as P. Gillis.

Gilm, J. J.   D Gate

Gis (I ?—?), J. C.   nt   **188 ?**
In paint in among many carved names.

Gish, J.C.   nt   **June 14, 52**
(*Ellison*, found) Name painted.

Glendinen, James   mt
(*Ellison*, found)

Glinnen, Hosky   n

Goddard, J.   s
Could possibly be a Mormon who traveled to the Great Salt Lake Valley in 1850. *Information from a descendant, 1997.*

Goncy, W.   s

Goodlow, N. S.   nt   **Rock Island County, Ill.**

Goodmere, D. L.   se

Goodwell, F. E.   s

Goodwill, F. L.   st
With E. B. Harrison.

Goover, C. S.   s   June 27, 49
(*Ellison*, nf)

GR—?Y   w, midway up
Huge letters, maybe three feet high, very weathered. Negative relief.

Gra???, A.   s   July

Graham, A.H.   swt
(*Ellison*, found) An Aaron H. Graham, living in Washington County, is
listed in the *1850 Oregon Territorial Census.*

Graham, J.M.   s
(*Ellison*, found) A Jeffrey Graham of Clackamas County is listed in the
1850 Oregon Territorial Census.

Graham, W. M.   D Gate
A William Graham is listed among the emigrant arrivals in Oregon in
1847. He was in the party led by Joel Palmer. This was Palmer's second
time to cross the trail to Oregon. *Flora, Emigrants in 1847.*
A Wm. Graham of Linn County or a Wm. Graham of Yamhill
County are both listed in the *1850 Oregon Territorial Census.*
A Wm. Grayham, and wife, are listed in the *Tuality County, Oregon
Territory 1849 Census. US Gen Web Archives.*

Graid   s   July 26, 184
D written backwards.

Grantham, J. M.   nt   June 11, 52
(*Ellison*, found)

Gray, A.   se   July

Gray, C.   s
A Dr. Charles Gary from Indiana traveled from St. Joseph to Oregon in
1852. He started out with the Crawford Company but switched to
another group along the trail. He left a diary of his journey. *Platte River
Narratives, pg. 360.*
Or it could be Charles Glass Gray, New York, who left Independence,
Missouri, bound for California on May 1, 1849. He was a member of

the Newark Overland Company. He left a diary of his trip. *Platte River Narrataives, pg. 161.* Charkes Glass Gray was born in New York in 1829. The Newark Overland Company was organized in New Jersey in early 1849 with General (Doctor) John Stevens Darcy as captain. General Darcy was Charles Gray's uncle. The party traveled via Lassen's Cutoff, arriving at their destination in California in November 1849. Charles Gray worked as a hotel clerk and returned to New York in 1852. *Gray, Off at Sunrise.*

Charles Glass Gray wrote this description of Independence Rock in his diary. "June 24. Off at 4 O'clock & came 8 miles before breakfast. Stop'd exactly opposite the celebrated Independence Rock, an enormous mass of stone & which has so often been described that I shall not attempt it, only I will say that it did not realize my expectations as to its shape & height. Where it was accessible it was literally cover'd with names, many years were represented but 1849 overwhelmed them all. Many ambitious mortals have here immortalized themselves in *tar & stone & paint*." This party continued on and traveled sixteen miles on this day. *Gray Off at Sunrise, p. 44.*

Also a C. Gray was in a party from Ogle County, Illinois who crossed at St. Joseph May 5, 1849 en route to California. *Rasmussen, p. 61.*

Gray, W. J.   se near cave   **63**
By J.R. Walton and S. Walton.

Gray, W. J.   s   **July 3, 1851**
(*Ellison*, found) A John W. Gray is listed among those who crossed to Oregon in 1851. *Oregon in 1851.*

Green, J. M.   s   **July 3, 1863 MO**
St also seen with name. A J. M. Green crossed the plains in 1863 as a member of the A. H. Patterson Company, an independent Mormon company. *LDS Crossing the Plains Index.*

Or a John Meeker Green, from New York, is listed in the *1890 California Census.* He lived in Lovelocks and was fifty-four years old when he registered for the census in 1886. He listed his occupation as a miner. *Butte County, California, 1890 Great Register, p. 98.*

Greenstreet   s   **July 8, 51 MO**
This Greenstreet's inscription could be on south top a few days earlier. See J. M. Greenstreet.

Greenstreet   nt   **1863 MO**
(*Ellison*, nt)

Greenstreet, J. M.   st   **July 3, 1851 MO**
Greenstreet is with E. B. Harrison. See Greenstreet on south. A large number of members of a Greenstreet family are listed as arrivals in Oregon in 1851. Some of these are, Absalon 1797-1856 and wife Sarah, John M. born in 1826, Mariah born in 1822, Matilda born in 1829 and others. *Oregon in 1851.*

Greer, G.   nt   **July 15, 1868**
(*Ellison*, nf)

Grier, J. S.   se   **June 17, 52**
(*Ellison*, nf) A Sylvester Grier, born in Pennsylvania, is listed as arriving in Oregon in October 1852. *Oregon Donation Land Claim Records.*

Griffith, W. M.   cave   **June 26, 1851**
(*Ellison*, found)

Grist, R. (P?)   nmt   **June 24, 62**

Griswold, A. W.   nt
An A. W. Griswold, Mormon, went from England to the Salt Lake Valley. He was probably in one of the handcart trains. *Information from a descendant, 1997.*

Groff, G. W., Dr.   nt   **June, 59**

Grubb, E. M.   st   **July, 89**
Probably with Chubley. There is a second E. M. Grubb inscription on the south side

Grubb, E. M.   s (midway up)

Guffy, Wm.   mt   **July, 20, 59**
(*Ellison*, found) A Wm. G. Guffy inscription surveyed at Emigrant Springs. *Kelly 1930 Survey of Emigrant Springs.*

H (a?)—??, T. R.   R. Pass w

H (e?) rrma—?   w   **J—y, 5 ?, 54 ?**
In tar. Seen best in color slide.

H (R?) ume, F.   s

H—???, J.   s   **July**

H., A.   s
   Very elegant initials.

H., A. C.   nt   **MO**

H., J. B.   mt
   Lovely lettering.

H., J. P.   se

H., J. W.   s
   In tar, very weathered.

H., P. J.   R. Pass n

H., R. I.   swt   **62**
   Almost gone.

H., S.   mt
   Definitely old.

H., S.   wt

H., S. W.   nt

HA, James R.   mt   **Aug 18, 52**

Haag   nmt
   (*Ellison*, nf)

Hacklenas ?, J. H.   sw
   Very large, very weathered, half way up on corner. Since this is difficult
   to read there is a possibility it could be Hackleman. A Hackleman family
   is listed among the emigrant arrivals to Oregon in 1847. *Flora,
   Emigrants in 1847.*

Hady, S.M.   s

Hagans, Wm. H.   nt   **July 2, 1862**
   (*Ellison*, found) Initials are Wm. **H. H.** Hagans.

Haines, F.   w

Haines, W. F.   D Gate   **Aug 17, 1881**
   A Wiley Haines inscription found at Register Cliff. *Scottsbluff Survey
   List.*

Hal—??, D. O.   cave

Hale, Jane   nmt
(*Ellison*, found)

Hale, Lillian A.   unknown   **July, 1852**
This name is found on a list of names surveyed June 5, 1927 by an unidentified person. Locations are not recorded. Although this list is found in the R. S. Ellison files, this name is not in his book. *Ellison Files, WY State Archives.* We have not found the name in recent surveying.

Hale, William   nmt
(*Ellison*, found) A W. F. Hale is listed in the *Tuality County, Oregon Territory, 1849 Census. US Gen Web Archives.*

Hales, Wm .H.   cave
(*Ellison*, found)

Haley, Max M.or W.   cave
(*Ellison*, nf)

Hall, G. H.   mt   **June, 59**
(*Ellison*, nf)

Hall, H . L.   st   **July**

Hall, John   mt   **July 4, 50**
(*Ellison*, found) A John Hall is listed as a member of the Union Company of Fairfield, Iowa encamped at Kanesville in late April 1850. This party was bound for California. *Rasmussen, p. 110.*

    Or a J. Hall, age twenty-nine, is listed in the *Island County, Washington Territory, 1860 Census.* He listed his occupation as a laborer. *US Gen Web Archives.*

Hall, Zoe   swt
(*Ellison*, found) We believe the last name is Holl. We see **ZOE HOLL.**

Ham, ??—   nt

Ham & family, E.   D Gate   **July 1- ?, 1859 ILL**

Hammond, Edward   s
(*Ellison*, found)

Hammond, John   unknown   **1844**
This name is included in a list of names compiled by D. W. Greenburg on August 22, 1926. Locations are not recorded. Although this list is found in the R. S. Ellison files, this name is not included in his book. *Ellison Files, WY State Archives.* We have not found the name in recent surveying.

Hamon, W. P.   s
(*Ellison*, nf)

Hankins, M. C.   R. Pass w   **1852**

Hanks, W. J.   mt   **1860 ILL**
(*Ellison*, found)

Hann (?), J. A.   w
An A. Hanna recorded at Emigrant Springs, WY. *BLM 1989 Survey of Emigrant Springs.*

Hanon, W. P.   unknown
This name is included on a list surveyed June 5, 1927 by an unidentified person. Locations are not recorded. Although this list is found in the R. S. Ellison files, this name is not in his book. *Ellison Files, WY State Archives.* We have not found the name in recent surveying. This could possibly be Ellison's W. P. Hamon.

Har—e-, E.   D Gate   **July 18, 1852 ILL**
Inscription reads **E. Har—?e—, & wife, family.** Cannot really read last name.

Harbum (n?), A. S.   s

Harddman, H. C.   swt
(*Ellison*, nf)

Haris, G.A.   s   **1854**

Harris, (W?) H.R   R. Pass n   **June, 59 Ohio**

Harris, Alice   w
Halfway up. Mar?? above it. An Alice Harris, 1866, inscription also found at Cache Cave. *Brown, Emigrant Inscriptions.*

Harris, B. B.   s
(*Ellison*, found)

Harris, J.   s   **1849 ?**

(*Ellison*, nf) A J. B. Harris was listed in the Independence, Missouri area April 5, 1849 as part of the early groups waiting to leave for California. He was part of a small group from Henry County, Indiana. *Rasmussen, p. 1.*

Or this could be James Harris of Washington County who is listed in the *1850 Oregon Territorial Census.*

A J. C. Harris inscription found at Register Cliff. *Scottsbluff Survey List.*

Harris, M. L.   unknown

This name is included in a survey list done June 5, 1927 by an unidentified person. Although this list is found in the R. S. Ellison files, this name is not included in his book. *Ellison Files, WY State Archives.* We have not found the name in recent surveying.

Harris, R.   nt

A Reuben Harris of Yamhill County is listed in the *1850 Oregon Territorial Census.*

Or this could be Robert Harris, a member of the Mormon Battalion, Company E, who was born in England in 1808. He emigrated to America in 1841 and went to Nauvoo. After serving with the Battalion, he went east by way of Fort Hall to get his family in 1847. He brought them to Utah in 1850. *LDS Biographical Encyclopedia, Vol. IV, p. 744.*

Harris, S.O.Sr.   w   **53**

(*Ellison*, nf) This could be Samuel Harris Sr. who came from Liverpool with his wife and children in 1853 and crossed the plains to the Salt Lake Valley. *LDS Crossing the Plains Index.*

Harrison, ARMU or J   mt

Harrison, E. B.   s   **July 2**

(*Ellison*, found) We read **July 21** or **27**. Backwards **J**. In a list of names included in a survey done June 5, 1927, they listed the year **51** as part of the inscription. *Ellison Files, WY State Archives.*

Harrison, J.   s

A J. M. Harrison left Birminghan, Iowa on April 1, 1846 going overland to St. Joseph and then crossed the Missouri at Savannah May 25. On May 26th they "organized a company...65 (men) strong, with 41 wagons and 500 head of stock." Their company was dubbed the Iowa Company. This party was at Fort Laramie on July 3 and while at Devil's Gate they killed a big horn sheep. This man left a diary but he discontinued it near Boise City. *Platte River Narratives, p. 80.*

Or a James Parry Harrison, born in London in 1846, emigrated to America and crossed the plains in 1861. He traveled in Joseph Harnes's wagon train and arrived in Salt Lake City in September of that year. *LDS Biographical Encyclopedia, Vol. II, pg. 133. Vol. III, p. 108.*

Or this could be John Harrison of Washington County, or James Harrison of Yamhill County, or John Harrison of Marion County who are all listed in the *1850 Oregon Territorial Census.*

Harrison, Jon   s   **July 24, 1851**
(*Ellison*, found)

Harrkison, E. B.   s

Harrow, J. G.   cave   **Iowa**
(*Ellison*, found) There is a J. G. Harrow also on north top with date of 185 (9?)

Harrow, J.G.   nt   **185 (9?)**
J. G. Harrow inscription also in cave with no date.

Harsh, W. H.   swt   **July 4, 59**
(*Ellison*, found)

Hart, H. F.   mt   **May 24, 1865**
(*Ellison*, found) H and F linked together so could possibly be HS. A Private H.S. Hart was a member of Company B, Eleventh Kansas Volunteer Cavalry. Several military men left their names on Independence Rock while stationed out here in the 1860s. The Kansas men arrived in the area in the spring of 1865 and most were mustered out in late summer, 1865. *Index to Kansas Volunteer Regiment Enlistments, 1861-1863.*

Hart, J.   s   **July, 49**
(*Ellison*, found) A John Hart, age fifteen, crossed the plains in 1849 going to the Salt Lake Valley as a member of Captain Benson's Fifth Company. *LDS Crossing the Plains Index.*

Also a J. T. Hart is listed as captain of a wagon train, Pawpaw Mining Company of Michigan, which was camped out of St. Joseph on April 10, 1849. *Rasmussen, p. 150.*

Hartley, H.   nt
(*Ellison*, nf) D. H. Hartley was a member of a party crossing to Oregon in 1852. *Webber, Comprehensive Index to Oregon Trail Diaries.*

Or this could be Henry H. Hartley from southern Illinois who traveled to Oregon in 1856. The train was under the leadership of his grandfather,

Joseph Hartley. Henry did not like the Oregon climate and returned to Illinois after eighteen months. *Mattes, Diary and Recollection Survey.*

Harves, D.   w   **52**
This is possibly what Ellison has as Harvey. In tar.

Harvey, D.   w   **52**
(*Ellison*, found) We think it might be Harves. A D. Harvey from Boone County, Illinois is listed among the party of emigrants arriving in Shasta, California on August 3, 1852. *Rasmussen, p. 149.*

Harvy   nt
A Daniel Harvey of Clackamas County, a J. Harvey of Washington County, and a John Harvey of Polk County are all listed in the *1850 Oregon Territorial Census.*

Harvy, J. H.   mt   **June 24, 62**
(*Ellison*, found)

Haskill x, Wm.   swt
x mark made under name. A William Haskell from Maine is listed among those using the Lander Cutoff in 1859. *House of Rep. Exec. Document #63, 1859.*

Hatch, Darnell   wt
Possibly not nineteenth century, however tails on L's.

Hatcher, W. T.   nmt

Hatcher, M. A.   nt   **July 4, 1862**
(*Ellison*, found) **XX** after name. We saw **Hatsher** in 1994. Also saw only **62** rather than **1862.**

M.A. Hatcher inscription. (Author's Photo)

Hatfield, W.   net
(*Ellison*, found)

Hau, H. L.   st   **July**

Hawes, B. D.   mt
E in last name put above the name, first attempt messed up. See other Hawes inscription.

Hawes, B. D.   mt   **June 52**
Second Hawes inscription in same vicinity. This one done correctly.

Hawk, W. M.   cave
(*Ellison*, nf) In 1848 William Hawk, a Mormon, advertised to carry mail from San Francisco to the Missouri River at fifty cents a letter. He met Brigham Young in the vicinity of Independence Rock in late August 1848. *LDS Biographical Encyclopedia, Vol. II, p. 131.*
Or this could be Wm. Hawk, who was living in Linn County when he was listed in the *1850 Oregon Territorial Census.*

Hawkins, A. H.   s   **July 11, 52**
This Hawkins is probably with B. T. and W. B. Hawkins whose inscriptions are close to this. An H. Hawkins is listed as arriving in Placerville during the last week of September 1852. *Rasmussen, p. 168.*
Another possibility is Arculus Hawkins, from Missouri, who settled in the Vacoville, California area. He had first gone out to California on his own earlier and then went back for his family. He crossed the trail again with them in 1852. *Information from descendant, 1999.*

Hawkins, B. T.   s   **July 11, 52**
See A. H. Hawkins note and M. C. Hawkins inscription at Rattlesnake Pass.

Hawkins, M. C.   R. Pass w   **1852**
There are two other 1852 Hawkins inscriptions on Independence Rock.

Hawkins, W. B.   s   **1852**
(*Ellison*, found) See A. H. Hawkins note. Another Hawkins inscription, 1852, in Rattlesnake Pass.

Hawley, D. O.   cave   **July 16, 1860 Fairmont, Iowa**
(*Ellison*, found) We saw Fairport, Iowa in 1994.

Hawley, A. D.   s   **59 (?)**
(*Ellison*, found) In a June 5, 1927 survey done by an unknown recorder the year '**51** was recorded instead of **59**. *Ellison Files, WY State Archives*

Hay R. Pass w **Ju, 55 ?**

Haydock, W. s
(*Ellison*, found)

Haynes, A. s **July 21, 49 Mass**
(*Ellison*, found) A Dr. A. Haynes is listed as a member of the Granite State & California Mining and Trading Company arriving in St. Louis April 28, 1849, bound for California. *Rasmussen, p. 40.*

Also an Asa Haynes, in 1849 left Knoxville, Illinois to go to the California mines. He was elected captain of the wagon train. On starting out this train had fifty wagons. This Asa Haynes was a member of the Jayhawkers Company. This party arrived in the Salt Lake City area late in summer and decided to travel south instead of trying to go over the Sierra so late in the season. They then made the ill fated decision to cross Death Valley thinking it would be a shortcut. He left a diary of this journey, "Captain Asa Haynes Diary". *Platte River Narratives, pg. 166.* also *Belden, Goodbye Death Valley.*

Hays, A. H. nt **61**
(*Ellison*, nf)

Hays, John s **June 3, 50**
(*Ellison*, found) The date might be **54**. A J. Hays is listed as member of one of the first organized units in St. Joseph, April 26, 1850. *Rasmussen, pg 104.*

A book believed to be a family project describes the journey of a Hayes family crossing the plains in 1850. *Mintz, The Trail, pg. 66.*

A John Hayes inscription found at Register Cliff. *Scottsbluff Survey List.*

HCR, A J. nmt

Heady, J. M. s **June 15, 62**

Heagen, J.? cave
(*Ellison*, found)

Heaitt, O. S. cave **May 25, 1850**
(*Ellison*, found)

Hea ?nns?d ?? e
Negative relief. Very difficult to read.

Heddrington   s   **59 ? Ohio**
(*Ellison*, nf) In a survey done June 5, 1927 by an unidentified person
W. Hedrington, Ohio, '57 or maybe '51 was included on their list.
Ellison Files, WY State Archives.

Heh ?, W. M.   w
Seen best on color slide.

Helm or(n), W. M.   w

Hena, H.   swt

Hepley   R. Pass n

Herbert, D. U.   nt   **July 8, 1897**
With H. T. Flelsaauer.

Herburne, M .A.   mt   **59**

Herreman, C. H.   mt   **60**

Herreman, O. H.   nmt   **56**
(*Ellison*, found)

Herse, H. J.   nt   **91**

Hesse (?), Ben   net
(written **Mr.** and **Mrs.**)

Hetty   nt   **54 (?)**
(could possibly be 82)

Hiatt, E.   net   **81**
(very weathered)

Hickok   sw
(on corner halfway up)

Higgins, J.?M.   near cave
(*Ellison*, found) A John Higgins of Richland County, Illinois is listed as
one of those who traveled the Lander Cutoff on the way to California
in 1859. There was one wagon and five people in his party. *House of
Rep. Exec. Document #63, 1859.*

Or this could be James Higgins who was born in 1820 in Kent, England. In 1862 he emigrated to America crossing the Atlantic in the ship Manchester. He and his wife, Martha, crossed the plains in Joseph Harnes's Company arriving in Salt Lake City in October 1862. *LDS Biographical Encyclopedia, Vol 2, p. 303.*

Martha Baines Higgins wife of James Higgins. (L.D.S. Family History Center, Casper.)

Higgins, L M.   se (in crevice east of cave)

Hiles, H. M.   D Gate

Hill, A. O.   D Gate summit   **/59**

Hill, Geo   mt   **June 18, 50 Pekin, ILL**
(*Ellison*, found) This inscription appears with F. B. Chapman.
     A G. A. Hill, 18?? inscription found at Emigrant Springs, WY. *BLM 1989 Survey of Emigrant Springs.*

Hill, H.   D Gate
An H. H. Hill is listed as one of those using the Lander Cutoff in 1859. He left from Wisconsin en route to California. There was one wagon and two people in the party. *House of Rep. Exec. Document #63, 1859.*
     Or this could be Henry Hill, born in 1829, who is listed among the emigrant arrivals in Oregon in 1847. *Flora, Emigrants in 1847.*
     A Humphrey Hill, age thirty-two, is listed in the *Island County, Washington Territory, 1860 Census.* He listed his occupation as a farmer. *US Gen Web Archives.*
     Or an H. Hill from Beloit, Wisconsin was a member of the Badger Gold Hunters party that arrived at St. Joseph April 25, 1850 prior to departing for the gold fields. *Rasmussen, p. 113.*
     Yet another possibility is H. Hill who is listed in the Iowa & Wisconsin Emigrant Company Number Three departing from Kanesville on May 9, 1859. *Rasmussen, p. 124.*
     A Hanks Nevil Hill, and wife Elizabeth traveled to Oregon in 1853. *Flora, Emigrants in 1853.*
     Or a Henry Hill of Polk County and a Henry C. Hill of Yamhill County are both listed in the *1850 Oregon Territorial Census.*

Hill, J.   s   **July 49 (?)**

This could be Jasper S. Hill who was a member of the Mount Pleasant Mining Company from Burlington, Iowa. Jasper was seventeen when he joined the company to go to the gold fields. They left St. Joseph May 11, 1849 bound for California There were fifteen wagons, forty-two men, one woman and one child in this company. This group followed the Sink of the Mary's River up the Carson River and reached Weaverville Dry Diggings August 25. See other J. Hill inscription. *Platte River Narratives, p. 167.*

A J. O. Hill is listed in a Kentucky wagon train camped at Independence, April 19, 1849. He was a member of the Green River Mining Company bound for California. *Rasmussen, p. 30.* J. H. Ingram was also a member of this same company. Ingram's inscription is on the south side with a July 6, 1849 date.

Or a John Birney Hill traveled to California in 1850, seeking gold. He was born in Indiana and went back east after his California adventures and settled in Coles County, Illinois. He left a journal of this trip and his descriptions of Independence Rock and Devil's Gate are quoted in the text of the first and third chapter of this book. *Annals of Wyoming, Vol. 9, #4, p. 25.*

A J. P. Hill was listed in the Iowa Company No. 1 of California Emigrants passing through Kanesville about May 16, 1849. *Rasmussen, p. 62.*

Or refer to Rasmussen for other J. Hill's, 1849.

Or a James Hill living in Linn County and a James Hill of Washington County are both listed in the *1850 Oregon Territorial Census.*

Hill, J.   nt   **61**

A J. W. Hill inscription recorded at Emigrant Springs, WY. *BLM 1989 Survey of Emigrant Springs*

Hill, W.   nt

(*Ellison,* found) A William Hill, going to California, is listed among those using the Lander Cutoff in 1859. *House of Rep. Exec. Document, #63 1859.*

Or this could be the Wm. Hill, who was living in Clark County, and is listed in the *1850 Oregon Territorial Census.*

Or a William Hill, born in Canada in 1840, crossed the plains with ox teams arriving in the Salt Lake Valley in October 1849. Since he was only nine at the time it is doubtful that this is his inscription. *LDS Biographical Encyclopedia, Vol. 1, p. 791.*

A possibility is W. J. Hill, listed among the arrivals at Placerville in early September 1852. *Rasmussen, pg. 156.*
A W. Hill, 1850 inscription can be found at Names Hill, WY. *Brown, Emigrant Inscriptions.*

Hill, W. B.   s
(*Ellison*, found) May be W. S. Hill

Hilt, B. R.   nt
(*Ellison*, found)

Hinchoon, R. W.   nt   Je 11

Hitchfield, S. C.   s   1860
With J. Winet.

Ho(or u)stetter, E.   e (at corner)

Hobart, R.E.   s   August 11, 49
(*Ellison*, found) In our recent surveying we saw only the initial **R**.
A Reverend Randall Hobart was a member of the Wolverine Rangers from Marshall, Michigan. They left Independence in early May 1849 and arrived at Lassen's Ranch in early November. *The Gold Rush Wolverine Rangers; Mattes, Diary and Recollection Survey.*
More information about the Wolverine Rangers and Randall Hobart is found in the book, *The World Rushed In*, by J.S. Holliday. The Reverend Randal Hobart, along with his son William, worked several mining claims along the South Fork of the Feather River until the early 1860s. Reverend Hobart then went into politics. He was elected sheriff and then auditor of Nevada County. Later he edited a newspaper. *Holliday, p. 448.*

Hobb, D. A.   s   June 19, 1849

Hobbs (or y), D.A.   s   June 18, 1840
(*Ellison*, found) Ellison says maybe Hobbs. 1995 survey says Hobby. The date should be **1849**.

Hobby, D A   s   June, 1849
A David Hobby is listed as a member of a wagon train from Michigan in the field out of St. Joseph April 10, 1849, headed to California. *Rasmussen, p.15.*

Hodal, G. W.   nt

Hoffman, R.   sw
(*Ellison*, found) Located in what we call west. A Rut. Hoffman of Ohio is listed among those using the Lander Cutoff in 1859, en route to California. *House of Rep. Exec. Document, 1859.*

Hoffman, R.O.   nwt   **81**

Hoig, A.   unknown
This name is included in a handwritten list of names surveyed June 5, 1927 by an unidentified person. Locations were not recorded. Although this list is found in the R. S. Ellison files, the name is not included in his book. *Ellison Files, WY State Archives.* We have not found the name in recent surveying.

Hok-??, A.   n

Holaday, D.   cave   **July, 1853**
(*Ellison*, found) We read **July 6, 1853** Several members of a Holaday family emigrated to the Great Salt Lake Valley. This could be a member of that family. *Information from descendant, 1999.*
    In a June 5, 1927 survey list the date July 6, 1853 is given. This coincides with our reading. *Ellison Files, WY State Archives.*

Holcomb, Guy   cave   **July 10, 5 (?)**
In crevice.

Holister, J. A.   nt   **59**
(*Ellison*, found) Maybe with J. Oliver.

Holl, Zoe   swt

Holland, J .L.   nt   **1862**
(*Ellison*, found)

Hollingsworth, J. J.   mt   **June 11, 1862 "6th OHIO VC"**
This is Jack J. Hollingsworth, Commissary Sergeant in Company A, Eleventh Ohio Volunteer Cavalry. Sergeant Hollingsworth was twenty-three when he enlisted on October 24, 1861. He mustered out with his company on April 1, 1865. *Roster of Ohio Soldiers, Vol. XI.*

Hollister, P.   R. Pass n   **July 4, 1862**

Holly (Holey)   mt   **— 13, 74 (?)**

Holmes, T.   mt   **July, 64**
A T. Holmes inscription found at Register Cliff. *Scottsbluff Survey List.*

Holson, G.   nt   June 18, 1860
Probably with J. W. Ellis, D. Antee.

Hon, R.   sw

Hon (Hor?), A. I.   mt

Hones, F. A.   w

Honsaker, J.   R. Pass s   July, 18—?
In tar. Another unreadable tar name by it. A Joseph Hunsaker, 1799-1869, along with his wife Elizabeth is listed among the emigrant arrivals in Oregon in 1847. *Flora, Emigrants in 1847.*

Hook, G. W.   s   1868
Box around two Hook names.

Hook, J. W.   s
Box around the two Hook names.

Hoover, G.W.   nmt   Je 11, 62
(*Ellison*, found) This is probably Sergeant George W. Hoover, Company A, of the Eleventh Ohio Volunteer Cavalry. He was eighteen years old at the time of his enlistment on October 10, 1861. Members of the Eleventh Volunteer Ohio Cavalry were stationed at Sweetwater Station one mile east of Independence Rock. *Roster of Ohio Soldiers, Vol. XI.*

Hormsbee   nmt   July 9, 53
Probably with A. Marsh and W. B. Selder.

Horton, W. J.   nmt   July 24, 53
(*Ellison*, found)

Hose (?), E. L.   mt
Last name very faint.

House, S. Carling   mt   1862
(*Ellison*, found)

Houghton,   s   48
Reading of year is not certain.

Houstter (u?), E.   e corner

Howard   s

Howard, E. W.   w   **July**
E. W. Howard, July inscriptions in two different places.

Howard, E. W.   sw corner   **July, 52**
This name is on a handwritten list of names surveyed June 27, 1927 by an unidentified person. Locations are not recorded on this list. Although this list is found in the R. S. Ellison files, this name is not in his book. *Ellison Files, WY State Archives.*

A Howard family from Wisconsin crossed the plains in 1852 going to California. The family left Kenosha, Wisconsin on March 29, 1852 and traveled to Council Bluffs. Instead of waiting in line for the crowded ferry, the family made their own one wagon raft in order to cross the Missouri and were swept two miles downstream. They were not part of an organized company, but were always near other companies. They traveled to Amador County, California. Fifteen year old Mary Elizabeth left recollections of the journey. *Platte River Narratives, p. 364.*

Howard, H. G.   mt   **July 4, 62 N. Y**
(*Ellison*, found) A Horace Howard inscription recorded at Register Cliff. *Henderson 1930 Survey of Register Cliff.*

Howell, J.   se   **July 11, 1850**
(*Ellison*, found)

Howes, B. D.   mt   **June, 52**
This is a second B. D. Howes inscription within twenty-five feet of the other. This one done correctly.

There is a B. D. Howes listed as arriving in Placerville the first week of August 1852. *Rasmussen, p. 148.*

Howes , B. D.   mt
(*Ellison*, found) There are two B. D. Howes inscriptions close together. On this one the **e** was left out and inserted above the **w** and **s**.

Hoyt   s

Hoyt, A. P.   D Gate   **8 2 03**

Hr?—??, S.   nt
Almost totally gone.

Hubber, Howard   R. Pass n   **June 20th, 1852 ?**

Huff, T.   s
There is a T. Huff inscription also in Rattlesnake Pass.

Huff, T.   R. Pass n
Another T. Huff inscription can be found on Independence Rock.

Huger, A.   nt   **May 21 ?, 1865**

Hugh, M. K.   smt   **1824**
(*Ellison*, nf)

Hughes, J. J.   nmt   **July 4, 1850**
(*Ellison*, found) We read I. J. Hughes.

Hughes, J .L.   w
(*Ellison*, nf) A J. L. Hughes was a lieutenant in a wagon train listed in
the *St. Joseph Gazette*, May 10, 1850, This company was bound for
California *Rasmussen, p. 116*

Hughes, J. R.   net   **July 8, 1853**
(*Ellison*, found) J. R. Hughes was probably traveling with W. S. Williams,
W. W. Gilbert, and A. E. Moody. Another J. R. Hughes inscription can
also be found at Cache Cave. *Brown, Emigrant Inscriptions.*

Hughes, Ralph   nt

Humbely, L. A.   nt   **May 28, 1895 Wauneta, NB**
Seven people all from Wauneta, Nebraska all together.

Humer, F.   s

Hunsaker, J.   R. Pass s   **J 8, ?.**
In tar. Almost gone. A Joseph Hunsaker is listed among the arrivals in
Oregon in 1851. *Oregon in 1851.*

Hunt, E.   mt
(*Ellison*, nf) This is possibly what we read as E. Hurst.

Hunt, F. M.   cave   **1861**
(*Ellison*, found) Ellison lists this in the cave. It is just outside the cave.

Hunt, H. C.   w
An H. Hunt of Iowa is one of those listed as using the Lander Cutoff
going to California in 1859. *House of Rep. Document #63, 1859.*

Hunt, Jas.   s   **Co. D 13th Inf. Powder**
                              River Exp. S.L.C.Y. U.T. Age 18
(*Ellison*, found) Ellison has this located on the south. It is actually on the

south top. It is a very large inscription spreading over a large area of Independence Rock. We read the inscription as **Co. D, 13th Inf, June, 74 Powder River Exp., S. L. City, U. T, Age 18**. There is something more in the inscription that we cannot read. The whole inscription shows up best in a photograph.

Hunt, Levie   nmt   **1884 Age 18**

Hunt (or Hart), J.   s   **July, 49**
(*Ellison*, nf) Another J. Hunt inscription is recorded at Register Cliff. *Henderson 1930 Survey of Register Cliff.*

A John Carpenter Hunt, from Vermont, lived in Chico at the time of the *1890 California Census*. He was fifty when he registered for the census in March 1884. He listed his occupation as miner. *Butte County, California, 1890 Great Register, p. 123.*

A James Hunt, single from Indiana, is listed in the *Sawamish County, Oregon Territory, 1857 Census. US Gen Web Archives.*

Hurley, J. B.   smt   **1859**
This name is found in an area all alone. This could possibly be the same as the Hurley on middle top, listed below.

Hurley, J. P. (R?)   mt   **1857 (9?)**
A J. P. Hurley, 1857, inscription is recorded at Register Cliff. *Henderson 1930 Survey of Register Cliff.*

Hurst, E.   mt
I had correspondence from the descendant of E. Hurst, but was unable to get any followup information

Hursted, E.   e corner

Hurter, D. W.   w
Could possibly be Purter.

Husted, C. E.   mt

Hustetter, E.   st

Huston   D Gate
This person might have been traveling with Wm Upton.

Huston, M.   D Gate   **June 22, 60**
Written M. and Wm. L Huston.

Huston, W.L. net **1860**
(*Ellison*, found) We saw a date of Je 30 or 20? We also read **ILL** in 1996.
W. L. Huston also in Devil's Gate.

Huston, Wm. L D Gate **June 22, 60**
This is written M. & Wm L. Huston. There are four chain links above
name. W. L. Huston also on Independence Rock.

Huxtable n boulder **ILLS**

I & A nt
(*Ellison*, nf)

Ilullu s **1852**

Inb-?-urb s **July 6, 62**

Incley?, N.R. s
(*Ellison*, found)

Ingram s

Ingram, J. H. (?) s **July 6, 49**
(*Ellison*, found) Boxed together with W. H. Stephens.
There was a J. H. Ingram listed as a member of a Kentucky wagon
train known as the Green River Mining Company of Kentuck. This
company was camped at Independence on April 19, 1849 and bound
for California. *Rasmussen, p. 31.* J. O. Hill was another member of this
wagon train and there is a J. Hill, July, 49 inscription also on the south
side. Refer also to W. H. Stephens entry.

Ingrim, C.C. mt
Initials might be G.C. instead of C.C. A Godfrey C. Ingrim from Ohio
traveled to California in 1852. He traveled from Cincinnati to St.
Louis, to St. Joseph. His party crossed the Missouri River on May 6,
1852. They traveled through Salt Lake City, took the Salt Lake Cutoff
and arrived at Sacramento on September 1. He described Independence
Rock as "so hard could not be cut with a cold chisel." *Platte River
Narratives, p. 365*

Irwin, G. mt
(*Ellison*, found) A Judge Robert Irwin and family left St. Joseph the second week of May 1852, bound for California. They were in a wagon
train led by Elias H.Perry. One thousand head of cattle accompanied

the Perry wagon train. This Irwin could be of this party. *Information from descendant, Tom Crews,*

Judge Irwin had an eleven year old grandson named George. This could be his inscription. *Brown, Wyoming Trails Newsletter.*

Ivey, C .C.   mt   **98 USA**

J., D. S.   wt

J., E.   st   **1860**

Two initials together. Says **RS + EJ ∞ H.** Very large letters. The inscription uses the oxbow symbol, probably meaning "with."

Jack, A. J.   nt   **June 11, 52**
(*Ellison*, found)

Jack, A. (?)   se

An A. Jack inscription is also found at Ayres Natural Bridge on La Prele Creek out of Douglas, WY. *Surveyed by the author.*

An A. Jack is listed as a member of the Missouri & Georgia Mining Company in the vicinity of Fort Childs, May 18, 1849 bound for California. *Rasmussen, p. 70.*

An Albina Adeline Jack is listed among the arrivals in Oregon in 1851. She died in 1896. A William A. Jack is also listed among the arrivals. It is assumed this was her husband. *Oregon in 1851.*

Jackson, Joe   D Gate

A Joseph Jackson is listed as a member of the Wayne County Company from Indiana traveling to California in 1850. They left St. Joseph on April 10. George Keller left a diary of this company's travels across the plains. *Company roster from Keller diary.* Refer to the Keller entry.

A J. B. Jackson is listed in the *Lewis County, Oregon, 1849 Territorial Census.* They were a family of six, he and his wife and four children. *US Gen Web Archives.*

Jackson, T.   mt   **59**
(*Ellison*, found)

Jacob, Norton   nt   **1847**

Large inscription. This inscription is the only one of the Pioneer Party that has been found. Norton Jacob was a member of the Brigham Young 1847 Pioneer Party traveling to the Great Salt Lake Valley. He was also one of the first to return to Winter Quarters in August 1847. His photo can be seen in Chapter One, page 33. He left a detailed journal of both trips, but he gave no details about putting his name on Independence Rock. The Pioneer Party did spend time at the Rock and the group held a prayer meeting on top of Independence Rock. Although he did not record anything about inscribing his name, like many other diariests Norton Jacob was quite descriptive about the saleratus lakes just to the east of Independence Rock. He writes:

"June 21 Mon. A beautiful clear morning moved on S West 7 1/2 miles and halted on the N bank of the Sweet-water one of the principal sources of Platte. this is a Beautiful Rivulet of clear water 50 yds wide I visited the Soda spring while we were halted here a mile & a half below. this Spring or more properly a Pool is a great Natural curiosity it is some 4 or 5 hundred yards in circumference, clear water without any outlet, & having the taste of Strong Lye, with a tincture of common Salt. As the water is diminished by evaporation the sand on the shore is covered with a substance white as the driven Snow. & that answers every purpose of Saleratus. I found it lying from 1/2 to 3 inches thick, & soon gathered us a bucket full—when I returned our camp had started, 1 1/4 miles came to the Southern Point of Independence rock on the bank of the Stream, this is a Pile of Granite standing in an Isolated position of a level grassy Plain & is 45 yards high & 600 b6 300 yards in extent & with a round cap licke summit on which there is Pools of water from five to ten feet in width several feet deep—High rocky ranges of Mountains on both sides of the Stream from 1/2 to a mile distant..." *Norton Jacob Journal.*

Jacobs, J. W.	mt	**June 10, 62**
(*Ellison*, found)		
Jadder, S. A.	nt	
Jaeson	D Gate	
James, M. M.	mt	

A James family from Lexington, Missouri traveled to California in 1851 or 1852. This was a family with four sons. *From James Family Records, descendant.*

Jaret, J. Hal.?	cave	
(*Ellison*, nf)		
Jemings, J. A.	nt	
Jenner, O.N.	mt	

Jepsoft, J.   mt
(*Ellison*, found)

Jerome, M. S.   mt
In this area it is hard to tell old names from 1920–30 Masonic names.

Jo ? la,   mt   **Sept. 5, 90**
The **5** is inscribed above **Sept.**

Joel   mt   **57**

John, G. (B?)   s
In tar. Could be part of the **Smahs** inscription, also in tar, but this is different printing, so they are probably two different inscriptions.

Johns, S (A?)   R. Pass s   **18 ??.**
Backwards **s** in name. A Johns family is listed in the *Tuality County, Oregon Territory, 1849 Census. US Gen Web Archives.*

Johnson, ?   se
(*Ellison*, nf)

Johnson, R.   w   **1840**
(*Ellison*, nf) A Robert Johnson, living in Clackamas County, is listed in the *1850 Oregon Territorial Census.*
   Or a Ruefus Johnson is listed in the *Champoeg County, Oregon Territory, 1849 Census. US Gen Web Archives.*

Johnson, V.   nmt
A Verna Johnson was a member of a party crossing to Oregon in 1852. *Webber, Comprehensive Index to Oregon Trail Diaries.*

Jon -(?) , J.   nt   **1827**
Date questionable.

Jones,—lty ?   R. Pass w   **Jun**

Jones, A.   mt
An Alexander Jones of Clark County is listed in the *1850 Oregon Territorial Census.*
   An A. Jones, 1850, inscription is at Names Hill. WY. *Brown, Emigrant Inscriptions.*

Jones, C.   w
A Charles Jones of Clackamas County and a Cyrus Jones of Washington County are both listed in the *1850 Oregon Territorial Census.*

A C. Jones, age twenty-seven, is listed in the *Island County, Washington Territory, 1860 Census*. He listed his occupation as laborer. *US Gen Web Archives*.

Jones, E. R.

This inscription is on a survey list dated June 5, 1927 done by an unidentified person. No locations are recorded on this list. Although this list is found in the R. S. Ellison files, the name is not in the Ellison book. *Ellison Files, WY State Archives*. This name has not shown up in our recent surveying. Refer to the Joseph Jones entry for possible initials of parents. *Information from a Jones descendant*.

Jones, E. S.   s   60

Jones, E. S.   s   60 ?

(*Ellison*, found) Two E. S. Jones inscriptions within twenty feet of each other.

Jones, F. A.   w

An F. A. Jones in the Green River Mining Company of Kentuck was camped at Independence, Missouri on April 19, 1849. This company was bound for California. *Rasmussen, p. 31*. Other members of this wagon train were W. H. Stephens, J. Hill, and J. H. Ingram all of whom left their names on the Rock.

Or this could be F. Jones, age thirty two, who is listed in the *Island County, Washington Territory, 1860 Census*. He listed his occupation as farm laborer. *US Gen Web Archives*.

Jones, F. R.   s   60 ?

Four Jones inscriptions are on south end dated **60**.

Jones, Joseph   nt   July 4, 1863

(*Ellison*, found) We read the date as **1863**, but in 1853 a Jones family traveled to Oregon and descendants have information that a Joseph Jones left his name on the Rock.

S. W. R. and Elizabeth Jones left in the spring of 1853 to make the long trip to Oregon Territory. They traveled with their ten children, one of whom was five year old Jesse Barrymore Jones. Fifty years after the trip, Jesse wrote down these memories of the crossing:

"Never since I saw it— Independence Rock, I mean—have I forgotten our camp there. I can give but a faint idea of the impression that is is so lasting, but it is a red rock eighty or a hundred feet high. Joe (his fourteen year old brother) got a scolding for climbing up to cut his name over all. I wonder if the rain and frost have left the marks of those early pioneers?" *Information from descendant, Jay Jones, Danville, PA.*

Jones, S.   s   **60 ?**

A Shadrach Jones, born in England in 1832, emigrated to the Great Salt Lake Valley. Date unknown. *LDS Biographical Encyclopedia, Vol. III, p. 660.*

Jones, W. M.   swt

A William Jones from Missouri is listed as having traveled the Lander Cutoff in 1859 en route to California. There were two wagons and nine people in this Jones party. *House of Rep. Exec. Document #63, 1859.*

Or refer to Rasmussen for other William Jones.

Or there are several Wm. Jones, different counties, listed in the *1850 Oregon Territorial Census.*

Jons, L .S.   s   **60**

Jor ?s, T.   swt

Very weathered. Almost gone.

Jordan, H. C.   D Gate

A H. W. Jordan inscription recorded at Emigrant Springs, WY. *BLM 1989 Survey of Emigrant Springs*

Juhl, K.L.   net

Justley, G.   cave

(*Ellison*, nf)

K., A. M.   mt

Tails on letters.

K., C. B.   w

K., D.   ne   **52**

With M.K., old style 2, halfway up.

K. , H.   nt

(*Ellison*, nf)

K., H. L.   sw (midway up)

K., J.   net   **52**

(*Ellison*,found) With initials M. R.

K., J. C.   s   July 8, 49
(*Ellison*, nf)

K., M.   ne   52
With D. K. It has an old style **2** on **52.**

K., M.   nt
(*Ellison*, nf)

K., W. R.   n
Behind fence.

Ka (O?) mr, C.   nt

Kamoly (Es?), C. C.   net   1871
Could be Kanoly or Kaholy?

Karr, M. B.   mt
(*Ellison*, found)

Keats   nw

Keck, H. H.   sw   June 09

Keele   Sent. Rock
Name in tar. Located on boulder on north ground.

Keller, George H.   s   1850
(*Ellison*, found) We saw **Gorge.** Inscription is in negative relief. He
records putting his name on Independence Rock with tar.

In 1850 George Keller from Wayne County, Indiana made the trip
across to California. He was physician to the Wayne County Company.
This group was able to leave early in the season for they jumped off from
St. Joseph on April 10, 1850 and had reached Fort Laramie by May third.
Early May was the usual starting time from the east for the emigrant parties in most years. This group went past Fort Bridger, Fort Hall, and took
the Lassen's Cutoff to California Cutoff. They arrived at Lassen's Ranch
on July 4th, very early in the season. He left a journal, *A Trip Across the
Plains and Life in California. Platte River Narratives, p. 270.*

George Keller left this description of the trip past Independence
Rock: "The Alkaline Lakes are about fourteen miles from 'Prospect
Hill'. The surface of the earth here, is covered with almost pure car-
bonate of soda, varying from two to ten inches in thickness. This salt
either for baking or any other use, is almost equal to the commercial

article.—Our fuel here, and for hundreds of miles farther, was the wild sage. This is an aromatic shrub differing considerable from the common garden sage. The stalks are found from one fourth of an inch, to three or four inches in diameter. It does not generally grow more than three or four feet high. After growing a few years, the stalks apparently break off at the surface of the earth, and seem entirely dead, while the tops are in full vigor.—In this condition it makes very good fuel.

"Independence Rock is five miles from the Alkaline Lakes. This rock stands 'solitary and alone' in the valley of Sweet Water River, entirely separated from the neighboring mountains. It is about five hundred feet long, two hundred broad, and about two hundred and fifty in height. It is composed of granite. We left our names in tar upon this rock, as thousands had done before us.—We encamped on the Sweet Water about a half mile above the rock." *Keller, WY Annals, p, 71.*

Author's note: We have found other names where diarists recorded that they painted their name and yet the name remains. Evidently the paint or tar wore away but due to chemical reaction on the Rock from the remaining residue, the inscription remains in what we call negative relief.

George Keller, 1850 inscription was also on Chimney Rock. *Information from Chimney Rock Historical Site*

Kelley, B. W.   mt
(*Ellison*, found)

Kellogg, W. H.   s
A William Kellogg is listed as a member of the Knox County Illinois Company, probably departing from Kanesville May 30, 1852. *Rasmussen, p. 65.*

Kelly, Henry   nt   53 Calloway Co. , MO
(*Ellison*, found)

Kenaston, A.T.   nt   Mercer Co., ILL
(*Ellison*, found)

Kendall, G.   w   81

Kendrick, L. D.   unknown
This name was included in a list of names recorded June 5, 1927. Locations were not identified. Although this list was found in the R. S. Ellison files, the name is not included in his book. *Ellison Files, WY State Archives.* We have not located the name in our recent surveying.

Kennauch (or n) , D. ne

Kennedy, H.L. nmt 7, 20—

Kennedy, J. net 52
(*Ellison*, found) With S. Forgert.
A J. M. Kennedy is listed among the arrivals at Placerville on September 21, 1852. *Rasmussen, pg. 166*

Kennedy, J. I. C. nt
With M. N. James.

Kennedy, J. K. cave July 26, 1850
(*Ellison*, nf) A John Kennedy is listed among the arrivals at St. Joseph by April 9, 1850, en route to California. *Rasmussen, p. 104.*

John Kennedy, from Ireland, is listed in the *1890 California Census.* He lived in Chico and was forty-eight when he registered for the census in May 1884. He listed his occupation as laborer. *Butte County, California, 1890 Great Register, p. 135.*

Or this could be John Kennedy, from Maryland, who lived in Nord and worked as an engineer at the time of the *1890 California Census.* He was sixty-six at the time of registration in 1884. *Butte County, California, 1890 Great Register, p. 136.*

A J. K. Kennedy inscription can be found at Names Hill, WY. *Brown, Emigrant Inscriptions.*

Kennedy, James mt
(*Ellison*, nf) A J. M. Kennedy is listed as arriving in Placerville the second week of September 1852. *Rasmussen, p. 164.*

This could possibly be Private James Kennedy of Company A of the Eleventh Ohio Volunteers. Private Kennedy was twenty-seven at the time of his enlistment on November 15, 1861. Members of the Eleventh were stationed at Sweetwater Bridge Station one mile east of Independence Rock. *Roster of Ohio Soldiers, Vol. XI.*

Kennedy. M. E. (?) mt
(*Ellison*, found) A Michael Kennedy, and wife Ellen, are listed among the arrivals in Oregon in 1851. *Oregon in 1851.*

Kennedy, W. M. F. cave
(*Ellison*, nf) A W. F. Kennedy, single from Illinois, is listed in the *Sawamish County, Oregon Territory, 1857 Census. US Gen Web Archives.*

Kenner, J. I. C. mt

Kennig, P. E. unknown **June 30, 1850**
This name appears on a list compiled by D. W. Greenburg on August
22, 1926. Locations were not recorded. Although this list is found in
the R. S. Ellison files, the name is not included in his book. *Ellison Files,
WY State Archives.* We have not found the name in recent surveying.

Kennsay (?), W. R. n **July ?**

Kenyon, P. D. Gate summit **1852**

Kern (e)?, J. mt **52 ??**
A John T. Kerns left Rensselaer, Indiana, March 15, 1852 en route to
Oregon. He crossed the Missouri River at Council Bluffs on May 19.
His company had to wait ten days at the crossing due to the congestion
and flimsy boats. They arrived at Ft. Laramie a month later on June 19.
His group traveled to Oregon via the Barlow Road and arrived in
Portland on October 13, 1852. He left a diary of the trip across the
plains. *Mattes, p. 368.*
    A similar inscription, **J. Kerns**, with no date, can also be found on
the middle top of the Rock. It may or may not be the same man.

Kerns, J. mt
(*Ellison*, found) A J. W. Kerns and wife Ann are listed among the
arrivals in Oregon in 1851. *Oregon in 1851.*
    Or this could be the same person as the J. Kern(e) listed above which
is also located on the middle top.

Kiel, Jr., John w **July 10, 1905**

Kiger, H E. nmt **June 15, 1853. Knoxville, ILL**
(*Ellison*, found) H. E. Kiger is with C. W. Lewis and C. W. Russell.

Kilgore, W. D. nw slope **1889 (99?)**

Kilgore, W. D. nw

Kimball nt
This inscription very weathered, large letters. This could be any one of
a number of Mormon Kimballs who crossed the plains over the years.
    Several members of a Kimball family are listed among the emigrant
arrivals in Oregon in 1847. *Flora, Emigrants in 1847.*
    Or a Nathan Kimball of Clatsop County and a Simamon Kimball
of Clackamas County are both listed in the *1850 Oregon Territorial
Census.*

Kimball, M.   R. Pass n   **June 17, 1859**
Could be Marshall Kimball who first crossed the plains in 1848 in Henry Harrison's Hundred. To date no records found if he traveled the trail in other years. *LDS Crossing the Plains Index*

King, Sue   nt   **MO**
Date very hard to read. Probably with Sue Park.

Kinman, S.   net   **52**
(*Ellison*, found) We'd say the location is more on north middle top.

A Seth Kinman from Pennsylvania is listed among those California bound emigrants arriving in Kanesville during the period of May 6 - 13, 1852. *Rasmussen, p. 136.*

A Seth Kinman, 1849 was also recorded on Chimney Rock. He had left Illinois for California in 1849. He possibly went to California in two different years. *Information from Chimney Rock State Historical Site.*

Kinne, G.   s
(*Ellison*, found) An Edwin G. Kinne party from Oconomowock, Wisconsin took the Lander Cutoff in 1859. This G. Kinne could be either Edwin G. or another member of the family. *House of Rep. Exec. Document #63, 1859.*

Kinnis, J. M.   s

Kinsela, T. J.   nt
(*Ellison*, found)

Kinsolla, T. K.   nt

Kionda (Kisnda), G.   w

Kirkpatrick, J. S.   cave
(*Ellison*, nf) A J. S. Kirkpatrick is listed as Colonel of the Wisconsin & Iowa Union Company organized near Council Bluffs on May 23, 1849. *Rasmussen, p. 66.*

In a survey list done June 5, 1927, the surveyor made the notation that this inscription was done in green paint. *Ellison Files, WY State Archives.*

Kite, J. W.   nt   **1863 ILL**
(*Ellison*, found)

Kite (?), Mrs. RAS   mt
Mrs. Ras inscribed below Kite

Kite, H.   mt   **June 29, 52**
(*Ellison*, found) This inscription is in the same box with FAOS Fox. Mrs. Ras under Kite.

Kl—b, L.   s
Could be Ko—bs.

Klimer (?)   s   **June, 52**
Near ground below cave.

Klines, C.   s   **J 17 52**
This inscription with G. Near.

Klingaman, Geo.   nt   **July 12, 59**
A George Klinagaman is listed among those using the Lander Cutoff in 1859 en route to Oregon. He was going alone and had three head of stock. *House of Rep. Exec. Document #63, 1859.*

Klinger, Ben   nmt   **July 2, 61**
(*Ellison*, found)

Koch, H.   net   **June, 65**

Koehne, H. L.   e boulder **64. Piqua, Ohio. Capt. 11th OVC**
Captain Koehne left another inscription on north west top.
 This is Henry L. Koehne of the Eleventh Ohio Volunteer Cavalry. Captain Koehne was thirty-two years old when he enlisted in Ohio on October 23, 1861 He was promoted to Captain of Company A on March 18, 1863. *Roster of Ohio Soldiers, Vol. XI*

Koehne, H. L.   nwt   **64 Piqua, Ohio Capt. 11th OVC**
(*Ellison*, found) This inscription also on e boulder. Refer to that entry.

Koff, M. B.   mt

Koku, L.   D Gate   **97**

Koms, D.   ne (midway up)   **52**

Koo (or Kon), G.   w

Kord, L.   D Gate   **USDS.**

Koruk ??   st

Krell ?, T.   s
  Badly weathered.

Krhurot, H. P.   se

Kropp, Geo.   sw
  A Mrs. Kropp, 1897 inscription also found on west side, midway up.

Kropp, Mrs.   w   **1897**
  Geo. Kropp also found in southwest area.

Kruger, A.   nt   **May (?)5, 1865**
  Date almost gone.

Kyes, A.   cave

L - ? Larly, M.   D Gate   **ILL**

L., C. C.   mt   **Aug. 11, 58**
  Written **Mr. & Mrs. C. C. L.** The **s** is backwards.

L., F.   nt

L., H.   mt
  Under Yaeger on middle top. Same type of printing.

L., M. A.   w

L., P. F.   w   **53**
  (*Ellison*, nf)

L., S. C.   s   **June 27, 1847**

LA, L. L.   mt

Lafex   e corner

Lamar—, M.   n
  May not be nineteenth century.

Lamb, D.   e   **July 5, ??.**
  See D. Lamb with a July 4, 1861 date. This person might have put his
  name on the Rock twice on different days while he was at
  Independence Rock

Lamb, D.   se   July 4, 1861

Lamb, M.D.   s   July 4, 1886

Lamb, V. L. (?)   swt   **UREA**
  (*Ellison*, found)

Lamooley   s

Lamoreaux, V. L.   nw (midway up)   **8, 10,—?**
                                                        Sioux City, IO

Lams, S.   swt
  Written **LAms**.

Lams (o?)urer,V. L.   swt

Lan, L.   unknown   **'49**
  This inscription is included in a survey list done June 5, 1927 by an
  unidentified person. Locations were not recorded. Although this list is
  found in the R. S. Ellison files, the name is not included in his book.
  Ellison Files, WY State Archives. We have not found the name in our
  recent surveying.

Lancaster, N.   sw   **May 9, 1850**
  (*Ellison*, found) Very large letters.

Lancet   w   **age 24**
  A **7** also visible. Not known if it is day, month, or year.

Lanenbarc, A.   net   **JE 21, 1860**
  Possibly Lanenbare. The date could be 1865.

Lang, L.   w   **52 (?)**
  An L. Lang is listed as arriving in Placerville the first week of September
  1852. Rasmussen, p. 157.

Lanog—?en   e

Lansing, L.   w   **49**
  (*Ellison*, found)

Lap, H. W.   nmt   **64**

Larken or Larner, T.   swt

Laron, L.   cave   **1852**
  (*Ellison*, nf)

Laron, L.   mt   **1858**
  (*Ellison*, found)

LaRue, A. & M.   nt   **5, 27, 36**
  This could be twentieth century.

Las - ??, U. or J.?   R. Pass n

Lauren   s

Laux, L. L.   n   **47**
  Behind fence.

Lawrence   n
  Behind fence.

Lawton, G. B.   s   **July 24, 49**
  (*Ellison*, found)

Lax, S.   nmt
  Old script.

Lea, I.   swt
  (*Ellison*, nf)

Lea, J.   mt
  J. Lea also on swt.

Lea, J.   swt

Lea, R.   swt
  (*Ellison*, found) R. Lea and T. Lea together.

Lea, T.   swt
  (*Ellison*, found) R. Lea and T. Lea together.

Lean, M. B.   s   **May 22, 1850**
  (*Ellison*, found) We think it could be May 29.

Lean, S.   s   **May 22, 1850**
  (*Ellison*, found)

Leason, C.   nt

C. Leason and E. Leason together. These may not be old, for some it is difficult to know.

Leason, E.   nt

See C. Leason

Leavitt, John   s

Difficult to read in most light. A J. H. Leavitt is listed among those going via St. Louis en route to California, April 1850. *Rasmussen, p. 99.*

Leck (Lock?), H. H.   s   **July 3**

Lee   net

(*Ellison*, nf)

Lee   s boulder

There is a J. C. Lee also on the same south boulder.

Lee, F. G.   cave

(*Ellison*, nf) A Francis Lee, living in Clackamas County, is listed in the *1850 Oregon Territorial Census.*

Lee, J. C.   s boulder   **June, 1852**

A J. Lee listed among those arriving in Placerville between August 1–8, 1852. *Rasmussen, p. 148.*

Lee, J. M.   s   **60**

Lee, J. S.   se   **June, 1850**

(*Ellison*, found)

Lee, W.   nmt

(*Ellison*, found) A William Lee of Ohio is listed among those using the Lander Cutoff in 1859. There were two wagons and seven people in this party going to California. *House of Rep. Exec. Document #63, 1859.*

Or a William Lee left Washington D. C. on April 11, 1858, going by boat to Fort Leavenworth. He was a member of the United States Corps of Topographical Engineers under Captain J. H. Simpson. He left notes of the 1858-59 reconnaissance. *Platte River Narratives, p. 488.*

Or a Washington Lee of Clark County and a Wilson Lee of Polk County are both listed in the *1850 Oregon Territorial Census.*

Or this could be Wesley Lee, from Illinois, who is listed in the *1890 California Census.* He was a druggist in Chico. He was age fifty-nine when he registered for the census in April 1884. *Butte County, California, 1890 Great Register, p. 144.*

Leeper, Miss M.I.(L.)   wt   **6, 95** (96?)
Seems to be with McCorkle and Chalfant.

Leeper, W. H.   mt   **July 3, 1863**

Leff, J. C.   s
Two different inscriptions.

Leff, J. C.   s   **June, 1850**
Halfway up, possibly J. Cleff.

Leggett, Mrs. T.   nt
Possibly related to a Thomas A. Leggett, from New York who lived in Oroville at the time of the *1890 California Census.* He was a farmer and was seventy-eight years old when he registered for the census in August 1884, *Butte County, California, 1890 Great Register, p. 145.*

Lemon, G.   mt   **Je 16, 52**
(*Ellison,* found) The inscription is boxed in with P. Miller, B. F. Norton, S.C. Carey, C.H. Ball.

Levert, A.   mt

Lewis, C.W.   nmt   **June 15, 1853**
                                                      Knoxville, Ill.
(*Ellison,* found) Three inscriptions together. Lewis, Kiger, and Russell.

Lewis, D. O.   s
(*Ellison,* nf) A David Lewis, from Platt County, Missouri, is listed as one of those who died along the trail on the way to Oregon in 1852. *US Gen Web Archives.*

   Or this could be D. C. Lewis who is listed among the arrivals to Oregon in 1851. *Oregon in 1851.*

Lewis (first L?), S.   R. Pass n   **June ???.**
Hard to read, in paint, name carved over it. A Stuart Lewis, living in Linn County, is listed in the *1850 Oregon Territorial Census.*

   A Samuel Lewis, from Missouri, is listed in the *1890 California Census.* He was a farmer who lived at Pence's Ranch and gave his age as fifty-six at the time he registered for the census in 1884. *Butte County, California, 1890 Great Register, p. 146.*

Ligget, H. M.   mt

Onder Hollingsworth.

Lindsay, E. J.   net

Linn, C. E.   mt   June 15, 52

(*Ellison*, found) This inscription written J. I. and C. E. Linn.

An E. Linn and a Homer Linn are listed among those who traveled to Oregon in 1851. *Flora, Emigrants in 1852.*

In 1852 Eliza Ann McCauley mentions seeing Linn's name on a bluff in the Green River area (Names Hill?) dated June 11. She states among the names, "Linn of New London" *Holmes, Vol 4., p. 62.*

Linn, J. M.   mt   July 17

A Jack Linn inscription recorded at Emigrant Springs, WY. *BLM 1989 Survey of Emigrant Springs.*

A John Linn, from Kentucky, is listed as living in Chico at the time of the *1890 California Census.* He was fifty-eight when he registered for the census in 1884, and listed his occupation as laborer. *Butte County, California, 1890 Great Register, p. 147.*

Linn, J.I. & C.E.   mt   June 15, 52

(*Ellison*, found) See notes under C. E. Linn.

Linn, W. M.   mt   July, 77

Name written over something under it.

Livingston, R.G.   mt   ILL

(*Ellison*, found)

Lloyd, B. F.   mt   June 10, 62

(*Ellison*, found) This is probably Benjamin F. Lloyd of Company A of the 11th Ohio Volunteer Cavalry. He was twenty-one when he enlisted on October 28, 1861. He was discharged on January 28, 1863 and then enlisted in the 4th U. S. Cavalry at that time. *Roster of Ohio Soldiers, Vol. XI.*

Lodrington, W.   s

Possibly Isodrington. Hard to read. Since this is so hard to read, this could possibly be A. N. Lundington of Dallas Co., Iowa who took the Lander Cutoff in 1859. *House of Rep. Exec. Doc. #63, 1859.*

Log—   se

Loga (n?)	nw	
Logan, J.	D Gate	June, 19, 52
Logan, J.	s	

This could be the James or Jim Logan who were members of a wagon party crossing to Oregon in 1853. *Webber, Comprehensive Index to Oregon Trail Diaries.*

A Joseph Logan and a James Logan both of Washington County are listed in the *1850 Oregon Territorial Census.*

Logue, Wilbur	n	Au, 1890
Loomis, H.	w	N.Y.
With E. Cameron.		
Lord, C. or G.	s	June 21, 60 or 69
Lovie, W.	s	
(*Ellison*, found)		
Lowry, E. S.	nt	55 Rochester, N.Y.
(*Ellison*, found)		
Lu—k, E.	s	54
Lucas, G. W.	s	
(*Ellison*, found)		
Lucas, J.	se	

A Joseph Lucas is listed in the *Champoeg County, Oregon Territory, 1849 Census. US Gen Web Archives.*

Lucas, T.   se

This could be read as **Louas**. A Thos. Lucas of Yamhill County is list-ed in the *1850 Oregon Territorial Census.*

Also Thomas Lucas is listed among those emigrants arriving by wagon train in Oregon in 1850. *The Oregonian, Dec 4, 1925.*

Lud—?, J.	s	July 4
Luding, J.	e corner	June 1849
Luellen, W.	s	July 11, 18 (5?)2

Luff or (p), J. C.   st   **June 16, 1860**
   This inscription is on a survey list done June 5, 1927 by an unidentified person. That listed inscription does not include a date. Although
this list is found in the R. S. Ellison files, this name is not included in
his book. *Ellison Files, WY State Archives.*

Lybyen, S. M.   nt

Lyn—s, D. B.   nt
   This is hard to read. It is possibly same as Ellison's D. B. Lynch.

Lynch, D. B.   nt
   (*Ellison*, nf) A David Lynch is listed among the arrivals in Oregon in
1851. *Oregon in 1851.*
   A D. Lynch, age twenty-eight, is listed in the *Island County, Washing-
ton Territory, 1860 Census.* He listed his occupation as a surveyor. *US
Gen Web Archives.*

Lyte   D Gate west   **84**
   Beautiful style printing.

M, Wm   swt   **1869**

M(h)oa (r)ley??, J.   w
   Could be McArley? Very difficult to read.

M—? I ? innes, Kate   e

M—???, John   w

M., A.   mt

M., A.   nmt   **1853**
   (*Ellison*, found) Beautiful lettering.

M., A. F.   swt
   The **F.** is backwards. Anchor drawn by initials.

M., B.   s   **1850**

M., B.   s

M., F.   se   **Ag??**
   The **Ag** is located underneath the initials **F.M.**

M., F.   s   **1850**

M., G.   e

M., N.   D Gate

M., N. T.   R. Pass w
Letters pecked.

M., R.   w
Together with L.D.

M., W.   swt   188—?

M., T. S.   Sent Rock
Located on boulder on north at ground level.

M., W.   swt   1849
(*Ellison*, found)

Maben, J. A.   net   June 2, 1881
(*Ellison*, found) We saw June 21 possibly. In a survey of Independence
Rock done August 22, 1926, by D. W. Greenburg he recorded J. A.
Maben but with a date of June 21, 1870. *Ellison Files, WY State Archives.*

Machin, T. N.   sw
(*Ellison*, found)

Mahar [—?]   nw
On corner ground.

Maher, M.   mt
(*Ellison*, found)

Mains, J. W. D.   D Gate   July, 62

Manchester   s boulder   Jun 15, /64
In cursive.

Maning, A.   cave   June 2, 1850
(*Ellison*, nf)

Manke, W. I.   mt   1860 ILL

Mann, M.?A.   mt   June 25, 50
(*Ellison*, found)

Marker, ??ricia   n
Written with Lynda Marker.

Marker, Lynda   n
Written Lynda & ????ricia Marker.

Marlin, P.   D Gate   July 4, 1861

Marrott   s

Marsh, A.   net   July 9, 53
(*Ellison*, found) This person was probably traveling with Hormsbee and
W. B. Selder.

Marsh, H.   mt   July 4
(*Ellison*, found)

Marshall   ne   July (??)—876
On ground.

Martin, Dawson A.   nmt   June 21, 58 ILL
(*Ellison*, found)

Martin, I.(J.?) P.   nt

Martin, L. P.   nt

Martin, P.   D Gate   July 14, 1861
P. Martin, Jul inscription is also on Independence Rock.

Martin, P.   net   Jul
(*Ellison*, found) P. Martin, July 14, 1861 inscription at Devil's Gate.

Mashek (r?), A. J.   n

Mason   e
Very faint.

Mason, B.   D Gate   May 25, 18

Mason, E. L.   mt   Jy 4, 55

(*Ellison*, found) E. L. Mason has his name on three locations on the Rock.
An E. Mason inscription found at Register Cliff. *Scottsbluff Survey List.*

Mason, E. L.   e   Jul 4, 55
This name can be found three times on the Rock.

Mason, E.L. (?)   emt   **Jul 4, 55**
(*Ellison*, found) We saw one inscription on east ground and also an E. L. Mason, same date on middle top. The one we saw on the middle top had Jy instead of Jul.

Mason, H.   emt
(*Ellison*, found)

Mason, J.   emt
(*Ellison*, found) A James Mason, from Cambridge, Ohio, traveled the plains with the Cambridge-California Mining Company No. 2 going to California in 1850. This party "jumped off" at Westport Landing on April 30, 1850 and was at Fort Laramie on June 13 and Fort Bridger on July 12. They traveled through Salt Lake City on the way to California. The company fell apart at Deer Creek and divided their property at that time. James Mason left a diary of the journey. Of Independence Rock he writes that he heard that Independence Rock, named by trappers, was the frequent scene of "mountain revelings." *Platte River Narratives, p. 280.*

Or this could be John A. Mason from Pike County, Illinois, who also traveled to California with the Pike Country Mining Company in 1850. This Mason wrote three letters, one from Fort Laramie, one from Salt Lake City, and one from California that gave details of the trip. *Platte River Narratives, p. 280.*

Or a Private James J. Mason was a member of Company F, Eleventh Kansas Volunteer Cavalry. There are several military inscriptions left on Independence Rock by soldiers stationed there in the 1860s. *Index to Kansas Volunteer Regiment Enlistments, 1861-1863.*

A John C. Mason is buried at the Chico, California, cemetery. He was born in 1815 and died in California in 1855.

Mason, L.E.   emt
(*Ellison*, nf)

Mason, M. M.   mt   **51? WIS**
(*Ellison*, found) We saw the **WIS** in 1994. Since the date is a question it could be M. M. Mason of Wisconsin who was listed among a small group of men who arrived in Downieville, California on August 14, 1852. The had crossed the Missouri River on May 15, 1852. *Rasmussen, p. 146.*

Masten, E. L.   mt   **54 (?)**

Masters, J.   n
Almost totally lichen covered. Behind fence.

Masters, John   nt
(*Ellison*, found) Very weathered. An A. J. Masters is listed in the *Tuality County, Oregon Territory, 1849 Census.* He lived there with his wife and two children. *US Gen Web Archives.*

Mastin, G.W.   nt   July 2, 62
(*Ellison*, found)

May, D.R. (D.F.?)   s   **May**

Ma^ce Sttots   saddle   July 4, 62
The **MA^Ce** could possibly be first initials.

Mc, B. F.   mt   **64**
Definitely old.

McAfee, A.D.   mt
(*Ellison*, found) An A. D. McAfee is listed among the arrivals at Placerville during the third week of September 1852. *Rasmussen, p. 167.*

McBride, J.   cave
(*Ellison*, found) Could be James McBride who went to Yamhill County Oregon in 1845.
     A Jas. McBride, living in Washington County, and a James McBride of Yamhill County are both listed in the *1850 Oregon Territorial Census*
     Or this could be John H. McBride who went to Oregon via the Barlow Road in 1846. His party crossed the Missouri River at St. Joseph on April 20 and followed the Platte Road to Fort Laramie, Fort Hall, and the Dalles. This party met Lansford Hastings in the South Pass area but the group ignored Hastings's sales pitch encouraging emigrants to try his new route. *Platte River Narratives, p. 82.*
     Or a James McBride from Iowa headed for the Great Salt Lake Valley with his family after his brother was hanged by an anti-Mormon mob. At the Missouri River the family joined a company of fifty wagons under the leadership of Captain Gardner Snow. In his autobiography James wrote that he inscribed his name at Chimney Rock so he may have left his inscription on Independence Rock also. *Platte River Narratives, pg 277.*
     Yet another possibility is J. C. McBride from North Carolina who crossed to California in 1850. He left a sketchy diary of his trip. He

writes that beyond "Rock Independence" the scenery "majestically romantic…huge piles of granite rise to a height sufficient to dizzy the head of a sailor." *Platte River Narratives, p. 277.*

McCallum, R. A.   nt   **May 28, 1895 Wauneta, NB**
Seven people all from Wauneta, Nebraska together.

McCam(l?)y, F. A.   s
Inscribed with an elegant script F See our McCamry, for this could be the same however Michigan not seen on this one.

McCamry., F. A.   s   **Mich**

McCord, R.   nt   **July 4, 1850**
(*Ellison,* found) A William R. McCord is listed among the emigrant arrivals in Oregon in 1850. *The Oregonian, Dec. 4, 1925.*

McCorkle, D. A.   wt   **— 6, 95 (96?)**
With Leeper & Chalfont. A young McCorkle child is buried in the small grave area on the west side of Independence Rock. His father was a worker in the soda works plant just east of Independence Rock. This was in the late 1890s. The person who left this inscription may be the father of the young child and lived in Johnstown while it was in existence. Refer to Chapter Four, "Saleratus, Emigrants' Baking Powder," for more on Johnstown.

McDowen, F. M.   e
This person probably traveling with J. R. Sites & Neweast.

McFall, D. P. (or F)   mt   **St. Mary's, Ohio**
This is probably an inscription of one of the soldiers from the 11th Ohio Volunteer Cavalry stationed at Sweetwater Station, although no information has been found on the official rosters to confirm this.

McFarland, F.   D Gate   **1881**
Could possibly be a Mormon going to Utah. *Information from descendant, 1999.*

McFarland, W.O.   nt   **June 19, 54 Perry, ILL**
(*Ellison,* found) McFarland traveled with J. M. Bradbury, J. Coon, and M. W. Fletcher. These men all wrote the same date and all are from Perry, Illinois. The destination of this party was probably California. Refer to J. Coon notes for explanation of this.

McGregor, R. S.   nt   **May 28, 189 Wauneta, NB.**
Seven people all from Wauneta, Nebraska together.

McH gceey ???   D Gate
Very difficult to read.

McHenry, J.   R. Pass n   **July 15, 60**
This person first inscribed **JUN**, then put the **L** above the **N** and then
added **Y**. One can see corrections made similar to this on several
inscriptions.

McIlroy, E. M.   mt   **1864**
(*Ellison*, found) The photo on page 113 shows only one **I** in this name.

McIlroy, W.D.   mt   **59**
(*Ellison*, found) A William D. McIlroy, from Iowa, is listed as having
traveled the Lander Cutoff on the way to Oregon in 1859. There were
fourteen wagons and thirty-seven people in this party. *House of Rep
Exec. Document #63, 1859.*

McK—???, F. R.   nt

McKee, F. F.   mt
(*Ellison*, found) This McKee could be traveling with A. E. Moody.
    A Fry Megee is listed among those who died along the trail on the
way to Oregon in 1852. He was from LaGrange County, Indiana. *US
Gen Web Archives.*

McKee, G. W.   nt   **July 2, 62**
(*Ellison*, found) A drawing of a dog is with the name. It also says **born
1842.**

McKennedy, L.   mt
A Leslie McKennedy was Captain of the Dixon Company from Dixon
County, Illinois, leaving St. Joseph April 27th, 1849, bound for
California. *Rasmussen, p. 41.*

McKinnis, A.T.E.?   s
(*Ellison*, found)

McKinnis, J.?   s   **Iowa**
(*Ellison*, found)

McKirre(McRisse?)D.   nw   **?8?9.**

McLain, D. P.   mt

Second inscription. Under Hollingsworth.

McLain, D .P.   mt   **St. Mary's, Ohio**

(*Ellison*, found) McLain put his name on the Rock in two places. It was not unusual for the soldiers stationed here to do this.

This is Daniel P. McLain, Company A, of the Sixth Ohio Volunteer Cavalry. *Brown, Emigrant Inscriptions.*

Note: The Sixth Ohio Volunteer Cavalry became the Eleventh Ohio Volunteer Cavalry in 1863 and many of these men were stationed at Sweetwater Bridge Station one mile east of Independence Rock.

McLellan, J.   nwt

(*Ellison*, nf) A John Jasper McClellan crossed the plains to the Salt Lake Valley and settled in Payson, Utah. His son, John Jasper McClellan, born in 1894 was an organist for the Tabernacle in Salt Lake City. *LDS Biographical Encyclopedia, Vol. I, p. 747*

McMeeker, Wm.J.   cave   **July 5, 1849**

(*Ellison*, found) This name could be McMeeken.

McOLBS, W   mt

Mc__?, A. A.   mt   **Mich**

(*Ellison*, nf)

Mc__?, B.F.   mt   **64**

(*Ellison*, nf)

Mc__?, W.S.M.   cave

(*Ellison*, found)

Mead, A.   nt   **June 59 Pitt, Pa**

(*Ellison*, found) A. Mead is listed as having traveled the Lander Cutoff in 1859. *House of Rep. Exec. Document #63, 1859.*

Mead, H. H.   st

(*Ellison*, found)

Mead—??, H. H.   st

Maybe another inscription over this. Hard to read.

Meck, Hiram   se   **July 12, 1850**

Ellison recorded this as Meek. This inscription is right above the cave.

Medina   n

Backwards **n**. Behind fence.

Meek, Hiram   se   **July 12, 1850**

(*Ellison*, found) This inscription is above the cave, so it is located on the southeast top. The name is Meck, not Meek as Ellison has it.

Mek, A.   mt

Mek, T (?) A.   mt

Mellis (Nellis?)   n

Merrill, J.M.   nmt   **June 27, 54**

(*Ellison*, found) Many members of the Merrill family traveled to the Salt Lake Valley. *Information from a descendant.*

Merrill, S. A.   nmt   **June 1, 1868**

(*Ellison*, found)

Middleton, W .A.   mt   **1861**

(*Ellison*, found) A William Middleton, from Kentucky, is listed in the *1890 California Census.* He was a farmer in the Chico area. He was sixty-five at the time of the registration for the census in 1884. *Butte County, California, 1890 Great Register, p. 170.*

Miller, E.R.   mt

(*Ellison*, found) We believe it could be F. R. Miller?

Miller, F. R.   mt

Date there but unreadable. An F. Miller, 52, inscription at Green River Bluffs. *Brown, Emigrant Inscriptions.*

Miller, H.   nt

A Private Hiram Miller was a member of Company A, Eleventh Kansas Volunteer Cavalry. Several of these military men left their names on Independence Rock while stationed out here guarding the telegraph lines and emigrant trails in the 1860s. *Index to Kansas Volunteer Regiment Enlistments, 1861-1863.*

Or a Henry J. Miller party is among those using the Lander Cutoff en route to Oregon in 1859. There was one wagon, nine people, and eleven head of stock in the party. *House of Rep. Exec. Document #63, 1859.*

Or another possibility is Hiram G. Miller who started out for California in 1846 as a member of the Donner Reed Party. This party left Springfield, Illinois and departed from Independence on May 12, 1846. Hiram left this party at about LaBonte Creek in Wyoming when he joined the pack train organized by Edwin Bryant at Fort Laramie. He had been keeping a diary of the journey, but when he left the wagon train James Reed started keeping up the entries. Mattes calls this a 'hybrid diary'. *Platte River Narratives, p. 82.*

Or an H. Miller is listed among the arrivals at Placerville in early August 1852. *Rasmussen, p.148*

Or a Henry Miller, born in 1807 in New York moved to Illinois in 1829 and was converted to Mormonism and then moved to Nauvoo. He crossed the plains to the Great Salt Lake Valley in 1850 with Apostle Orson Hyde. He returned to Council Bluffs and crossed the plains again with his family in 1852. He was captain of a company on this trip. *LDS Biographical Encyclopedia Vol. III, p. 165.*

Miller, John   mt

A J. M. Miller, 1857 inscription recorded at Register Cliff. *Henderson 1930 Survey of Register Cliff.*

A John Miller is listed among those who used the Lander Cutoff in 1859 en route to California. *House of Rep. Exec. Document #63, 1859.*

A John C. Miller is listed among the emigrant arrivals in Oregon in 1850. *The Oregonian, Dec. 4, 1925.*

Four different John Millers, in different counties, are listed in the *1850 Oregon Territorial Census.*

Or refer to Rasmussen for other John Millers.

A Jonithan A. Miller is buried in the Chico, California cemetery. He was a native of Indiana, born in 1825 and died in 1899.

Miller, M.   s   Jun 11, 50

Below cave. In tar. N. Miller made his inscription on same date.

A Mart. Miller is listed among the emigrant arrivals in Oregon in 1850. *The Oregonian, Dec. 4, 1925.*

Miller, N.   se   June 11, 1850?

(*Ellison*, nf) M. Miller made an inscription on the same date.

Miller, N.   unknown   June 11, 1844

This name and date is included in a list compiled by D. W. Greenburg on August 22, 1926. It is possible it is the same as the N. Miller above but it is doubtful a reading of 1850 could be mistaken for 1844. *Ellison Files, WY State Archives.* This person may have gone over the trail more than once. We have not found the name in recent surveying.

Miller, Orin   s   **June 8, 1850**
In tar; very weathered.

Miller, P.   mt   **Je 16, 52**
This inscription is boxed in with B. F Norton, C. H. Ball, S. C. Caery, G. Lemon. See R. Miller same date on middle top.

    In a survey done August 22, 1926, D. W. Greenburg saw the initials P. E. Miller in this inscription. *Ellison Files, WY State Archives.*

    A Peter Miller, from Wisconsin, is listed among those preparing to depart from Kanesville prior to May 20, 1852. *Rasmussen, p. 140.*

    A P. H. Miller, age twenty-eight is listed in the *Island County, Washington Territory 1860 Census.* He listed his occupation as farmer. *US Gen Web Archives.*

Miller, R.   mt   **Je 16, 52**
(*Ellison*, found) See P. Miller same date on mt. An R. Miller arrived in Downieville, California prior to September 1852. *Rasmussen, p. 160*

Miller, Sidney H .   nt
Written Sidney H. & H. Miller.

Mills, John   mt
(*Ellison*, found) A John Mills, living in Clackamas County, is listed in the *1850 Oregon Territorial Census.*

    Or this could be Private John H. Mills who was a member of Company E, Eleventh Kansas Volunteer Cavalry. Several of these military men left their names on Independence Rock while stationed out here in the 1860s. *Index to Kansas Volunteer Regiment Enlistments, 1861-1863.*

Mine, John H.   D Gate

Miner, A. E.   nt   **41 ?**
(*Ellison*, nf)

Miner, J.   nt   **ILL**
(*Ellison*, found)

Mixer, S. P.   st

Mobley, J.   w
Very weathered. A John Mobley from Fulton, Ohio was reported on the trail to California leaving Ohio in early April 1849. *Rasmussen, pg. 199*

Moffat?, W. H.   s   **49**
(*Ellison*, nf)

Moffitt, Miss & L.   nt   **July 4, 1862**
(*Ellison*, found)

Moll??   s

Could be of the Mormon Mollen family. Several Mollens had crossed the plains to Salt Lake. *Information from descendant.*

Additional information: a Simpson Montgomery Molen, born in Jacksonville, Illinois in 1832, moved several times with his family ending up in Nauvoo and Winter Quarters. He crossed the plains in 1847. *LDS Biographical Encyclopedia, Vol. I, p. 408.*

Simpson Montgomery Molen. (L.D.S. Family History Center, Casper.)

Monchen, M.
nmt   **1864 (?)**

Mond, A.   w
Might possibly be twentieth century inscription.

Monday, W.   nt   **55**
(*Ellison*, nf)

Monkrin   nt

Monohan, S.S.   mt   **66**
Written M & SS Monohan.

Monohon, M.?   nmt   **June, 1866**
(*Ellison*, found) Ellison has a question mark by the initial. We believe it is definitely an M. The inscription says M & SS. In a survey list compiled by D. W. Greenburg on August 22, 1926 he shows the inscription as reading M. Monohon but he read the date as June, 1862. *Ellison Files, WY State Archives.*

Montgomery, A.   swt   **July 20, 49**
(*Ellison*, found)

Moo? ey, (D or L) K   s

Moodie, S.?   nt
(*Ellison*, nf)

Moody, A. E.   nt   **July 9, 1853**

A second A. E. Moody inscription on middle top. It has a July 8, 1853 date. He may have been traveling with W. S. Williams, W. W. Gilbert, and J. R. Hughes.

Moody, A.E.   mt   **July 8, 53 New York**

(*Ellison*, found) Inscription also on north east top with a July 9, 1853 date.

Moody, V. D.   mt   **July 24, 49**

(*Ellison*, found) A Joseph Moody from Pennsylvania went to California in 1849 as a member of the Diamond K Company. This V. D. Moody could possibly be a relative. The Diamond K Company was from Pittsburgh and each member subscribed two hundred and fifty dollars for expenses. *Platte River Narratives, p. 191.*

Moolin, Dawson A.   nmt   **June 21, 58 ILL**

In script.

Moons, W.   swt

A William Moon is listed among those using the Lander Cutoff en route to California in 1859. *House of Rep. Exec. Document #63, 1859.*

A W. Moon inscription found at Register Cliff. *Scottsbluff Survey List.*

Moore, H.   mt

(*Ellison*, found) A John H. Moore from Franklin County, Massachusetts arrived in Oregon in November 1850. He settled in Clackamas County. *Oregon Donation Land Claim Records*

An H. C. Moore, 1865, inscription is recorded at Register Cliff. *Henderson 1930 Survey of Register Cliff.*

An H. C. Moore, 1852, inscription is recorded at Register Cliff. *Scottsbluff Survey List.*

Moore, L. N.   s

Moore, M.   mt   **July, 1850**

(*Ellison*, found) An Edwin Marshall Moore is listed among the arrivals in Oregon in 1850. *The Oregonian, Dec. 4, 1925.*

Moore, W.   cave

A William Lee Moore, from Kentucky, was a farmer in Kentucky Ranch, California at the time of the *1890 California Census.* He was forty-eight years old when he registered for the census in March 1884. *Butte County, California, 1890 Great Register, p. 175.*

A William Moore and Melinda Moore are among those who died somewhere along the trail on the way to Oregon in 1852. They were from Chariton County, Missouri. *US Gen Web Archives.*

Moores, S.E.   nt   **6,28, 59**

(*Ellison*, found) Ellison has **S. E.** but the initials could be **S. F.** Ellison also has 6, 28, 59 but the month **June** is printed out. In the list of Independence Rock names compiled by D. W. Greenburg August 22, 1926, he has S. F. Moores, June 28, 1852. *Greenburg List, Ellison Files, WY State Archives.*

Moreley, C.C.?   s   **July, 49**

(*Ellison*, found)

Morey, D   mt

(*Ellison*,found)

Morey, G.   s   **50**

Moreys, E.   s

Morgan, J. W.   mt

A Jenkins Morgan, born in Glamorganshire, Wales September 2, 1829 was raised and educated in Wales. Upon hearing of the discovery of gold, he traveled to California in 1849. He first settled in Nevada County and then settled in Cherokee, California. *Mansfield, History of Butte County, p. 1134.*

Or this could be Joseph Morgan, from Cass County, Missouri who is listed among those who died along the trail on the way to Oregon in 1852. There were three Morgans from Cass County who died on the trail that year. *US Gen Web Archives.*

Morgan, J. W.   nt

(*Ellison*, found) A Jesse Morgan left St. Joseph May 24, 1849 going to the Salt Lake Valley. He and his wife, Martha, left St. Joseph on May 24 and traveled overland to Council Bluffs. From there they took the upper ferry and traveled on the north side of the Platte River until Fort Laramie. His wife Martha left a diary of their trip. After wintering in the Salt Lake Valley, the following year Jesse and Martha journeyed on to California and Martha became a widow when Jesse Morgan at age forty-five was murdered in Sacramento. *Platte River Narratives, p. 191.* Lannon Mintz writes that the original journal was kept by Jesse Morgan. *Mintz, The Trail, p. 97.*

Martha Morgan's diary records indicate that they were traveling in the Captain Allred and Captain Taylor wagon train. This was a Mormon company crossing to the Salt Lake Valley. The Allred and Taylor inscriptions are on the south side of Independence Rock with a September 10, 1849 date. Martha wrote the following in her diary: "Sunday, Sept. 9th—Traveled sixteen and a half miles over some very sandy roads. Here we passed the Saleratus Heads, presumed to be 100 acres, white as snow. It was a windy day, and the saleratus would drift like snow before the wind. We gathered what we wanted, went on and encamped near Independence Rock. The Rock is notorious for size and is a great curiosity. I presume the names of more than 3000 people are recorded on it." *Morgan, p. 5.*

A John Morgan is listed among the arrivals in Oregon in 1851. *Oregon in 1851.*

Morley, I.D.B.G.S.   mt

(*Ellison*, found) We believe the initials B.G.S. are a separate inscription.

An I. D. Morley is buried in the cemetery at Chico, California. He died August 25, 1885, "aged 72 years, 6 mo. and 6 ds." The cemetery records show this is Israel Dodge Morley who was born in New York on February 19, 1813. He was a farmer in the Chico area. His wife Samantha, 1812-1882, and his daughter, Harriet born in Michigan in 1840 are also buried there.

The I. D. Morley could be Isaac Morley, Mormon, who crossed to the Salt Lake Valley. *Bennett, pg 275.*

This I.D. Morley headstone is located in the Chico, California, cemetery. (Author's Photo)

Morris, C.W.   nt

(*Ellison*, found) A Charles Morris, from Ohio, is listed in the *1890 California Census*. He lived in Magalia and was forty-five at the time of the census registration in 1884. He listed his occupation as a teamster. *Butte County, California, 1890 Great Register, p. 177.*

Morris, Claborn   s   **June 25, 1851**
(*Ellison*, found)

Morris, Elias & Mary   nt   **Sept. 12, 1852**
                                                North Wales, Pa.

(*Ellison,* found) Ellison has North spelled out but the inscription says N. Wales. We saw no **Pa**.

Elias & Mary Morris inscription. (Photo by author.)

Elias Morris was seventh Bishop of the Fifteenth Ward in Salt Lake City. He was born in 1825 in Denbigshire, North Wales. In early 1852 he sent his betrothed, Mary Parry, to America on the ship, "Ellen Maria". Mary was from Newmarket, England. He was with the Sugar Company and sailed from Liverpool on March 28. He and Mary were married May 23, 1852 in Council Bluffs and crossed the plains with the Sugar Company. They arrived in Salt Lake City in late November. *LDS Biographical Encyclopedia, Vol. I, p. 636.*

The question arose concerning this party as to what caused them to arrive in the Salt Lake Valley so late when they were at Independence Rock on September 12. Correspondence with the LDS Historical Department gives this information concerning the party:

"This company left Fort Leavenworth, Kansas on July 4th with Philip De La Mare, a French emigrant, as captain. He was in charge of bringing the first beet sugar refining machinery across the plains to

Elias Morris. (L.D.S. Family History Center, Casper.)

Utah. The sugar machinery which was being transported weighed between two and four tons. At the Sweetwater, a severe snow storm befell the company with temperatures below zero and two feet of snow. The company lost some cattle and their food supplies were reduced necessitating the killing of more cattle. Beyond the Bear River, since the mountains were too rough, they had to leave several of the largest boilers in the mountains until the following spring. Supplies and additional men were sent out by Brigham Young to help them get to the Valley, but they

didn't arrive at their final destination of Provo until late November."
*Correspondence from Melvin Bashore, LDS Historical Department, dated
June 2, 2000.*

Author's note: If the severe storm hit them somewhere on the Sweetwater, and with the date of September 12th on Independence Rock,
this storm probably hit them sometime in mid to late September.

Morris, G. W. s **J, 1859**

Morris, G.W. sw **185—**

A G. W. Morris is listed among arrivals at Placerville during the first
week of September 1852. *Rasmussen, pg. 157.*

Another possibility is a G. W. Morris who came from England to
Nauvoo in 1846 and then went on to the Great Salt Lake Valley sometime in the 1850s. *Information from a descendant.*

Morriss (?), E. H. s

An Eliam Morris, and wife Susannah, are listed among the arrivals in
Oregon in 1851. *Oregon in 1851.*

Morrs(?),W. R.(or M) e **June 4 or 14**

Could possibly be Mirrs.

Morsen, J. E. e **Aug ?**

Inscription in negative relief.

Morton, B. P. mt

Mosley, J. w

Backwards **s**.

Motel st **50**

Name almost gone.

Moxley, C. C. s **Jly, 49**

A C. G. Moxley, age twenty-one, is listed as a member of the J.
Goldsborough Bruff 1849 party headed for the goldfields. The Bruff
party was at Independence Rock in July of 1849. This could be the
same person. C. G. Moxley was from Anne Arundel Co., Maryland.
Bruff Diary, p. xi

Moxley, C.C. sw

(*Ellison*, found) No date on this C.C. Moxley.

Moyer, C.   s   **June 19, 1850**
Box around the name.

Moyer, C.   s   **June 7, 1850 Pa**
(*Ellison*, found)

Moynahan, F. V.   mt

Ms, B. F.   nt   **64**

Mullins, W.   nt   **June 19, 1858.**
(*Ellison*, found) Probably with S. E. Dennis.

Munger, L.   D Gate   **1861**

Munson, M.? H.   s   **June 6**
(*Ellison*, nf) In a survey done June 5, 1927 the date June 6, 1850 was
recorded. The surveyor just recorded the initial H. Munson. *Ellison
Files, WY State Archives.*

Muonens ??, Kate   e

Murphy, C. L.   unknown   **July**
This inscription was included in a list of names surveyed June 5, 1927
by an unidentified person. Locations were not recorded. Although this
list is in the R. S. Ellison files, this name was not included in his book.
Ellison Files, WY State Archives. We have not found the name in recent
surveying.

Murphy, C. P.   nt   **June 22, 1859**
(*Ellison*, found) We read the date in 1995. Ellison had no date.

Murphy, W. J.?   sw
(*Ellison*, nf) A William C. Murphey and wife Elvira Ann are listed
among the emigrant arrivals in Oregon in 1847. He was born in 1818
and died in 1906. *Flora, Emigrants in 1847.*

    Another William Murphy is also listed among the emigrant arrivals
in Oregon in 1847. *Flora, Oregon in 1847.*

Murray, C. P.   nt

Myers, Bess   mt   **June 15, 1890**

Myers, Bourk   D Gate

N—?(or APN?), A P   R. Pass South
In tar, almost gone.

N., J.   s   **July**

N., M. J.   mt
(*Ellison*, nf)

N, W. B.   nt   **59**

Nabs?, John   s
This could be **Nahs.** Written in tar, hard to read.

Neal, M.   mt   **June 15, 1852 ILLs**
(*Ellison*, found) An M. Neal of Illinois is listed as a member of a small group who arrived in Downieville, California prior to August 14, 1852. *Rasmussen, p. 146.*

Neal, M & HW   mt   **July 20, 1859 ILLs**
(*Ellison*, found) This Neal boxed with M. Neal and M. N. VanHorn. In a survey done August 22, 1926 by D. W. Greenburg he read the date as July 20, 1852. *Ellison Files, WY State Archives.*

Neal, M.   R. Pass n   **June x2, 1852**
M. Neal, A.B.P. Wood, O. Babcox, J.D. Barnard are all together. See other Neal inscriptions on Independence Rock.

Near, G.   s   **June x 7, /52.**
With C. Klines.

Near, J. L.   nwt   **May**
In between big rocks on top.

Near, D.   mt   **July 4, 1850**
(*Ellison*, found) **X X** after Near.

Neely, M.   D Gate

Neils (?), J.D.   ?
Very faint.

Nelson. A.   nt   **July 17, 64**
(*Ellison*, found) It is written **Juy** not the July that Ellison lists. We saw the state **IO** in 1995.

Nelson, D.   e   **1895**

Nelson, D.   nt
A D. Nelson, 1895, also on east side. A D. Nelson, 6/4/1855, N. Y. inscription at Register Cliff. *Scottsbluff Survey List.*

Nelson, K. J.   mt

Nelson, K. J.   nmt   **July 1**
(*Ellison*, found)

Nelson, N.   nm   **18(46?)**
Backwards **n**. A Nels C. Nelson, from Denmark, is buried in the Chico, California cemetery. He was born November 4, 1836 and died December 31, 1907.

Nelson, W.   se
A W. Nelson from Suffield, Ohio is listed in a party leaving in early April 1850 en route to California. *Rasmussen, p. 100.*

A Private William Nelson was a member of Company D, Eleventh Kansas Volunteer Cavalry. Several of these military men who were stationed out here in the 1860s put their names on Independence Rock. *Index to Kansas Volunteer Regiment Enlistments, 1861-1863.*

Another William Friendly Nelson, originally from New York, is listed in the *1890 California Census*. He was a farmer in Bangor and was seventy-two at the time of census registration in 1884. *Butte County, California, 1890 Great Register, p. 183.*

A William Nelson 5/4/1850 inscription is recorded at Register Cliff. *Scottsbluff Survey List.*

Nelson, W. D.   net
A date is there, but it is very weathered and cannot be read.

Nevin, O. W.   mt   **1863**
(*Ellison*, found)

Nevin, W.   mt
(*Ellison*, found)

Nevins, B. F.   D Gate

Neweast   e
Probably with Sites and McDowen.

Newell, W.C.? (S?)   s
(*Ellison*, found)

Newsom   cave   **July 9, 1857?**
(*Ellison*, found) We saw the year 1851. Refer also to the Newsom, 1851, on the west side.

Newsom,   w   **J, 51**
(*Ellison*, found) We saw the initial **S** with this name. Note also the Newsom in the cave.

A David Newsom (1805-1882), and his wife Polly are listed among the arrivals in Oregon in 1851. They aided the Clark party after they were attacked by Indians in the Raft River area. See T. Clark entry. *Oregon in 1851.*

Nich, J. T.   st   **June 13, 1862 P. Iowa.**

Nicholas   nwt

In boulders, midway up.

Nigh, J. T.   mt
(*Ellison*, found) This is probably John T. Nigh of Company A of the 11th Ohio Volunteer Cavalry. He was eighteen when he enlisted on November 14, 1861 and came west with his Company in 1862. *Roster of Ohio Soldiers, Vol. XI.*

Noll family   e

Nollen, W. N.   cave   **Iowa**
(*Ellison*, nf) There are two Nollen families listed in the *Tuality County, Oregon Territory, 1849 Census.* This Nollen could be one of this family. *US Gen Web Archives.*

Norr   se

Norris, F. K. (H K?)   D Gate   **Ohio**

Norris, L.T. J.   mt
(*Ellison*, found)

Northrop, T. E.   R. Pass n   **July 2, /50 (60?)**

Norton, B.F.   mt   **Je 16, 52**
(*Ellison*, found) This inscription is boxed in with P. Miller, C.H. Ball, S.C. Caery, G. Lemon. Could be Col. Norton of the Rough and Ready Party in 1852. *Mattes, Diary and Recollection Survey.*

Norton, B. L.   mt

A Norton inscription (no initials, no date) is recorded at Emigrant Springs, WY. *BLM 1989 Survey of Emigrant Springs.*

Norton, J. W.   nt   **July 24, 55 Wis**
(*Ellison*, found)

Now(Noll), B. S.   net   **June 10, 1853**

Noyes, M. J.   swt

(*Ellison*, found) Name all by itself. No other names near it.

A Mormon family Noyes went to the Salt Lake Valley. *Information from descendant*

O., H. N.   Sentinal Rock

On nw corner.

O., U. N.   D Gate   **June (?) 14, 64**
The month is not clear.

O Conner, D.J.   s   **1860**

O'Connor, D. J.   s   **60**
There are two different D. J. O'Connor (O'Conner) inscriptions on the south.

O'Connor, J. J.   s

A John O'Connor, originally from Ireland, is listed in the *1890 California Census.* He was a merchant in Chico, and was sixty years old when he registered for the census in 1884. *Butte County, California, 1890 Great Register, p. 187.*

O Dell, C.   D Gate

A Charlotte ODell is listed among the arrivals in Oregon in 1851 *Oregon in 1851.*

O'Mara   unknown   **1823**

The notation "Date Indistinct as to the **8**" is included in a list of names surveyed June 5, 1927 by an unidentified person. Locations were not recorded. Although this list is found in the R. S. Ellison book, the name is not included in his book. *Ellison Files, WY State Archives.* We have not found the name in recent surveying.

Author's note: The notation about the indistinct date was included as part of the survey by the unidentified party. Although this is a very early date, if it were 1923 instead of 1823 the **8** should not be indistinct by 1927.

O Riley, H. H.   nt

Oemer, D. P.   mt   **June 27, /59**

Ogle, A. H.   unknown   **1887**
This name was on a list of names surveyed June 5, 1927. Locations were not identified. Although this list was found in the R. S. Ellison files, the name is not included in the Ellison book. *Ellison Files, WY State Archives.* We have not found the name in recent surveying.

Olds, F. G.   mt   **91**

Oliver, J.   nt   **59**
(*Ellison*, found) Maybe traveling with Holister.

Olson, Arlo   mt   **90**

Onable?, Alva S.P.   mt   **64**
(*Ellison*, nf)

Onger (s?)   R. Pass n   **18 ??**

Oolgard, Ws D.   s   **60**

Oregon & Calif Trail   R. Pass n   **1843-1914**
Written in large letters with the inclusive dates. These inscriptions were hand carved at various sites along the trail by H. G. Nickerson of Lander, Wyoming in the early 1900s.

Oregon & Calif Trail   n
Behind the fence. Only a portion of this is visible. Part of this inscription is covered by the bronze Grace Raymond Hebard plaque.

OREGON TRAIL OLD   nw
Faint in most light. Near ground.

Orley (Oakley?), J.M.   w

Ormsbee, H.   net   **July 9, 53**
(*Ellison*, found)

Orrin, L. & D.   cave

Osby, Carl   cave
(*Ellison*, found)

Oster ne
> May be **C. Ter** rather than Oster. Very worn date.

Owen, J. M. unknown
> This name was included on a list of names surveyed June 5, 1927. Locations were not recorded. Although this list was found in the R. S. Ellison files, the name was not included in his book. *Ellison Files, WY State Archives.* We have not found the name in recent surveying.

P—???, J. H. R. Pass n

P. B. H. D. Gate top
> Unsure of date. Maybe something 9. Tails on letters.

P., C. E. w

P., D. D. Gate

P., I. nmt
> (*Ellison*, found)

P., J. L. sw

P., M (?) R. n

P., P. D Gate 1860

P.O.B., B. mt
> (*Ellison*, nf)

Pa-—?, W. D Gate 1859

Paine, C.A. emt 1862
> (*Ellison*, found) This is probably Pvt. Charles A. Paine of Company A of the 6th Ohio Volunteer Cavalry. He was twenty-two at the time of his enlistment on October 26, 1861 and he mustered out on April 1, 1865. *Roster of Ohio Soldiers, Vol. XI.*

Paine, W.H. nt
> (*Ellison*, found) A Wm. Paine, Clackamas County, is listed in the *1850 Oregon Territorial Census.*

Palmer, J. & E. R. Pass n Sep 11th, 18(6?)2
> The **11th** is written under the date. A John Turner Palmer, from New York is listed in the *1890 California Census.* He was a farmer living at

Central House and was fifty-eight years old at the time he registered for the census in 1884. *Butte County, California, 1890 Great Register, p. 191.*

A James Lewis Palmer, originally from Denmark is listed in the *1890 California Census.* He lived in Thompson's Flat. He was sixty-six at the time of the census registration in May 1884. He listed his occupation as a miner. *Butte County, California, 1890 Great Register, p. 191.*

An E. J. Palmer inscription is recorded at Register Cliff. *Henderson 1930 Survey of Register Cliff.*

Pane—?, John   s

Paprott, A.   s   **June**
Very hard to read.

Pardet, S.   cave   **June, 49**
(*Ellison*, nf)

Park, Sue   nt
Elaborate old fashioned **P.** Possibly with Sue King. **MO** by Sue King's name.

Members of a Park family traveled over the trails from Missouri. Descendants still live in the Sweetwater Valley. *Information from descendants.*

An A. L. Park, 1858, inscription is recorded at Register Cliff. *Scottsbluff Survey List.*

Parker   R. Pass n   **une**
Another Parker name is in Devil's Gate. A T. Parker 6/2/40 inscription recorded at Register Cliff. This could coincide with the June date of this inscription at Rattlesnake Pass. *Scottsbluff Survey List.*

An L. Parker, age twenty, is listed in the *Island County, Washington Territory, 1860 Census.* He listed his occupation as a machinist. *US Gen Web Archives.*

Parker, L. M.   nt.   **July 9, 1859**
(*Ellison*, found)

Parker, S (?)   R. Pass n
Another Parker also in Rattlesnake Pass. An S. Parker, 52 inscription at Green River Bluffs. *Brown, Emigrant Inscriptions.*

A Samuel Parker, Marion County, and a Saml. Parker, Washington County are listed in the *1850 Oregon Territorial Census.*

A Parker family travelled across the trail going to Oregon in 1850. *Flora, Emigrants in 1850.*

Parkert, H   s

Parkhurst, H   s

Parkin, B. P.   s   **49**
(*Ellison*, found) Could possibly be what we read as Rankin. See Rankin.

Parks   sw   **64**

Parlet, S.   cave   **June 16, 66.**
(*Ellison*, found) We read Jaret S. Parlet. However, in a survey list done
on June 5, 1927 by unidentified persons, they list S. Parlet and a J. Hal
Jaret so our reading of the name could be wrong. This list connects S.
Parlet, J. Hal Jaret, and Adam F. Ridley as probably together on this
date of June 16, '66. *Ellison Files, WY State Archives.*

Parmelee, S. J.   mt   **— 31, 89. Michigan**
With Wm Vreelant.

Parr, A.   nt

Parrh(u or n)rot, H.   e corner

Parris, W. H.   R. Pass n   **June, 59 Ohio**

Parrish, P (?) R   st   **June 25, 54**

Parrish, Sampson   st   **June 25, 1? 4 ?**
Hard to read the date. This man is probably with P. Parrish on the same
date 54.
      Or a large number of Parrish family members traveled to Oregon in
1844. Could possibly be of this party. *Webber, Comprehensive Index to
Oregon Trail Diaries.*

Parrott, A.P.   sw   **July 4, 45**
(*Ellison*, nf)

Patch-uhin, W.   s   **New York**

Patchin, T. W.   e

Paterson, W. C.   se   **July 4, 40**

Patterson, W. C.   e
Possibly a **J** instead of a **P** on Patterson. A Patterson name is recorded at
Register Cliff. *Henderson 1930 Survey of Register Cliff.*

A William Patterson is listed among the emigrant arrivals in Oregon in 1850. *The Oregonian, Dec. 4, 1925.*

Patteson, W. W.   e corner

Could be Pattison. A William Pattison left St. Louis April 10, 1849. His party crossed the Missouri River at Duncan's Ferry on May 18th. They arrived in the Willamette Valley, Oregon November third of that year. He left a diary of their trip. He wrote of the trip after Fort Laramie, "the rode was Literally Streued with Possessions". From Willow Springs to South Pass he wrote that dead cattle also strewed the road. *Platte River Narratives, p. 197.*

William's daughter-in-law, Rachel, died of cholera and is buried at Ash Hollow. She was eighteen years old and died in June 1849. *Information from Chimney Rock Historical Site.* She and Nathan Pattison had been married just eight days before their trip. *Platte River Narratives, p. 197.*

Patton, R.E.   mt   **June, 62 ?**
(*Ellison*, found)

Paul, S.   w
(*Ellison*, nf)

Paulsen, T.   nmt
See other Paulsen inscription. No date seen on this one.

Paulsen, T.   nmt   **1850**
(*Ellison*, found) There are two Paulsen inscriptions on north middle top.

Pavaden   D Gate

Peak, L.   s

Peak, L.   sw boulder
Two L. Peak inscriptions on the Rock.

Pearce, A.   nmt   **June 15, 1852**
(*Ellison*, found) An **X** between the initial and the last name.

Pearce, S.O.   nmt   **June 15, 1852**
(*Ellison*, found) An **X** between the initial and last name. Two Pearces on this date.

Peck, Nancy   D Gate   **1850**

A C. S. Peck & Lady, 1850 inscription found at City of Rocks. *Brown, Emigrant Inscriptions.*

A Washington Peck went to California in 1850. *Mattes, Platte River Narratives, p. 288.*

Pemberthy, H.   s   **May 29, 1850**

Could be Penberthy. H. Penberthy, May 1850 inscription is included in a June 5, 1927 survey list done by an unidentified person. Although this list is found in the R. S. Ellison files, the name is not in his book. *Ellison Files, WY State Archives.*

Pence, A . C.   nt   **May 28, 1895 Wauneta, NB**

Seven people all from Wauneta, Nebraska all in the same place.

Pence, R. M.   nt   **May 28, 1895 Wauneta, NB**

Seven people all from Wauneta, Nebraska all in the same place.

Perist, T. G.   nt   **Age 17**

Possibly with Clark and Dickson.

Perry, P.C.   sw

(*Ellison*, found)

Peters ??, Floyd   cave   **MTY**

Pettit, A.   swt

(*Ellison*, found) An Andrew Pettit, Mormon, crossed the plains to the Salt Lake Valley in 1860. He was a member of Captain Warren Walling's ox train company. *LDS Crossing the Plains Index.*

An Amable Petit, living in Marion County, is listed in the *1850 Oregon Territorial Census.*

Phenn, George   unknown

This name is included in a list of names surveyed June 5, 1927 by an unidentified person. Locations were not given. Although this list is found in the R. S. Ellison files, the name is not included in his book. *Ellison Files, WY State Archives.* We have not found the name in recent surveying.

Phenn, J. R.   unknown

See note under George Phenn.

Phillip, C. E.   s

Phillips, J.   nmt

(*Ellison*, found) A J. Phillips is listed in a group of California emigrants arriving in Kanesville, May 13-20, 1852. *Rasmussen, p. 140*

Several J. Philips (James, John, Joseph, etc.), Mormons, crossed to the Salt Lake Valley in different years. *LDS Crossing the Plains Index.*

A John Phillips, from Benton County, a John Phillips, of Yamhill County, and a John Phillips, living in Polk County, are listed in the *1850 Oregon Territorial Census.*

A Joseph Phillips is buried in the Chico, California cemetery. He was born in New York in 1814 and died in 1893.

Probably this same Joseph Phillips is listed in the *1890 California Census.* He was originally from New York and was a laborer by trade. He was seventy at the time of census registration in 1884. *Butte County, California, 1890 Great Register, p. 197.*

Phorigh, A.   w   **18??.**

Phy, R.   sw

On corner between ground and top.

Pidge, D. P.   sw

(*Ellison*, found)

Pierce, W.   nt   **Ju 2, 1861**

With J. Ware, W. R. R. Thompson, J. S. O. Ward.

A William Madison Pierce, from North Carolina, is listed in the *1890 California Census.* He was a miner living in Lovelock and was fifty-three at the time of census registration in July 1884. *Butte County, California, 1890 Great Register, p. 198.*

Pimall (?), N. S.   R. Pass w

Backwards **N**. Could be Bimall or even Farrell.

Pitt., J. W.   D gate   **64**

Same year and vicinity as T. P. Baker.

Pittman   Sent Rock   **July 8, 1863**

Name in tar. Located on boulder on n. ground.

Place, F. E.   nmt   **1884**

Platt, G. W.   cave   **June 2, 59**

The **G** and **W** are upside down. The last name, Platt, is mirror image.

It could be Calvin Warner Platt, from Ohio, who is listed in the *1890 California Census.* He was a hotelkeeper living in Pine Grove. He was fifty-seven at the time he registered in June 1884. *Butte County, California, 1890 Great Register, p. 199.*

Plu, C. F.   e corner

Po—r-dy?, P.   s

Pod?—y, C. E.   w   18—

Poe   nt   NZ
Tails on letters.

Pom, C. A.   nmt   1862
This could be a soldier stationed at Sweetwater Station just east of Independence Rock. His name is next to D. Stout and C.A, Paine who were both soldiers out here. The year is also the same. However his name was not found in a search of the official rosters.

Poole, S.   swt   NJ
Lovely printing.

Poplin, P. (or R)   w   J ?? 18 ?
Backwards n. Year could be 18 instead of the day.

Porter, D. U.   unknown
This name was included on a survey list done June 5, 1927 by an unspecified person. Locations were not identified on this list. *Ellison Files, WY State Archives.* It is possible it could be the same as our D. W. Porter. Recent surveying has not found this name.

Porter, D. W.   sw
Two D. W. Porters within fifty feet of each other. A D. W. Porter found at Holden Hill and at Names Hill. *Brown, Emigrant Inscriptions.*

Porter, D. W.   sw
(*Ellison,* found) Two D. W. Porters within fifty feet of each other.

Porter, J.,Inc.,?   nmt
(*Ellison,* found) A J. R. Porter inscription recorded at Emigrant Springs, WY. *BLM 1989 Survey of Emigrant Springs.*
    A James A. Porter, Clark County; a John Porter, Lewis County; and a John E. Porter, Benton County are all listed in the *1850 Oregon Territorial Census.*

Or a John P. Porter family, including his son Joseph Rich Porter, went to Utah in 1847. Joseph was born in Iowa March 29, 1844. Since he did mission work, he crossed the plains more that once. He was a major in the Utah militia and later settled in Porterville, Utah. He was the first school teacher in Morgan County. *LDS Biographical Encyclopedia, Vol II, p. 148.*

Joseph Porter was the son of John P Porter. (L.D.S. Family History Center, Casper.)

A Jno. Porter, Sr. and family, and a Jno. Porter, Jr. are both listed in the *Tuality County, Oregon Territory, 1849 Census. US Gen Web Archives.*

Or this could be John Porter of Company I, Eleventh Kansas Volunteer Cavalry who was one of those soldiers killed at the Platte Bridge Battle in July of 1865. *Index to Kansas Volunteer Regiment Enlistments, 1861-1865*

Potter, A.   st   **July 5, 60**
A gun drawn by the name.

Powell, A. ??   D Gate   **1864**
With M. L. Powell. An Abraham Powell, coming from England, crossed the plains in 1864 going to the Salt Lake Valley. He and his family were in Captain William S. Warren's Company. *LDS Crossing the Plains Index.*

Powell, M. L.   D Gate   **1864**
With A. Powell.

Power, Wm.   mt   **June, 1862 Troy, Ohio**
This had to have been one of the soldiers who came to the territory in 1862 with the Sixth Ohio Volunteer Cavalry. Several of these men were stationed at Sweetwater Station, one mile east of Independence Rock until 1865 when they were mustered out.

Powers, A.   R. Pass n   **July 4, 1859**
Backwards S. backwards 9.

Pratt, E. D.   nt   **61**
(*Ellison*, found) An Elmer Pratt, originally from Illinois, was living in Chico at the time of the *1890 California Census.* He was forty-seven at

the time that he registered for the census. He listed his occupation as engineer. *Butte County, California, 1890 Great Register, p. 201.*

Prothero, Samuel   sw   **July 2, 1850**
(*Ellison*, found)

Putnam, —er   ne   **MO**
Several members of a Putnam family are listed among the emigrant arrivals in Oregon in 1847. They were traveling in the Buell train. *Flora, Emigrants in 1847.* See O.E. Buell entry.

Putney, C. M.   nmt   **May 9, 1850**
(*Ellison*, found) A C. M. Putney, from Wisconsin, was listed among the emigrant arrivals in Kanesville by May 1, 1850, en route to California. *Rasmussen, p. 105.*

Putney, J. M. & M.   mt   **June 9, 1850**
(*Ellison*, found)

R—???, G.   n   **74**
Right below Berth, 74. Probably with them. This is hard to read.

R., B. M.   st

R., B. P.   w

R., C. H.   set
(*Ellison*, nf)

R., H.   nwt
Midway up. Big letters.

R., H. D.   mt   **52**
(*Ellison*, nf)

R., H.H.E.N.   swt
(*Ellison*, nf)

R., J. D.   mt   **52**

R., J. D.   nt   **52**

R., M.   mt   **52**
Two initials written together with an &.

R.?, H. M.   st
  (*Ellison*, nf)

RA, T. F.   w
  Above Lancaster.

RA ???, James R.   mt   **Aug 52**

Raerbon, J. M.   se

Raines, J. H.   cave   **June 18, 60**
  Located just outside the cave.

Ramsey, R. D.   R. Pass w   **1?50**
  A Mary Ann Ramsey traveled to the Salt Lake Valley in the early 1850s.
  She came from England. This might be one of her family members.
  Information from descendant, 1998.

Rand, R.   nt   **59**
  (*Ellison*, found)

Rankin, B. P.   s   **CA 49**
  This inscription could possibly be Ellison's B. P. Parkin.

Rankin, H.   D. Gate summit

Rannell, A. C.   nt   **July 2, 1861**
  (*Ellison*, nf)

Rathbun, J.   nt
  (*Ellison*, found) A Dr. J. H. Rathbun was listed as a member of the
  Buckeye Rovers from Ohio en route to California. They left St. Joseph
  May 10, 1849. *Rasmussen, p. 55.* When the group from Ohio reached
  St. Joseph they purchased three wagons, eleven yoke of oxen, one yoke
  of cows, and in early May formed a train to leave for the gold fields.
  Scarnehorne, pg. xiii.

  A good account of this party's trip is in the book *The Buckeye Rovers
  in the Gold Rush* a diary kept by John Banks and J. E. Armstrong. In the
  list of members of the Buckeye Rovers in this book Dr. Rathbun's name
  is spelled Rathburn. *Scamehorn, p. xiii.*

Rawlings, I. T.   D Gate   **1866 (?)**

Reach, Miss E. L.   st
  Beautiful printing on the Miss.

Read, S.   mt   **June, 1852.**
(*Ellison*, nf) An S. P. Read is listed among California emigrants arriving in Kanesville between May 6-13, 1852. *Rasmussen, p. 136.*

Redd, S.S.   mt   **June 15, 1852**

Redner, R .P.   n   **June 6, 1898**
The numbers **94** are also inscribed under the 1898.

Reed, F.   cave
(*Ellison*, found) An E. Reed recorded at Emigrant Springs, WY. *BLM 1989 Survey of Emigrant Springs.*

Reid, B.   net

Bernard J. Reid in about 1850 or 51. He was a Forty-niner. (Santa Clara University Archives.)

(underneath it **M.R., T.R., S.R.**) This could be Bernard J. Reid who was a passenger on the 1849 Pioneer Line going to California. The promoters of the Pioneer Line promised to deliver the one hundred twenty passengers to California via mule drawn carriages. They left Independence, Missouri on May 15 and arrived in California September 21. Bernard Joseph Reid was born April 24, 1823. He grew up in western Pennsylvania. His father's name was Marietta and he had a brother named Simon. Although they themselves did not make the trip, Bernard might have put their initials by his name. He left a diary detailing this unfortunate trip by stagecoach now in print as *Overland to California with the Pioneer Line. Gordon, p. 5.*

The Pioneer Line management did not live up to their promises concerning the overland journey and the passengers had to discard possessions, just as many of the wagon train people did. Bernard Reid writes this account of the scene a few miles east of Independence Rock. "Thursday, July 12 (1849) A scene of destruction began. Trunks, bags, boxes were brought out, opened, and ransacked. Cut down to 75 lbs. per man. The scene can easily be imagined. In the evening the plain was scattered with waifs (stray articles) and fragments, looking as though a whirlwind had scattered about the contents of several dry goods, hardware and variety shops. Men and boys from three or four other trains camped nearby were loitering around like vultures waiting for their prey and not even did they wait, but handled and snatched and begged and eyed curiously the various objects of their desire before they were cast from their baggage. Some 30 lbs. we concluded to pack on the pony— 162 going into the wagons...Most of the train appeared dressed out in their newest and best, having discarded their old suits....Moved 5 miles up the river after dark." *Gordon, p. 81.*

The next day the group came to Independence Rock. Bernard Reid wrote this in his diary. "Friday, July 13. Roused up early and off before breakfast...About two miles to Independence Rock, remarkable only for its isolated position and for the thousands of names carved and painted on its surface. The southerly end of it is pretty close to the river where the trail crosses it. Saw a very few names that I knew. Among them those of Fathers DeSmet, Point, and Mengarini put there under the monogram 'IHS' 8 years ago." *Gordon, p. 84.*

Reilly, J.E. or S.   s   **June? 21, 60**
(*Ellison*, found) We find **S** to be correct. June is correct, though Ellison questioned it. We saw Reily.

Reisellis?   s
(*Ellison*, found)

REX   se corner
Letters twelve inches high.

Rey ??, H.   cave (entrance)

Reynolds, J. N.   D. Gate summit

Rhoades, John&GB   mt   **1882**

Ribeou, D.   sw   **1850**
This could be what Ellison has as D. Riblont. We believe it is Ribeou. In a June 5, 1927 list of names recorded by an unknown person(s), they recorded Ribeout. This seems to agree with our reading. *Ellison files, WY State Archives.*

Riblont, D.   sw   **1850**
(*Ellison*, found ?) See Ribeou.

Rice ?, E.   w
An Elta Jane Rice is listed among the arrivals in Oregon in 1851. *Oregon in 1851.*

Rich (y?), A. W.   nmt

Rich, L. H.   unknown
This inscription is included in a list of names surveyed June 5, 1927. Locations were not identified. Although this list is found in the R. S. Ellison files, the name is not included in his book. *Ellison Files, WY State Archives.* We have not found the inscription in our recent surveying.

Richards, L.H.   s
Very close to and similar writing as D. Richardson.

Richardson, W. H.   nt   **June 22, 59**
(*Ellison*, found) A William Richardson from Iowa is listed among those using the Lander Cutoff in 1859 en route to Oregon. There were two wagons and five people in this Richardson party. *House of Rep. Exec. Document, #63, 1859.*

  Or this could be the Wm. H. Richardson who is buried in the Chico, California, Cemetery. He was born April 25, 1832 in Morgan County, Indiana. He died at age forty-eight on August 16, 1880. There are a number of Richardsons buried in the family plot.

Richardson MD, D.   s   **Aug 25, 1847**
Probably with I. H. Brown. This is Darwin Richardson who was a member of Captain Perrigrine Sessions' Fifty who crossed the plains in 1847 en route to the Salt Lake Valley. The P. G. Sessions inscription and the Brown inscriptions are very close to this inscription.

Richy, John W.   cave   **60**
(*Ellison*, nf)

Ridley, Adam F.   cave   **June 16, 66**
(*Ellison*, nf) In a survey list done June 5, 1927, the surveyor lists Adam Ridley, S. Parlet, and J. Hal Jaret as probably traveling together. *Ellison Files, WY State Archives.*

Ridley, F.   cave
(*Ellison*, nf)

Rigg, J.   mt   **July 3, 1850**
(*Ellison*, found)

Riggs, E.   s
A Mrs. Evaline H. Riggs is listed among the emigrant arrivals in Oregon in 1850. There is a possibility she could be related to the J. Rigg above. *The Oregonian, Dec. 4, 1925.*

Riley, R. D.   D Gate   **July 2, 1853**

A Riley family crossed the Oregon in 1853. *Webber, Comprehensive Guide to Oregon Trail Diaries.*

Rinehart, J.   s   **June 17, 52**

This could have been John Rinehart, eldest son of Lewis and Elizabeth Rinehart. John and his brother George, with their wives, crossed the plains to Oregon in 1852. John's wife was Sarah Elizabeth Edwards. John and Sarah had an arduous journey on their trip across the plains, for their oxen died about half way along. They had to abandon their wagons, and therefore endured many hardships and privations before they reached their destination. For a thousand miles, Sarah rode a cayuse pony on a saddle improvised by herself. On their arrival in Oregon, Lewis had a cash capital of eight dollars. Sarah Rinehart died in 1886 and John died in 1894.

John Rinehart and his wife Sarah. (Courtesy Paula Lantz)

Lewis and Elizabeth, John's parents, were originally from Tennessee and moved to Illinois in 1829. They lived in Illinois fifteen or sixteen years, then moved to Mahaska County, Iowa. In 1854 they then traveled overland to Oregon with nine of their thirteen children. The Rinehart family has a large book covering the history of the Rinehart family and their descendants. *Information from descendant, Paula Lantz.*

Rio, E.   w

Ro???, R. W.   s boulder

Could possibly be Bo.

Ro?n   st   **18 ?0**

In tar, almost gone.

Robb, R. H.   nt   **June 14, 1853**

(*Ellison*, found) M. Robb 1924, beside this inscription.

Roberts, E.   s

An Edward Roberts and family crossed the plains in 1849 en route to the Salt Lake Valley. They were members of Captain Ezra Benson's Company. *LDS Crossing the Plains Index.*

Or this could be Edgar Roberts from Indiana who arrived in Kanesville on April 29, 1852, en route to California. *Rasmussen, p. 134.*

Roberts, W.P.   mt

William D. Roberts. (L.D.S. Family History Center, Casper.)

Very faint. Probably with W. H. Leeper. A W. Roberts, from Iowa, is among those listed as using the Lander Cutoff en route to California in 1859. *House of Representatives Executive Document #63, 1859.*

Or could be W. P. Roberts, who was born in Illinois in 1835, left Missouri in 1851 crossing the plains to Utah. He then moved directly to Provo. *LDS Biographical Encyclopedia, Vol. I, p. 498.*

Or a William Roberts, living in Marion County, is listed in the *1850 Oregon Territorial Census.*

Robins, J.M T   mt   July 6, 69 Wis
(*Ellison*, found) Almost gone.

Robison, J. P.   D Gate   July 4, 59
J. B. Boomer on same date. Below is information related to various Robinson parties that went through. Sometimes spellings were different during trail times so there could be a tie in.

A Robinson party of three people from Illinois is listed as having traveled the Lander Cutoff en route to California in 1859.

Or another Robinson party of thirteen from Iowa also took the Lander Cutoff to California in 1859.

Or a William H. Robinson party of ten wagons and twenty-one people took the Lander Cutoff en route to California in 1859. This party was from Illinois. *House of Rep. Exec. Document #63, 1859.*

Robson, Kurt   nt

Rolf, E.   se

Romic, S.   D Gate   June 28, 58

Ross, C. T.   mt   June 9, 1850
(*Ellison*, found) The date **ninth** is written out. A Charles T. Ross, Wisconsin, is listed among the California emigrants who had arrived at Kanesville prior to May 15, 1850. *Rasmussen, p. 117.*

Ross, J. M.   s

(*Ellison*, found) A John M. Ross, Lewis County, is listed in the *1850 Oregon Territorial Census.*

A James Ross is listed in the *Champoeg County, Oregon Territory, 1849 Census. US Gen Web Archives.*

Ross, W.   net   **July, 60**

(*Ellison*, nf)

Ross, W. G.   unknown

This name is included in a survey list done June 5, 1927 by an unidentified person. Locations are not given. Although this list is found in the R. S. Ellison files, this name is not included in his book. *Ellison Files, WY State Archives.* We have not found the name in recent surveying.

Rothis, C.,   mt   **81**

Could possibly be **Bothis**.

Rotter, Jack   net

This could be a twentieth century inscription?

Rounds, B.   nt

Roundtree   s

A Major Roundtree was part of a small group who left Platteville, Wisconsin for California during the early part of 1849. *Rasmussen, p. 90.*

A Charles Roundtree, from Louisiana, is listed in the *1890 California Census.* He was a laborer living in Chico and was fifty-four years old at the time he registered for the census in 1884. *Butte County, California, 1890 Great Register, p. 215.*

A P. H. Roundtree was listed in a company of wagons going to Oregon and Washington in 1859. They left from Knox County, Illinois on March 21st. They crossed the Missouri River at Omaha. At the start from the Missouri bottoms this was a large company of one hundred five wagons going to Oregon and Washington. Roundtree was lieutenant of this company. P. H. Roundtree was going to join relatives in Washington. An account of this trip is in "Autobiography of P. H. Roundtree". *Platte River Narratives, p. 512.*

Roundtree, J. H.   s   **June 19, 52**

(*Ellison*, found) A J. M. Roundtee, Illinois inscription recorded at Register Cliff. *Henderson 1930 Survey of Register Cliff*

Rover, Bates   nt   **June, 53**

(*Ellison*, nf)

Row, Alfred   R. Pass n   **June the 12, 1852**
J.L. Stewart, Geo. Freeman, Row, Adam Acker are all on the same boulder, same date.

An Alfred Row from Stevenson County, Illinois is listed among the arrivals in Shasta, California in early August 1852. *Rasmussen, p. 149.*

Rowlo?ue, A.   s

Ru (?)ll   s

Rualy???, O. ?   nw

Rugger, Ed & Emma   nt   **64 MO Telegraph opr**
(*Ellison*, found) Ellison wrote north top but it is on the west top.

He must have been the telegraph operator at the Sweetwater Bridge Station one mile east of Independence Rock. Some of the Eleventh Ohio Volunteer Cavalry were stationed at Sweetwater Station in 1864.

Author's note: These posts established along the trail were very small posts of usually no more than twenty to twenty-five men. Some women did live on these posts.

Runsby, W.   w
Possibly Ransby.

Russell, C. W.   nmt   **Knoxville, ILL**
(*Ellison*, found) With Kiger and Lewis.

A Charles Russell, Lewis County, is listed in the *1850 Oregon Territorial Census.*

Or this could be Cyrus W. Russell who is buried in the Chico, California cemetery. He was born in 1839 and died in 1914.

Russell, R.   nmt   **July 59**
(*Ellison*, found)

Rutheford, R. V.   D Gate   **July 2, 18 ?**

Ryan, E. D.   mt   **June 18, 1854**
(*Ellison*, found)

Ryan, W. T.   mt   **July 4, 62 ? Indp, Ind**
(*Ellison*, found)

Ryanon (??), J. A.   nt
Elegant Y in name. Hard to read.

Ryle, A.   s

S., B. G.   mt
(*Ellison*, found) Ellison has this as part of the I. D. Morley inscription. We believe it should be separate.

S, Earl   ne

S, Willr   w
Near graves.

S —?, C. H.   nt

S., E.   below cave   **1867**

S., G. W.   mt

S., G. W.   wt

S., H. M.   nmt   **1852**
(*Ellison*, found)

S., M.   wt   **Jun 8, 63**
Three sets of initials—**C.C.**, **T.W.** and **M.S.**—are all together.

S., M.   s   **June 29, 1849**

S., M.   wt

S., Mrs. R.A.   mt
(*Ellison*, found)

S., R.   st   **1860**
Says **R S + E J** with (ox bow symbol here) **H**. Very large letters.

S., T. J.   mt
(*Ellison*, nf)

S., W. H.   mt
These initials appear twice on middle top within twenty-five feet of each other.

S., W. H.   mt

Sage, S.A.S.   mt   **June 1862**
(*Ellison*, nf)

Salkers   mt   **June 21, 59 ILL**
This is possibly what Ellison has as Saller.

Saller?, J.E.&J.A.   mt   **June 21, 59 ILL**
(*Ellison*, found) We read Salkers. Possibly with Dawson Moolin.

Samer, D. D.   w   **Jul 30 ?**

Sampson   st
A Benjamin Sampson is mentioned as being in the party of Thomas and
Frances Sawyer going to California in 1852. *Holmes, Vol. 4, p. 86.*
Or see various other Sampsons in Rasmussen.

Sampson, Ephriam A.   cave
(*Ellison*, found)

Samuel, Stephen   mt
S's written backwards.

Sanborn, A.   nt   **June 19, 1859**
(*Ellison*, found) A Henry Alphonso Sanborn, from Maine, is listed in
the *1890 California Census.* He was a lumberman living in Chico and
was forty-nine years old at the time of census registration in 1886. *Butte
County, California, 1890 Great Register, p,. 218.*

Saph, E.   nmt   **July 9, 1853**
(*Ellison*, found) The month is written in beautiful script.

Sasry, Jas.   s
Sasry seems to be together with J. Cappen and Vincent. Cappen and
Vincent have a date of May 29, 1850. See Vincent note.

Saudo-??, Oscar   nw
Midway up. An old style S. Almost gone.

Saunders, L.   s
Another L. Saunders on se.

Saunders, L.   se

Savage(Sausage?),S.A.   mt   **June 27, 186 ?**

Sawyer, D. D.   w   **July, 90**

Sawyers, B. F.   mt   **July 15, 1890**
Upside down L in July.

Sayre, S. D.　　　　　　　mt
　(*Ellison*, nf)

Scarlet, W. A.　　　　　　mt
　(*Ellison*, found) Name almost gone.

Schenan (LT.), S.A.　　　　sw
　This could be Scheman. **LT** may be separate initials and not part of the Schenan.

Schmidt, T. A.　　　　　　nt
　A T. Schmidt is listed as a member of a New York wagon train called the German California Mining Company camped out at Independence, Missouri April 20, 1849. *Rasmussen, p. 35.*

Schnur, John　　　　　　nt　　　　　　　　　　**July 10, 59**

Schott, C.　　　　　　　R. Pass w

Scott, J.W.　　　　　　　s

Scott, S. A.　　　　　　s　　　　　　　　　　**July 28, 1860**
　(*Ellison*, found)

Scou—?ir, G.　　　　　　e

Sc__?, W.　　　　　　　se
　Near Baker on ground. Very faint.

Seamands, W. G.　　　　　nt　　　**July 2, 1862 Platteville, Iowa**
　(*Ellison*, found)

Seamonds, MOT　　　　　nt　　　　　　　　　　**July 2, 62**
　Boxed with design all around the box. **J.** backwards. Probably with W. G. Seamands whose inscription gives a hometown. Even with the different spellings of the last names, since they have the same date and are found so close together they are possibly related.

Searl, O.H.P.　　　　　　mt
　(*Ellison*, found) There was a Searl (no first name given) of Massillon, Ohio who was a member of a wagon train leaving Stuebenville, Ohio about April 1, 1849, bound for California. *Rasmussen, p. 199.*

Seaton, J. H.　　　　　　nt　　　　　　　　　　**1891**
　Could possibly be Searon.

Secrist, J.   nt   **1855**

(*Ellison*, found) Quite faint. A Jacob F. Secrist, Mormon was the original Captain of the Second Company in 1855 which departed from Kansas June 13, 1855. Research shows he died July 2 and the party did not arrive in Salt Lake until September 7 so it is doubtful this could be Jacob's inscription on this return trip. He first crossed the plains with his family in 1847, arriving in Salt Lake Valley in September. *LDS Crossing the Plains Index.*

Further research shows Jacob Secrist was born in Pennsylvania in 1818. After first crossing the plains, he resided in the Salt Lake Valley until he was called on a mission in Europe in 1852. On returning to America in 1855, he was chosen Captain of the Second Company then assembling for crossing the plains. He was stricken with cholera and died July 2, 1855 and was buried on the Little Blue River. *LDS Biographical Encyclopedia, Vol. II, p. 711.* This inscription could possibly be of a member of his family traveling in that wagon train or put there on the Rock in memory of Jacob Secrist.

Sedley, J.E. & J.A.   nmt

This inscription is right under Dawson Moolin, 58, with an ox yoke symbol.

Segmonds, Matt   nt   **July 2, 62**

(*Ellison*, found) A drawing of a heart is found with the inscription.

Selder, W. B.   net   **July 9, 53**

(*Ellison*, found) Probably with Hormsbee and A. Marsh.

Senster, A.   nmt   **63 NY**

(*Ellison*, nf)

Sergam ??, D. L.   e

Service, J.   ne

A John Service crossed the plains in 1859. He left from Warsaw, Indiana and traveled overland to Council Bluffs during a very rainy season that took ten weeks to cover this distance. He was going with his family to California. He left diaries of his trip which were later lost in the Berkeley fire of 1923. Recollections remain. *Platte River Narratives, p. 513.*

Sessions, P. G.   s

(*Ellison*, found) This is Perrigrine Sessions, (who was called P. G.), a Mormon, who went across to the Salt Lake Valley with his parents and family in 1847. They were in the company coming through later in the summer after the Brigham Young Pioneer Party. He was Captain of the First Fifty. His mother Patty Sessions, the famous Mormon midwife, was a member of this party. *LDS Crossing the Plains Index.*

Perrigrine Sessions was born June 15, 1814 in Newry, Oxford, Maine. He died June 3, 1893, in Bountiful Davis, Utah. *Information from descendant.*

Sg (o) ??, T. S.   D Gate   **Jul**

Sh??nn?, J. R.   w   **Jne 2, 18—?**
Seen best on color slide.

Shaefer, N.G.   nt   **50**
(*Ellison*, found) Possibly Shaffer. J. H. Shaffer, 1900 is right below this inscription. In the D. W. Greenburg list of names compiled August 22, 1926, he lists N. G. Shaffer, 1850, which agrees with our reading. *Greenburg List, Ellison Files, WY State Archives.*

Shaffer, J. H.   nt   **1900**
Right under Shaefer, 1850. Possibly a relationship.

Sharp   s   **June**
(*Ellison*, nf) A Sharp family traveled to Oregon in 1852. They left at two P.M. on May 5. The parents traveled with two children and arrived in the middle of October. *Oregon Trail Lore & Early Life in Oregon.*

A James Meikle Sharp left an account of an 1852 overland trip to Oregon. He could be of the same Sharp family as listed above. *Mintz, The Trail, p. 120.*

A C. Sharp, male, is listed in the *Tuality County, Oregon Territory, 1849 Census. US Gen Web Archives.*

Or another possibility is Albert Sharp who was a member of Company D of the Mormon Battalion. In October 1846, Colonel Philip St. George Cooke sent women, children, and sick soldiers back to Pueblo from Santa Fe under the leadership of Captain James Brown. This group was known as the Brown Sick Detachment. In the spring of 1847, this group traveled to Fort Laramie and followed the Brigham Young Pioneer Party to the Salt Lake Valley arriving at the Valley just a few days after the Pioneer Party. The Pioneer Party was at Independence Rock in June. *Utah Crossroads Newsletter.*

Or three Sharp brothers, born in Scotland, converted to Mormonism and emigrated to America in 1848. In 1850 they crossed the plains to the Salt Lake Valley. One of them, Joseph Sharp, traveled back and

forth as a freighter and died September 15, 1864 at Willow Springs in Wyoming. *LDS Biographical Encyclopedia, Vol. 2, p. 479.*

John Sharp, from Scotland, was another one of these brothers who crossed the plains in 1850. *LDS Biographical Encyclopedia, Vol. I, p. 677.*

John Sharp. (L.D.S. Family History Center, Casper.)

Shaw, P.	s	**July 24, 59 ?**

(*Ellison*, found)

Shawk, W. B.	s	**, 60**

(*Ellison*, found) We saw the date of **J. 29, 60** in 1995.

Shedd, S.	nt	**June 15, 52**

(*Ellison*, found)

Shelby, J. B.	D Gate	**81**
Sheppner, J. A.	w	**1884**
Sherburne, M. A.	mt	**59**

Very large letters.

Sherwood, J. F.	D Gate	**July 12,—5?**

A John Sherwood, living in Marion County, is listed in the *1850 Oregon Territorial Census.*

A J. Ely Sherwood crossed the plains in 1849. He wrote *The Pocket Guide to California, a Land and Sea Route Book.* His guide was unique in that he claimed overland travel by air was possible due to a new invention, the "revoidal spindle". *Mintz The Trail, pg. 121.*

A Joseph Sherwood, single and age twenty-five, is listed in the *Champoeg County, Oregon Territory, 1849 Census.* He listed his occupation as lumberman. *US Gen Web Archives.*

Shinner	D Gate

Shipley, Captn.	mt	**June 09, 62**

(*Ellison*, found) Ellison has **Bt M.O.V.C.** as part of the inscription. We read **M.** in the name and **6th O.V.C.** instead of Bt.

This is Francis Shipley, Captain of Company A., 11th Ohio Volunteer Cavalry. He was twenty-eight years old when he enlisted on October 9, 1861. He mustered out on April 1, 1865. *Roster of Ohio Soldiers, Vol. XI.*

Captain Francis M. Shipley was in the original Lt. Col. W. O. Collins's expedition of 1862. *Casper Collins, A.W. Spring*

Shipley, J. M.   mt   **1862**
This could possibly be a second inscription of Captain Shipley even though the first initial is wrong. Some of the men stationed at Sweetwater Station one mile east of here put their names on Independence Rock more than once.

Shortridge, S.?R.   nt   **July 4, 1863**
(*Ellison*, nf)

Shriver, R.   nmt

Shufelt, C. P.   D Gate

Shulte, Dora   s   **July**
(*Ellison*, nf)

Shulte, Herb   s   **July**
(*Ellison*, nf)

Sillihan, S.   nt   **June 11, 52**
(*Ellison*, found)

Silovich (?)   nt

Simmons, C. H.   unknown   **Oct. 31, 1861 (or 1881), Monroe, Wis**
This inscription was included on a list of names recorded June 5, 1927 by an unidentified person. Locations were not recorded. It could possibly be the same as or related to what we have just below this entry. Although this list was found in the R. S. Ellison files, this name was not included in his book. *Ellison Files, WY State Archives.* We have not located the name in our recent surveying although we did find an E. R. and E. H. Simmons from Monroe on the same date, different year.

Simmons, E R & E H   w   **Oct 31, 1880 Monroe, Wisconsin**

Simpson, J. F.   se   **July 18**

(*Ellison*, found) A J. F. Simpson is recorded as a member of an 1852 wagon train which was the same party as Sarah Pratt. This was a Mormon train, some going to California. *Holmes, Vol. 4, p. 188.*

A J. F. Simpson, June 25, 1851, inscription can be found at Register Cliff. *Brown, Emigrant Inscriptions.*

Simpson, J. M.   mt   **1868**

Singer (s?), M.   mt

Name in negative relief. Name stands out surrounded by lichen.

Sir—??, Oscar   nw

Sires, W.   sw   **89**

(*Ellison*, nf)

Sites, J. R.   e

A large F. under the name. With McDowen and Neweast.

Skinman   nt

Sl—?e,, J. A   e

Slack, ??   cave

Chamberlain name written over this one. A C. Slack, Michigan, is listed as one of those taking the Lander Cutoff in 1859. *House of Rep. Exec. Document, #63 1859.* However since it appears that the Chamberlain name with 1849 date was painted over the Slack name, it is doubtful that this could be the C. Slack of 1859.

Or this could be Henry Slack, from Kentucky, who is listed in the *1890 California Census.* He was a laborer in Honcut and was seventy-one at the time he registered for the census in 1884. *Butte, County, California, 1890 Great Register, p. 229.*

Slater, E. N.   nmt

An Elisha W. Slater, from New York, is listed in the *1890 California Census.* He was a miner living in Enterprise and was fifty-six at the time he registered in 1884. *Butte County, California, 1890 Great Register, p. 229.*

Slater, F. N.   nt

Slater, H. T.   nmt   **1902**

(Written **Son of S.S. Slater.**)

Also on same panel is **Don Slater, 1960** with the words **Great Clan.**

Slater, S. S.   nmt   **1849**

(*Ellison*, found) Directional symbol drawn by name. See H. T. Slater. In a survey done by D. W. Greenburg August 22, 1926, he listed Slater, F. M. Edwards, P. W. Edwards, and J. K. Waller as possibly being all together. *Ellison Files, WY State Archives.*

Smahs   s   **44**

This is below the cave. It is written in tar. The name John could be part of this inscription.

Smer (Smea?) Mary   mt   **1882**

Mary very plain to see.

Smih   s

Small, in cursive, possibly more letters after it.

Smith   w   **22 (?)**

Smith, A. R. or (B?)   net

Difficult to read. An Andrew Smith was a member of James G. Willie's Handcart Party in 1856. Since the bad weather had not hit this party at this point, he possibly could have inscribed his name. *LDS Biographical Encyclopedia, Vol. I, p. 599.*

Andrew Smith was a member of the Willie Handcart party but they still had good weather while at Independence Rock. (L.D.S. Family History Center, Casper.)

Or an A. B. Smith in Clark County and an A. P. Smith in Clackamas County are listed in the *1850 Oregon Territorial Census.*

Or an Alfred Smith, born in Birmingham, Warwickshire, England, on May 21, 1836, arrived near Portland, Oregon in 1865. When he was four years old his family came to the United States and settled on a farm in

Alfred Smith who went to Oregon in 1864. (Courtesy of Steve von Hitrix, descendant.)

Wisconsin. In 1864, Alfred joined an emigrant train bound for the west. After a journey of six months they arrived at Boise City, Idaho and Mr. Smith worked several months in the mines in that locality. In the fall of 1865 he went on to Oregon and became a farmer. *Portrait and Biographical Record of Willamette Valley, pp. 660-661.*

Smith, Ames   s

An Amos Smith of Wisconsin is listed among those using the Lander Cutoff in 1859. *House of Rep. Exec. Document #63, 1859.*

There are two different A. Smith's listed in the *Tuality County, Oregon Territory, 1849 Census. US Gen Web Archives.*

An A. J. Smith, 8/9/1856 inscription recorded at Register Cliff. *Scottsbluff Survey List.*

Smith, C. B.   s

A C. B. Smith, Hillsdale County, Michigan is listed among the arrivals at Placerville in the first two weeks of August 1851. *Rasmussen, p. 133.*

Smith, C. H.   cave   **1860**

(*Ellison*, found) We believe this is an error in Ellison's list. The second letter in the last name is **W**. This could be an upside down **M** but improbable.

Smith, C. S.   n   —0, 75

Smith, Drange (?)   nt   Jne, 186—?
Shows up in photo, technical pan film.

Smith, E.   s boulder   **June 19, 52**
An Edward Smith, age fifty, of Tennessee was listed in the Sacramento Union as one of those who died on the trail in 1852. *Rasmussen, p. 161.*

Or an E. Smith is listed among those who died somewhere along the trail on the way to Oregon in 1852. He was from Jackson, County, Iowa. *US Gen Web Archives.*

Another possibility is Edwin D. Smith, from Illinois, who is listed in the *1890 California Census.* He was a farmer living at Biggs and was forty-seven years old when he registered for the census in March 1884. *Butte County, California, 1890 Great Register, p. 230.*

An Edmund Smith, from Virginia, is listed in the *1890 California Census.* He was a miner living in Wyandotte and was seventy-two at the time he registered in 1884. *Butte County, California, 1890 Great Register, p. 231.*

Smith, E. A.   mt   **1852**

Another **E. A. Smith, 1859**, can be found on middle top and another on the south area with an **1852** date.

Smith, E. A.   mt   **June 7, 1859**
(*Ellison*, found)

Smith, E .A.   se corner   **June 19, 52 (?)**

An E. A. Smith of Alton, Illinois crossed on the trail going to the Salt Lake Valley in 1852. He was a member of Captain Thomas Howell's Third Company. *LDS Crossing the Plains Index.*

Smith, E. H.   s   **June 2, 60**
(*Ellison*, found)

Smith, F.   mt   **Ohio**

(*Ellison*, found) This is probably Private Fletcher Smith of Company A of the 11th Ohio Volunteer Cavalry. He was nineteen years old when he enlisted on October 15, 1861 and he mustered out with his company on April 1, 1865. *Roster of Ohio Soldiers, Vol. XI.*

Smith, G. L.   net   **1861**
(*Ellison*, found)

Smith, H.   swt

(*Ellison*, found) A H. M. Smith, of Linn County, or a Henry Smith, Marion County, are listed in the *1850 Oregon Territorial Census.*

An H. D. Smith is listed in the *Tuality County, Oregon Territory, 1849 Census. US Gen Web Archives.*

Or a Hiram Smith, from Vermont, is listed in the *1890 California Census.* He was a surveyor and lived at Fall Creek. He was fifty-five at the time of census registration in 1884. *Butte County, California, 1890 Great Register, p. 231.*

A Private Henry H. Smith was a member of Company E, Eleventh Kansas Volunteer Cavalry. Several of the military men who were stationed out here in the 1860s left their inscriptions on Independence Rock. *Index to Kansas Volunteer Regiment Enlistments, 1861-1865*

Smith, I. A.   s boulder   **of Mich**

I. A. Smith, W. M. Foreman and S.Taft all together. Refer to W. M. Foreman notes.

Smith, J.A.   s

Quite faint.

Smith, J.   swt   **July, 1860**

(*Ellison*, found) We saw this date in 1995. This person is with I. F. Sweeney.

A J. Smith inscription is recorded at Register Cliff. *Henderson 1930 Survey of Register Cliff.*

A Jonathan P. Smith, native of Ohio, is buried in the Pioneer Cemetery at Georgetown, California. He died July 9, 1883 at the age of fifty-two years.

A John McKinstry Smith, from New York, is listed in the *1890 California Census.* He was a miner living at Thompson's Flat and was sixty-six at the time of census registration in 1884. *Butte County, California, 1890 Great Register, p. 230.*

A John James Smith, from England, and a James Schuyler Smith, from New York are also listed in the *Butte County 1890 Great Register, p. 231.*

Smith, J. A.   s boulder   **June 17, 59 (2?)**

A James A. Smith of Iowa is listed as having used the Lander Cutoff en route to California in 1859. He listed one wagon and six people in his party. *House of Rep. Exec. Document, 1859.*

Smith, J. W.   swt

A J. W. Smith recorded at Emigrant Springs, WY. *Kelly 1930 Survey of Emigrant Springs*

A Joseph Smith, age twenty-five, is listed in the *Island County, Washington Territory, 1860 Census.* He listed his occupation as a laborer. *US Gen Web Archives.*

Smith, James   unknown   **52**

This name is included in a list of names surveyed June 5, 1927 by an unidentified person. Locations were not recorded. Although this list is in the R. S. Ellison files, this name is not in his book. *Ellison Files, WY State Archives.* We have not found the name in recent surveying.

Smith, James   s   **Mar 28, 1850**

(*Ellison*, found) Ellison has Mar 28 but it is **May**.

There was a James Smith listed in the Des Moines Company No. 1 organized to leave for California, May 2, 1850. *Rasmussen, p. 107.*

A J. C. Smith is listed among the emigrant arrivals in Oregon in 1850. *The Oregonian, Dec. 4, 1925.*

Smith, John   n   **June 18, 68**
                                                          CALAWAY CO, MO

Smith, M. A.   D Gate

A Macky Smith, of Marion County or a Markham Smith, Washington County, or a Moses Smith, in Washington County are listed in the *1850 Oregon Territorial Census.*

An M. Smith, male, is listed in the *Tuality County, Oregon Territory, 1849 Census. US Gen Web Archives.*

Smith, P.—?   n

Morrison, 1924 over this inscription. The name P. A. Smith, June 22, 1846 is included in a list of names surveyed June 5, 1927 by an unidentified person. Locations are not recorded. Although this list is found in the R. S. Ellison files, this name is not in his book. *Ellison Files, WY State Archives.*

A Peter Smith from Missouri is listed as filing a land claim in Yamhill County, Oregon in 1845. *Oregon Donation Land Claim Records.*

Another possibility is Peter Smith and his wife Rachel who are listed among the arrivals in Oregon in 1851. *Oregon in 1851.*

Or a P. C. Smith, age twenty-eight, and his wife, Margaret, age twenty-six, are listed in the *Island County, Washington, Territory, 1860 Census.* He listed his occupation as a laborer. *US Gen Web Archives.*

Smith, R. I.   n

Behind fence. There was a Richard Smith in the 1849 Pioneer Line party. B. Reid's inscription is just above this inscription on north east top *Bernard Reid Diary* Bernard Reid was a member of the Pioneer Line Party.

Or this could be Richard Smith who was a member of the Mormon Battalion, Company C. He was a member of the Brown Sick Detachment, under the leadership of Captain James Brown. This group was sent back to Pueblo from Santa Fe in October 1846. In the spring of 1847 they then traveled to Fort Laramie and followed the Brigham Young Pioneer Party into the Salt Lake Valley. *Utah Crossroads Newsletter.*

Smith, S.   e corner

Second S backwards. A Simeon Smith, Marion County, or a Stephen Smith, Washington County, or a Sydney Smith, Yamhill County are listed in the *1850 Oregon Territorial Census.*

Smith, S. A.   nmt   **Ju 27, 1850**

A Samuel Smith, Mormon, was a member of Captain Aaron Johnson's Company crossing to the Salt Lake Valley in 1850. *LDS Crossing the Plains Index.*

Smith, S. I.   swt   **54**

(*Ellison,* found)

Smith, W.   D Gate   **1881**
A W. D. Smith inscription recorded at Register Cliff. *Henderson 1930 Survey of Register Cliff.*

Smith, ? dranite   nt   **June, 1862**
S on its side.

Sn—??e, L.d.   w   **J. , 18—**
In tar, almost gone.

Snow, B.   nw   **June 10, 1853**
Midway up, in reddish circle. This could possibly be Bernard Snow, Mormon who crossed the plains to the Great Salt Lake Valley. *Information from descendant, 1997.*

Snow, Hannah   se   **1844**
(*Ellison*, nf) A John Snow and L. Snow living in Washington County, are listed in the *1850 Oregon Territorial Census.* This early date could be of this Snow family.

Snow, John   unknown   **'44**
Probably southeast. See Hannah Snow. John Snow along with Hannah Snow is included in a survey list done June 5, 1927 by an unidentified person. No locations are given in this list. Although this list is found in the R. S. Ellison files, the name John Snow, '44, is not included in his book although Hannah Snow is listed in his book. *Ellison Files, WY State Archives.* We have not found either name in recent surveying.

So—?, J.   s

Soper, Jno.   s   **July**
(*Ellison*, nf)

Sopper, H. P.   s
Says H. P. Sopper & Son.

Sotheenberth, W.   s   **May 29, 1859**

Sound, J.   nt
(*Ellison*, found)

South, A. R.   s
Two initials together. A R and W M South.

South, J. W.   s boulder

South, W. M.   s
(*Ellison*, found)

South, W. M.   s   1864

South, W. M.   s
Two initials together. A R and W M South.

Spalding, J. B.   s
A Josiah B. Spalding is buried in the Georgetown, California Pioneer Cemetery. He was born in Plainfield, New Hampshire on December 12, 1829 and died in Garden Valley, California on June 5, 1864. A Masonic symbol is carved on his tombstone.

Spaulding, D.?B.   s
(*Ellison*, found) A Benjamin F. Spaulding, from Maine, is listed in the *1890 California Census.* He was a farmer living at Berry Creek and was sixty-seven at the time he registered for the census in 1888. *Butte County, California, 1890 Great Register, p. 236.*

Spencer   s   J 29, 49
An Orson Spencer, originally from Massachusetts, went to Nauvoo and left in 1846. At that time he went to England to sign up converts. His children went to Utah in 1848. He then crossed in 1849 as Captain of the First Company. *Information from descendants in 1997.*

Or an O. Spencer led a group of men going to California in 1849. *Rasmussen, p. 73.*

Or an R. Spencer is listed as a member of the Pittsburgh and California Enterprise Company encamped at St. Joseph in early April 1849. *Rasmussen, p. 17.*

Three Spencers are listed in three different counties in the *1850 Oregon Territorial Census.*

Spencer, C. G.   sw

Spere, J.   nt   July, 59
(*Ellison*, found)

Sponaele?, Hlua ??   s
XXXX inscribed under name.

Staley, H.   mt   June 11, 52
(*Ellison*, found) A H. Staley is listed among the overland emigrants who had arrived at Placerville during the week of August 16-19, 1852. *Rasmussen, pg 153.*

In a list of names compiled by D. W. Greenburg on August 22, 1926, a J. H. Staley is listed along with an H. Staley. Greenburg read this party as being from Richmond, Indiana with the date June 11, 1852. See the entry JNPC & RM Staley of the same date. Greenburg had the initials NPG and RM as separate inscriptions that were with the Staley party. *Ellison Files, WY State Archives.*

Staley, J. H.   unknown   **June 11, 1852**
                                                               Richmond, Ind
See entry above for explanation.

Staley, J N P C & R M   mt   **June 11, 52 Richmond,**
                                                               Ind
(*Ellison*, found) We read BM. See H. Staley, same date. This could possibly be some other initials inscribed on top of the Staley inscription.

Stam—??, S. B.   s

Standing, J.   s   **June 3, 50**
(*Ellison*, found) Standing could be traveling with John Hays.

A Joseph Standing, Mormon, probably went to the Great Salt Lake Valley. An Elder Joseph Standing was killed in Georgia while on missionary work in 1879. *Information from descendant.*

Or, James Standing, born in 1815 in England, emigrated with his family to America. He moved with the Mormons to Missouri and then to Nauvoo. He traveled to the Salt Lake Valley in 1849 crossing in Reddick Allred's Fifty of Allen Taylor's Hundred. Allen Taylor's 1849 inscription also on the south side of Independence Rock.

Stansbie, J. A.   mt   **Ju, 1859?**
(*Ellison*, found) Ellison could not read the date, but in 1995 we read this date.

Stansbury, W.   ne

Star, C.   mt   **59 Troy, NY**
(*Ellison*, found) This inscription is possibly **Start** since a **T** is under the **R**.

Starr   n

Starr, J. A.   mt   **July 4, 62 Iowa**
(*Ellison*, found)

Starr, L.   net   **52**
(*Ellison*, found) There was a Starr family who traveled to Oregon in the emigration of 1852. *Comprehensive Index to Oregon Trail Diaries.*

Starr, S. B.   s
(*Ellison*, found) A Sarah Starr was a member of a party traveling to Oregon in 1852. *Comprehensive Index to Oregon Trail Diaries.*

Another possibility is Samuel S. Starr, living in Benton County, who is listed in the *1850 Oregon Territorial Census.*

Staton, J. H.   nt   **1891**

Steele, L. V.   R. Pass w   **Ju 20, 1859**
Backwards S. A Steel party of one wagon traveled the Lander Cutoff en route to Oregon in 1859. *House of Rep. Exec.Document, 1859.*

Stehson, T.   mt
The first **s** and the **n** are backwards.

Stephen, Samuel   mt
(*Ellison*, found) The two **s**'s are written backwards.

Stephen, T (J)   nmt
A Thos. Stephens, and family, are listed in the *Tuality County, Oregon Territory, 1849 Census. US Gen Web Archives.*

W.H. Stephens inscription. (Author's Photo)

Stephens, W. H.   s   **July 6, 49**
(*Ellison*, found) Must be traveling with J. H. Ingram for the two names are boxed together and both have the July 6, 1849 date. W. H. Stephens name also at Rock Avenue one day prior to this.

This could be William H. Stephens from southern Indiana who traveled across maybe going to California. Members of this same family from Missouri later traveled across going to Oregon in 1851. *Information from the Hileman family, descendants.* See the J. H. Ingram notes that could tie these two together as going to California.

Or perhaps this is William Stephens, native of England, who is buried in the Pioneer Cemetery at Georgetown, California. He died July 9, 1883 at age fifty-two.

Or a William Stephens, living in Clark County, is listed in the *1850 Oregon Territorial Census.*

Stephson, T.   nemt
   (*Ellison*, found)

Stetl, T.D.E.   s   July ?, 1850

Stetl (?), S. T. E.   s   1850

Stevenson, H. O.   net   June 14, 58
   (*Ellison*, found)

Stewart, J. L.   R. Pass n   **June the 12 A. D., 1852**
Stewart, Geo. Freeman, Alfred Row, Adam Acker all on same boulder, same date.

A James Stewart is listed among the arrivals in Shasta, California in early August 1852. Alfred Row and Geo. Freeman also listed among those arrivals at the same time. *Rasmussen, p. 149.*

Stierle, J.   nmt   **Ohio**
(*Ellison*, found) We found this on mt. This is probably John Stierle of Company A, Eleventh Ohio Volunteer Cavalry. He was forty-four years old at the time of his enlistment on November 15, 1861 and mustered out with the rest of his Company on April 1, 1865. *Roster of Ohio Soldiers, Vol. XI.*

Stines   nt   **1850**
Written above R. Stines. Very weathered.

Stines, R.   nt
Probably with Stines, 1850. Both inscriptions are very weathered.

Stoc (r?), T.   sw   June (18?), -85-

Stockdale, F.   sw corner   June ?, 49

Stockdale, T.   w   June, 49
See F. Stockdale, They are probably together in the same company.

Stockdale, T. or F.   sw   June 10 ?, 49
See other Stockdale inscriptions, same date.

Stoo—?, D. R.   w
Seen best on color slide.

Stotts, M. A.   wmt
(*Ellison*, nf)

Stotts, M. A.   nmt
Ellison recorded an M.A. Stotts on wmt; this could possibly be the same.

This D. Stout inscription is carefully embellished. (Author's Photo)

Stout, D.   mt   **1862 6 OVC, Co. A.**
(*Ellison*, found) Drew rectangular sign around his name, has scroll legs on the sign. An inscription of another soldier, C. A. Paine, is very close to this one.

    This is David Stout of Company A of the Ohio Volunteer Cavalry. He was nineteen years old when he enlisted on November 16, 1861. He mustered out with his company in April 1865. *Roster of Ohio Soldiers, Vol. XI.*

Strong, R.T. & R.W.   mt
Initials connected by old Masonic symbol. R. corrected on first initial.

Stume (y?), J. K.   mt   **June 29, /52**

Stump, T.   swt   **52**
(*Ellison*, nf)

Stuoiosus   D Gate   **Chicagonis**
This is in script with a definite left hand slant to the writing.

Sturtevant, A.I.& I.K.   mt   **June 29, 52**
(*Ellison*, found)

Stuwds ??   D Gate
Probably a member of the United States Department of Surveyors. There are other early day U. S. surveyors inscriptions here.

Sudam, D. L.   e

Sun, Thos. E.   D Gate summit
The original Tom Sun set up ranch headquarters on the Sweetwater River just west of Devil's Gate in the 1870s. This could be his inscription or the inscription of his son or grandson. The portion of the Sun Ranch that housed the ranch headquarters is now the site of the Mormon Handcart Visitor's Center.

Sunter, A.   nmt   **63 NY**
A. Sunter is also included in a list of names on Independence Rock compiled by D. W. Greenburg, August 22, 1926. Greenburg did not have the state NY on his list. Although this list is found in the R. S. Ellison files, this name is not included in his book. It is still visible. *Ellison Files, WY State Archives.*

Supv ???   D Gate   **July 4, 1881**

Surdam, D. L.   e

Susrte —???   nt
Very difficult to read.

Sw—?, L. D.   w   **July,**
In tar, almost gone.

Swartout, T.   s   **July 4, 49**
(*Ellison*, found)

Sweeney, T. F.   swt   **July, 1860**
(*Ellison*, found) In 1995 the **F** looks like an upside down **L**. With J. Smith.

A Timothy Sweeney, from Ireland, is listed in the *1890 California Census.* He lived at Chico and listed his occupation as marble polisher. He was fifty-three at the time of census registration in 1890. *Butte County, California, 1890 Great Register, p. 245.*

Swigare, G. W.   nt
(*Ellison*, nf)

Swilm, C. H.   cave   **1848**
This could be Ellison's C. H. Smith. Our reading seems correct.

Sx —??   nw

T—?ale, W. E. nt **July 13, 18 ??**
Very difficult to read.

T—?e, S. R. Pass n
Boxed.

T., A.N. R. Pass n

T. H. n
Tails on letters.

T., R. se
In a survey done June 5, 1927 these initials were recorded. Locations
are not given. At the time of the 1927 survey USGS was also seen along
with the initials. *Ellison Files, WY State Archives.* This shows that this
person was a member of the United States Geological Surveyors. There
are some USGS inscriptions in Devil's Gate. Ellison did not have this
inscription in his book.

T., W. A. s
Quite old and weathered.

T., W. L. mt
(*Ellison*, nf)

Taber, H. mt
(*Ellison*, found) A Horace Taber, Michigan, departed June 1, 1852 with
a small group from Kanesville, Iowa bound for California. *Rasmussen,
p. 141.*

Tafsot, T. nt
This could be T. Talbot. If so, a Theodore Talbot was attached to John
C. Fremont's expedition. This expedition was to map the country to the
coast. He was on more than one Fremont expedition as a member of
the Topographical Engineers. *The Journals of Theodore Talbot 1843 &
1859-52., Merrill J. Mattes Research Library.*

Taft, S. s boulder **Mich**
With W. M. Foreman and I.A. Smith. See the notes under W. M.
Foreman. These three men were probably all going to California.

Talmadge, R. W. w **May, ?8**
Near graves. A J. Talmadge inscription recorded at Register Cliff. Could
possibly be of the same family. *Scottsbluff Survey List.*

A Talmadge family went to Utah in the late 1850s. The family originally came from England. *Information from descendant, 1998.*

Tamarack	mt		**76**

Tanding, J. S.	s		**June 8, 54**

Tannebill, S. W.	nt	May 28, 1895	**Wauneta, NB**

Seven people all from Wauneta, Nebraska together.

Tanner, Hal	w		**June 9, 50**

(*Ellison,* found) Near graves.

Tate, A.?	s		

(*Ellison,* found) An Alexander Tate, from Michigan, is listed in the
1890 California Census. He was a farmer living in Magalia and was fifty-
three at the time he registered for the census in 1884. *Butte County,
California, 1890 Great Register, p. 246.*

Tate, Jas.	s		**June 29, 49**

James Tate inscription. (Author's Photo)

(*Ellison,* found) Colonel James Tate left Saline County, Missouri April 5,
1849, when he was fifty-three. His party traveled overland to St. Joseph
and crossed the Missouri River at St. Joseph on May 3. He reported a terrible jam at the St. Joseph ferry with fights and killings among the emigrants. After the crossing they formed a party of fifteen wagons, fifty-eight
men, and two women. They were at Fort Laramie on June 6 and South
Pass on July 6. They traveled via the Humboldt and Truckee Rivers and
and arrived in Sacramento September 27, 1849. He left a diary, "One
Who Went West: Letters of James Tate." *Platte River Narratives, p. 217.*

From the diary of James Tate in the vicinity of Independence Rock: "Friday, 29th. Three miles to the alkali Ponds where abundance of sallaratus may be obtained. Six—further to Independence Rock. The Sweet water sweeps along two angles of it Leaving a narrow space between. Here a vast number of names are inscribed, it is of granite, it stands in plane covered with a coat of fine grass, the rock rises high and is three quarters of a mile in circumference. I have cut my name with Mr. George with a chisel where it will stand for ages. the rock is solid and smooth and but few places perpendicular." *Tate Diary, Merrill J. Mattes Research Library.*

Author's note: James Tate evidently had a sense of history when he inscribed his name "for ages". His name is still easily read one hundred fifty years later. However, he may have insured fate would keep his name visible, for he put a second inscription, with the same date, also on the south side a little further towards the southwest corner. This inscription of "Mr. George" is still visible with this first inscription, but it is not inscribed with the second Jas. Tate inscription.

Tate, Jas.　　　　　　　　　SSW　　　　　　　　**June 29, 49**

Tate, W. (?)　　　　　　　　S

A W. Tate is listed among the arrivals at Placerville in early August 1852. *Rasmussen, p. 149.*

Taylor　　　　　　　　　S

Taylor, A.　　　　　　　　S　　　　　　　**Sept. 10. 49**

(*Ellison*, found) Inscription says **R.W. Allred, A. Taylor & Co.** with the date. Allred and date are not in Ellison's list.

This is Allen Taylor, Mormon, who first crossed to the Salt Lake Valley in 1848 in the First Division of Brigham Young's Company. He then crossed again as Captain of the Second Company in 1849. *LDS Crossing the Plains Index.*

The Allen Taylor Company left Kanesville, Iowa, on July 5-6, 1849. This was a large group with 137 wagons and 445 people. They arrived in Salt Lake between the times of October 10-20, 1849. The group divided into smaller groups upon reaching the mountains and set their own pace, thus continuing to arrive until October 20th. There were two deaths in the company, one of these deaths occurred during a stampede in R. W. Allred's Fifty. The group experienced several stampedes during their journey. Over a dozen trail narratives were left by members of this large group. *Correspondence from Melvin Bashore, LDS Historical Department, June 19, 2000.*

Taylor ?, J. B.   nmt

Photo of John Taylor, early day Mormon, whose inscription could be on the Rock. (L.D.S. Family History Center, Casper.)

A J. D. Taylor, Mormon, emigrated to the Great Salt Lake Valley. *Information from descendant.*

More possibilities on this Taylor: A John Taylor was an Elder in the early Mormon Church. He journeyed with the first company to Winter Quarters and helped organize the Mormon Battalion. After being called on a mission in Great Britain, he returned to Winter Quarters in 1847 and had charge of a large company going to the Great Salt Lake Valley in that year. *LDS Biographical Encyclopedia, Vol. I, p. 17.*

Or a Joseph Taylor, born in Sussex, England in 1830 sailed from Liverpool in 1851. He left Winter Quarters June 12, 1851 in Captain Joseph Outhouse' Company and arrived in Salt Lake City in September. *LDS Biographical Encyclopedia, Vol. I, p. 295.*

Or a Private John B. Taylor was a member of Company B, Eleventh Kansas Volunteer Cavalry. This unit was stationed out here in 1865 and several of the military left their names on Independence Rock. *Index to Kansas Volunteer Regiment Enlistments, 1861-1863.*

A John Taylor, June 8, 62, from Wappello Co. Iowa inscription recorded at Emigrant Springs, WY. *Kelly 1930 Survey of Emigrant Springs.* Inscription still visible in 1989 BLM survey.

A J. Taylor inscription recorded at Register Cliff. *Scottsbluff Survey List.*

Or a Joseph Taylor, 6/7/1859 from PA inscription recorded at Register Cliff. *Scottsbluff Survey List.*

Taylor, R.   s

This could be Rachel Taylor, a member of a family traveling from Illinois to California in 1853. *Holmes, Vol 6.*

Or it could be Robert Taylor whose family is listed in the *1850 Oregon Territorial Census,* living in Washington County.

An R. Taylor, 1853 inscription can be found at Names Hill. *Brown, Emigrant Inscriptions.*

Taylor, W.   se

Tennant, J. M.   nt   **Aug. 24, 87**

It is possible this date is not with this name.

Th (a?) m, N.   nt

Thager, T (or H?)   . nt
Very weathered.

Than ??, W.E.   nt   July 13, 18 ??

Thatcher, W.   net   June,—9 (?)
A William Henry Thatcher, from New York, is listed in the *1890 California Census*. He was a farmer living in Wyandotte and was fifty-two at the time for census registration in 1884. *Butte County, California, 1890 Great Register, p. 248.*
A William M. Thatcher, 1853 inscription can be found at Names Hill. *Brown, Emigrant Inscriptions.*

Thatcher, Wm.   sw   1862. Co.F—4th Cav. U.S.A.
(*Ellison*, found) There is another soldier from the 4th U. S. A. Cavalry, 1862 inscription on the southwest side. See Nic H. Tonney. Part of the 4th U.S. A. Cavalry could have accompanied the Colonel Collins Sixth Ohio Volunteer expedition out here in 1862. *Robrock, The Eleventh Ohio Volunteer Cavalry, p. 27.*

Thayer   nw   72
Another Thayer, date 72, in same area. This one shows up well.

Thayer, (H?)   nw   72
Very weathered.

Thayer, H. ?   nwt   June 10, 188?

Then—t?, Jarro(d?)   w   J 3 or 9

Thobals, W. L.   se

Thomas   st
(above cave)

Thomas   cave

Thomas, W.B.R.   nt
(*Ellison*, nf) A W.H.R. Thomas, Lieutenant, of Louisa County, Iowa is listed as being part of the California Banner Company departing from Kanesville, Iowa May 9, 1850. It is possible the **B** Ellison recorded is **W.H.R.** (typo or misreading). We could not find it in recent surveying to verify. *Rasmussen, p. 121.*

Or another possibility is this is Dr. William Thomas who was in a company of Kentuckians bound for California in 1849. They traveled by boat to Independence and left overland from there. They were at Fort Laramie on June 3. The were at the Humboldt Sink on July 24 and arrived at Hangtown August 11, 1849. After having the grueling journey with mean spirited mules, climaxed by the Humboldt region Thomas exclaimed, "All the gold in California would not induce me to return by this route." He was traveling with the same party as James Pritchard. He left a diary of the trip. *Mattes, Platte River Narratives, p. 217.*

Thompson, C. (?)   s   **29, 51**
Two names in a rectangle. One too faint to read.

A Charles Thompson traveled from Nebraska to California. *Mattes, Diary and Recollections Survey.*

Carroll Thompson, from Illinois, is listed in the *1890 California Census.* He was a teamster living at Rock Creek and was forty-nine at the time of census registration in 1884. *Butte County, California, 1890 Great Register, p. 249.*

Thompson, E. S.   swt
(*Ellison,* found) An Estella Thompson is listed among the arrivals in Oregon in 1851. She later married A. F. Peterson. *Oregon in 1851.*

Thompson, J.   s   **June, Ottawa, ILL**
(*Ellison,* found) There are a J. P. Thompson and a J. B. Thompson, both from Illinois, listed among emigrant arrivals in Kanesville on May 1, 1850. *Rasmussen, p. 106.*

Related to above data: A John Thompson, from Illinois, is listed in the *1890 California Census.* He was a farmer living in Nord and was fifty-seven at the time of registration in 1884. *Butte County, California, 1890 Great Register, pg. 249.*

A John Thompson is buried in the Chico, California cemetery. He was born in Franklin County, Illinois on February 1, 1827 and died March 31, 1899.

J. Thompson is listed in the *1850 Oregon Territorial Census,* living in Clatsop County.

A John Thomson, of Illinois, is listed among those using the Lander Cutoff en route to Oregon in 1859. *House of Rep. Exec. Document, #63, 1859.*

A J. Thompson July inscription can be found at Raven Rock, Nevada. *Brown, Emigrant Inscriptions.*

A James Thompson, June 30, 1861 inscription is recorded at Emigrant Springs, WY. *Kelly 1930 Survey of Emigrant Springs.* Inscription still visible in 1989 BLM survey.

Thompson, J. B. D Gate **Iowa**

Thompson, W .R. R. nt **Ju 2, 1861**
With W. Pierce, J. Ware, and J.S.O. Ward. This group possibly went to California. See note under W. Pierce.

Throne, A.? X. s **July, 49**
(*Ellison*, found) We saw an **X** by the name and a date of **1849**.

Tibbals, W. L.? sw **June 4, 1865**
(*Ellison*, nf)

Tippetts, W. J. mt

Todd, A .C nmt **65 Co. I, 11th K.V.C.**
(*Ellison*, found) A Private Andrew G. Todd is listed as a member of Company I, Eleventh Kansas Volunteer Cavalry. The Eleventh Kansas Volunteer Cavalry came out to the west in the early spring of 1865. Most of them mustered out in the fall of 1865. Many of these men were stationed at Sweetwater Bridge Station located one mile east of Independence Rock. *Index to Kansas Volunteer Regiment Enlistment Lists, 1861-1865.*

Tolman e
Definitely old. In 1848, a Judson Tolman, Cyrus Tolman, and Benjamin Tolman, all in Brigham Young's Second Company, traveled to the Great Salt Lake Valley. These men were grandsons of Allen Taylor and William Draper whose names are also on Independence Rock. *Information from descendants, 1997.*
  More on these Tolmans: Judson Tolman was born in 1826 in Maine. In 1846 they moved to Nauvoo and he was in Hosea Stout's company helping build bridges and roads. He then wintered at Winter Quarters. In 1848, he crossed to the Salt Lake Valley in Brighan Young's Company and was in Daniel Garn's Fifty. *LDS Biographical Encyclopedia, Vol. II, p. 78.*
  Or an S. W. Tolman is listed in Clatsop County in the *1850 Oregon Territorial Census.*
  Also refer to Tolmans in Rasmussen entry.

Tombenson mt **June 18th, 1861 BEL., ILL**

Tonney, Nic H. sw **1862 S. Co.F 4th Cav, U.S.A.**
(*Ellison*, found) In 1995 we read **Nicies Tormey**. See Cudhiy and Wm. Thatcher.

In the fall of 1862, Lieutenant Colonel William O. Collins assumed command of operations in the west for the area between Julesburg and South Pass. Besides his Sixth Ohio Volunteer Cavalry, he also had at his disposal at Fort Laramie two undermanned companies of the Fourth U. S. Cavalry. This soldier must have been out here with some of the Sixth Ohio Volunteers at the time he left his inscription on Independence Rock. *Robrock, The 11th Ohio Volunteer Cavalry, p. 27.*

Tormey, Niceis   sw   **1862**
See Ellison's Tonney, Nic. H.

Tower, O. L.   nt   **July 4, 1859 ?**
(*Ellison*, found)

Tower, O. L.   w   **49**
(*Ellison*, found)

Towl, W.   s
(*Ellison*, nf)

Tram   se

TRAVERSE ROCK   Sent Rock
Looks like old tar. Drawing of a figure in a canoe?

Trotter, J.   s   **50**
(*Ellison*, found) The date is possibly **59**.

Trowski, E.   mt

Tru—???, W.   wt   **July, ??**
Reverse negative image. In 1847, a William Alexander Trubody wrote of an overland excursion by ox team and reported in the California Historical Quarterly. *Mattes, Diary and Recollection Survey.*

Truax, Olive   net
With John Valdez.

Tu(i), E.   R. Pass n
Letters just quit, so could be all the name there is. E. Turner, VA is just under this inscription in much larger letters, so the guess is that the E. Turner started his name in smaller letters and then decided to make the inscription in larger letters. The printing is almost identical.

Tur(k?)er, John or H.H? w   **18 (79?)**

Turnor, E.   R. Pass n   **VA**

Tyrrell   s

A T. Tyrrell also on s side.

Tyrrell, T.   s   **60**

(*Ellison*, found) Maybe traveling with J. Willis.

U., J.   R. Pass w

Ullin, I. L.   st   **1852**

Uneirig (Unerng?),S.   s

Upton, Wm. L. I.   D Gate   **June 22, 60 IL**

V(W?)attles, P.   D Gate   **July 4, 1857**

V., D.H.U.   nmt

(*Ellison*, nf?) See next entry.

V., Dr. H. V.   nt

Could possibly be what Ellison has as D.H.U.V.

V., I. W.   D. Gate summit

Vaden, P. A.   D Gate

Valde, John   net

Due to the appearance of the rock after the **e** in Valde, the surveyors believe that due to weathering the last letter of the surname has flaked off. If this is the case, the last letter could possibly have been a **z**.

Vam— a—?   D Gate

Van Cleave, Sarah E.   nmt   **June, 66**

(*Ellison*, found) In a survey done by D. W. Greenburg on August 22, 1926, he believed that Sarah Van Cleave and Sarah Brumbaugh might be together. Their names are close together with the same date. *Ellison Files, WY State Archives.*

Van Hobson, G.   nt   **Aug 24, 87 ILL**

It's possible this date is with another name.

Van Horn, M. N.   mt   **Iowa.**

Boxed with M. Neal, M & H W Neal. In a survey done on August 22, 1926 by D. W. Greenburg he read the date July 15, 1852 with this inscription.

Van Horn, M. N.   mt   **Iowa**
(*Ellison*, found) Possibly with the two Neals. A second inscription also on middle top. See the other M. N. Van Horn entry.

Van Leuden, D. P   sw   **Au 12,—2 ?**

Van Wie, J. H.   cave
(*Ellison*, nf)

Van Wit   unknown
This name is included in a survey list done June 5, 1927 by an unidentified person. Locations are not recorded in this list. Although this list is found in the R. S. Ellison files, this name is not included in his book. *Ellison Files, WY State Archives.* We have not found this name in recent surveying although it is possible this could be what Ellison has as Van Wie.

VanVleet, R. E.   sw

Vangunday, A. J.   nt   **(?)-L-D-V-C**
(*Ellison*, found)

Vangunday, A. W.   nt   **(?)-L-D-V-C**
(*Ellison*, found)

Vans, J. E.   s

Varden, L. P.   s

Vasponable, A. L.   mt.
Backwards s and n.

Vickery, T.   nt

Vincent   s   **May 29, 1850**
Together with J. Cappen and Jas. Sasry. Two Vincents, George and Dow, from Illinois are listed among the emigrant arrivals at Kanesville May 1, 1850. A William Vincent also listed at the same time. *Rasmussen, pp. 105, 106.*

Two Vincent inscriptions can be found on the south side within twenty-five feet of each other.

Vincent, J.   s   **July 10, 49**
(*Ellison*, found) A J. Vincent is listed as being a member of the Wisconsin & Iowa Union Company leaving Kanesville in May 1849. *Rasmussen, p. 67.*

Vincent, V. (I?)   s   **July 10, 49**
Very close to J. Vincent, July 10, 49. This one is spelled Vincnt with the **e** inserted above the last name.

Vincent, W. A.   s
(*Ellison*, found) There are two Vincents on south side within twenty-five feet of each other. In 1996 we could see only the initial A.
    See notes under Vincent for information on a William Vincent.

Vincint, J.   s

Vinton, Charles   nt
Date unreadable.

Vircks, Paul   st   **19 /86**
Name almost all lichen covered.

Vise, J. A.   s   **25 NE ?**
We believe the 25 is day of month.

Voh ??, J.   s   **June**
In tar, below cave.

Vosburgh, L. N.   s   **July 18, 50**
(*Ellison*, nf)

Vreeland, Wm   mt   **31, 89 Michigan**
With S. J. Parmelee.

Vurch, I. N.   s   **July, 62**

W (?) amey, John   nt   **1878**

W—???, J. B.   swt
Very weathered.

W—?, ???   w   **1—?**

W-?er (Walker?), J.K.   n

W., A.   D Gate

W., A.   nt   **69**

W., E.   st
Big letters.

W., E. A. mt J— (??)
Very elaborate J follows initials.

W., H. L. D Gate **Millard, ILL**
Two inscriptions from Millard, Illinois. The other is the single initial **E**.

W., I. E. mt **56**

W., J. swt

W., J. B. s **51**

W., L. w

W., L. w

W., T. wt **Jun 8, 63**
Three sets of initials—**C.C., T. W.** and **M.S.**—are all together with same date.

W., W. nt **64**

Wagner, J. net **52**
A John Wagner, originally from Germany, is listed in the *1890 California Census*. He was a merchant at Mountain Home and was forty-nine years old at the time of census registration in 1884. *Butte County, California, 1890 Great Register, p. 259.*

Wald cave

Walker, D. C. ne
Same inscription also on net.

Walker, D. C. net
Same inscription also on ne.

Wall, E. A. nmt
(*Ellison*, nf)

Wall, J. K. net
(*Ellison*, nf) A John Wall, from Ireland, is listed in the *1890 California Census*. He was a farmer in Evansville, and his age was fifty-two at the time he registered for the census in August 1884. *Butte County, California, 1890 Great Register, pg. 261.*

Wallace, J.   mt   **56**
(*Ellison*, found) This date was read in 1995.

Wallace, J. J.   mt
(*Ellison*, nf) There were several Wallaces who emigrated to California.
They were of the same family as General Lew Wallace. *Information from descendants.*

A J. Wallace and a Martha Ann Wallace, from Illinois, are among
those who died somewhere along the trail on the way to Oregon in
1852. *US Gen Web Archives.*

Wallace, M. H.   R. Pass n
Probably with T. D. Wallace. A Michel Haw Wallace, from New York,
is listed in the *1890 California Census.* He was a carpenter living in
Chico and his age was sixty-four at the time he registered for the census in 1884. *Butte County, California, 1890 Great Register, pg. 261.*

Wallace, T. D.   R. Pass n
Large letters. Probably traveling with M.H. Wallace and going to
California. See note under M. H. Wallace.

Wallage Famdl-y   se
Could say Family but looks like Famdl-y?

Wallage, GEO   mt
A George B. Wallace was Captain of a Fifty crossing the plains with ox
teams going to the Salt Lake Valley in 1847. *LDS Biographical
Encyclopedia, Vol. I. pg. 782.*

Waller, J. K.   unknown
This name is found on a list compiled by D. W. Greenburg August 22,
1926. He listed Waller, F. M. Edwards, P. W. Edwards, and S. S. Slater
as together. Although he saw no date, the S. S. Slater inscription has an
1849 date. S. S. Slater and F. M. Edwards are on north middle top.
Although this list is found in the R. S. Ellison files, this name in not in
his book. *Ellison Files, WY State Archives.* We have not found the name
in recent surveying but this panel has names over names.

Wallis, J. I.   mt

Wallis, J. K.   nt

Walton, E.   cave
(*Ellison*, found)

Walton, J. se near cave **1863**
(*Ellison*, nf) In 1863 a Joseph Walton, Mormon, crossed the plains to the Salt Lake Valley as a member of Captain Moses Clouson's Company. *LDS Crossing the Plains Index.*

Walton, J. E. cave **1871**
(*Ellison*, found) A second J. E. Walton, 1871 inscription also on north east top.

Walton, J. E. net **May, 1871**
(*Ellison*, found) A second J. E. Walton, 1871 inscription in the cave.

Walton, J. R. se near cave **1863**
(*Ellison*, found)

Walton, S. se near cave **63**

Walton, S. W. se
(*Ellison*, found)

Wam?(e maybe), R. sw
Written **Mr. and Mrs.**

Wampler, W. mt **59**
(*Ellison*, found)

Wanemakr, H. nt **59**
Very weathered.

Wanins, R. nt **May ??, 81**

Wankrim mt

Ward, J.S.O. nt
(*Ellison*, found) Traveling with W. Pierce, J. Ware, and W. R. R. Thompson, probably going to California.

Ward, J. W. nt **59**
(*Ellison*, nf)

Ward, W. mt **July 1**
A William Ward, originally from Virginia, is listed in the *1890 California Census.* He was a butcher living in Ophir, and was fifty-nine when he registered for the census in 1884. *Butte County, California, 1890 Great Register, pg. 262.*

Wards, Jed   mt   **Sep 4th, 79**

Ware, J .   nt   **Ju 2, 1861**
With W. Pierce, W. R. R. Thompson, and J.S.O. Ward, probably going
to California.

Ware, R.   D Gate

Warner, L. S.   s
(*Ellison*, nf)

Warner, W. C.   ne
Backwards **n** in name. Midway up. A William Warner left Navarre,
Ohio and traveled to Council Bluffs. He then left Council Bluffs with
a group on May 17, 1853. This party consisted of four men, two
women, and one baby. They traveled to Salt Lake City and laid over one
week before traveling on to California. Starvation threatened them
before their arrival in California. They arrived in Nevada City on
September 17. He left a letter, "Overland to California: Letter from an
Ohio Argonaut." *Platte River Narratives, pg.429.*

Warner, W. G.   net
(*Ellison*, found)

Warner, W. O.   ne   **66**
With J.J. Brooks. It is located midway way up the Rock.

Warren, Elza   **49**
Written along with Rena Warren, same date.

Warran, J. S.   R. Pass w   **June 20, 1859**
                                                                       Iowa City
A J.S. Warren Iowa City same date also in Independence Rock.

Warren, J. S.   s   **June 20, 1859**
                                                                       Iowa City
J. S. Warren, Iowa City, also on same date at Rattlesnake Pass.

Warren, Rena   w   **49**
Written along with Elza Warren.

Wasson, Jonathan   cave   **July 17, 1846**
(*Ellison*, found) It is definitely **Wassom** with an **m** and not an **n** as the
last letter. Ellison seems to be wrong.

Watkins, J. H.   nt   **July 64**
(*Ellison*, found) Date almost gone.
    A J. E. F. Watkins inscription recorded at Register Cliff. *Henderson 1930 Survey of Register Cliff.*

Watts, D.   s

Weatherington, Ira (?)   nt   **July 4, 1849   Cole**
    Boxed.   **Co., ILL**

Weaver, D.   s
    A Dr. D. Weaver is listed as a member of the Wayne County Company from Indiana who crossed to California in 1850. He was from Wooster, Ohio. This group left St. Joseph on April 10. George Keller left a diary of the trip across the plain by this company. *Company roster from Keller diary.*

Weaver, J. A.   s   **July 4, 50**
    (*Ellison*, nf) A James Weaver and a John Weaver are among the emigrant arrivals in Oregon in 1850. *The Oregonian, Dec. 4, 1925.*

Webb, P.   s   **Aug. 11, 49**
    (*Ellison*, found) In 1848, a Pardon Webb, Mormon, went across to the Salt Lake Valley in Brigham Young's Company. With all the back and forth travel of the Mormon men on the trail, it is possible that he traveled across again in 1849. *LDS Crossing the Plains Index.*

Webster, A.   et   **1891**

Webster, A. D.   net   **July, 50**
    (*Ellison*, nf)

Webster, P.   net   **July, 50**
    (*Ellison*, found)

Webster, W. L (?)   se
    Very faint. A W. C. Webster inscription at Register Cliff. *Brown, Emigrant Inscriptions.*

Wei (n), W.   st

Wel (e) or (c), C.   swt

Wel—? (Welch?), W.   cave above

Welch, C.   mt
(*Ellison*, found) A C. B. Welch party is listed as having crossed the Lander Cutoff en route to California in 1859. There were four wagons and eleven people in this party. *House of Rep. Exec. Document #63, 1859.*

Or a C. W. Welch is listed among the arrivals at Placerville, California in early September 1852. *Rasmussen, pg. 163.*

Welch, H.   mt   **52**
(*Ellison*, found) We saw the initials **AAMC**, also **MICH** in 1996. The initials could be the inscription of someone else.

Wellman, W. W.   mt   **July 4, 62 Iowa**
(*Ellison*, found) He could possibly have been traveling with John Beck.

Wellman, W.   mt

Wells, Floyd   unknown
This inscription is on a list of names surveyed June 5, 1927 by an unidentified person. Locations of names are not recorded. Although this list is found in the R. S. Ellison files, this name is not in his book. *Ellison Files, WY State Archives.* We have not found the name in recent surveying.

Wells, J. K.   s   **July 4, 64**
(*Ellison*, found)

We(r?) -t zio-?, H. M.   s   **May/49**
Very difficult to read due to names over names.

Wertz, H. M.   s   **May 12, 50**
(*Ellison*, found) We think the date may be **May 19, 50**.

A Henry Wertz is listed as a member of the Wayne County Company taken on board the steamship Consignee prior to their jumping off for California. This group was from Indiana and left from St. Joseph on April 10, 1850. George Keller left a diary of this company's travels. *Company roster from Keller diary.*

West, J. H.   mt
(*Ellison*, found) A Jeptha West, 1857, inscription recorded at Register Cliff. *Henderson 1930 Survey of Register Cliff.*

A T. H. West, Ohio, 1859 inscription recorded at Emigrant Springs, WY. *Kelly 1930 Survey of Emigrant Springs.*

Westbott, V.   R. Pass s

This inscription could be made by the same person as V. Westgott on north side of the Pass.

Westgott, V.   R. Pass n   **May 27, 1864**

The same name also on Independence Rock two days earlier.

Westgott, V.   n   **May 25, 64**

The same name also at Rattlesnake Pass two days later.

Wh—, E. R.   s

Wh—??—lock, B.   sw   **Ju (?) 26th, 49**

Very weathered.

Wharton, D. J.   nmt   **64**

(*Ellison*, found ?) We read **Wheaton**.

Wheaton, D. J   nmt.   **64**

Possibly what Ellison has as Wharton.

Whey, John   s   **June**

(*Ellison*, found)

Whi—??, S. R.   se   **60**

White, A. L.   unknown   **May 9, 50 ILL's**

This name is included on a survey list that was done June 5, 1927 by an unidentified person. Although this list is found in the R. S. Ellison files, this name is not in his book. Locations were not recorded on this list. Whoever did the surveying had D. B. Gillam, A. L. White, and J. B. Brian probably all traveling together with a joint date. Gillam is on the south side of the Rock. *Ellison Files, WY State Archives*. We have not found this name in recent surveying.

White, ANDW (?)   nt   **Ju 9, 1861**

White, C. J.   nt

White, I.   nt   **Jue, 60**

Shows up in photograph.

White, J.   net   **July, 60**

(*Ellison*, found) A J. White went to Idaho sometime in the early 1860s to avoid family conflict during the Civil War. *Information from descendant, 1997*.

White, J.   nt

Seen with use of b/w technical pan film. A J. White is listed among the arrivals in Placerville in early August 1852. *Rasmussen, pg 147.*

Or another J. White is among the arrivals in Placerville between August 16 -19, 1852. *Rasmussen, pg.153.*

Or there are two different J. White's listed in the *Tuality County, Oregon Territory, 1849 Census.* One was Jno. M. White and family; the other was Jno. S. White and family. *US Gen Web Archives.*

White, Jawn   nt   **Ju 2, 61**

(*Ellison*, nf)

White, L. H.   cave

White's inscription is in the cave twice. No date on this one. Inscription seen on digital photo.

White, L. H.   cave   **July 3, 1860**

(*Ellison*, found) This is a second L. H. White in the cave, this one with a 1860 inscription on the southwest top.

White, L. H.   swt   **1860**

(*Ellison*, found) Two L. H. White inscriptions are also in the cave.

White, P.   w   **—19, ?**

This could be a twentieth century inscription, but there are tails on the letters and an elaborate W in White.

Whitmore, Hildreth   w   **1904 (?)**

Date almost gone.

WHNE, C. J.   nt

WI T E, T. G.   st

Wil ???ires   w   **59**

Name almost covered with lichen. Located near the graves.

Wil—?, H.   s

Wilber, S.   nt

Date unreadable.

Wilbur, S. R.   nmt   **Sept., 52**

(*Ellison*, found) In 1996 we saw the inscription is probably S. K. Wilbur.

In 1852 an S. Wilbur, Mormon, crossed the plains going to Utah. He was a member of Captain Eli B. Kelsey's Nineteenth Company. *LDS Crossing the Plains Index.*

Wilcox, F. W.   nt

An unnamed Wilcox is mentioned in the Bernard Reid diary of the 1849 Pioneer Line crossing. He was guide for the Mounted Riflemen who marched across the plains in 1849. *Reid diary, pg 207*

A Frederick Wilcox, from Rhode Island, is listed in the *1890 California Census.* He was a miner living in Enterprise, and was sixty-one at the time of census registration in 1884. *Butte County, California, 1890 Great Register, pg. 269.*

An F. Wilcox, wife and children, are listed in the *Tuality County, Oregon Territory, 1849 Census. US Gen Web Archives.*

Wilde, H. W.   s

Wilder, J. D.   mt

This Wilder inscription on Independence Rock twice. There is no date on this one.

Wilder, J. D.   mt   **June 18, 1854 (?)**

(*Ellison*, found) J. D. Wilder name on Independence Rock twice.

Wile, H. W.   s

Box around name.

Wiley, J. H.   se

(*Ellison*, found)

Wiley, John   s   **June, 1850**

Wilkerson, Bobby   emt   **7, 31, 49**

Together with Jimmy Wilkerson. This could be a twentieth century inscription however see Jimmy Wilkerson note.

Wilkerson, Jimmy   emt   **7, 31, 49**

This could be a twentieth century inscription, but the inscription has a backwards **n**. Note: In 1859 a Jimmy Wilkinson left a diary of his trip across the plains, so this nickname was in use in the nineteenth century. *Mattes, Diary and Recollection Survey.*

Wilkin, R. S.   nt

(*Ellison*, found) An R. S. Wilkin, from Indiana, is listed among those using the Lander Cutoff en route to California in 1859. There were seven wagons and nineteen people in this party. *House of Rep. Exec. Document #63, 1859.*

Willett, A. L.   s   **March 6, 50 ILL**

(*Ellison*, found) We believe the date reads **May**. Ellison has other inscriptions that are along with this name dated May 6, 50. March would have been very early to be here.

Willey, John   s   **June 21 NH**

Williams, Allie   nt

(*Ellison*, found) An A. Williams, male, is listed in the *Tuality County, Oregon Territory, 1849 Census. US Gen Web Archives.*

Williams, C.   mt

(*Ellison*, found)

Williams, G.   mt   **June, 61**

A George Williams, from Pennsylvania, is listed in the *1890 California Census.* He was a miner living at Yankee Hill and was age fifty-two at the time he registered for the census in 1884. *Butte County, California, 1890 Great Register, pg. 271.*

Williams, H.   s

(*Ellison*, nf) An H. D. Williams left from Viroqua, Wisconsin and traveled overland to St. Joseph in 1859. He crossed the Missouri at St. Joseph. The party was at Fort Laramie on May 29 and at South Pass on June 16th. This party was originally bound for Pikes' Peak but on meeting the disillusioned miners returning from the fizzled gold rush they traveled to California instead. H. D. Williams left a diary that is rated a superior account by Merrill Mattes. *Platte River Narratives, pg. 517.*

Refer to the W. F. Williams entry. He was also from Wisconsin traveling in 1859.

Or this could be Henrietta C. Williams who traveled from Boston to Council Bluffs and then to Salt Lake in George Albert Smith's wagon train in 1849. They left Winter Quarters on July 4, 1849 and arrived in Salt Lake City in late October. This party was caught in a snowstorm at South Pass. Refer to the Bishop W. Draper entry for details of this storm. *Platte River Narratives, pg. 224.*

Or a Henry F. Williams traveled from the District of Columbia to California in 1848. *Mattes, Diary and Recollection Survey.*

A Henry Henry Williams, originally from Wales, is listed in the *1890 California Census.* He was an engineer living in Magalia and was forty-five years old at the time of census registration in 1884. *Butte County, California, 1890 Great Register, pg. 271.*

Williams, J.   mt   **June 29, 1852**
(*Ellison,* found) A James Stevens Williams left Ottuma, Iowa arriving at Council Bluffs April 6, 1852. He and his wife, Frances, started out in a company of five horse drawn wagons, fourteen men, three women, and three children. This party was ahead of the worst of the cholera, arriving at Fort Laramie on May 29. They arrived at Oregon City on July 31, 1852. He had gone to California on an earlier crossing in 1850 but came back to get his family. Letters were handed down in the family. *Platte River Narratives, pg. 398.*

Or a J. Williams was in a Michigan/Wisconsin party that left Kanesville May 7, 1852 en route to California. *Rasmussen, pg. 138.*

Also a J. Williams is listed among the arrivals at Placerville in mid August 1852. This could be the J. Williams of the Michigan/ Wisconsin party. *Rasmussen, pg. 153.*

A James Williams inscription recorded at Register Cliff. *Henderson 1930 Survey of Register Cliff.*

Williams, J.   nt   **1864 (?)**
(*Ellison,* nf) A James Madison Williams, from Tennessee, is listed in the *1890 California Census.* He was a farmer living in Pence's Ranch and was sixty-five at the time he registered for the census in 1884. *Butte County, California, 1890 Great Register, pg. 271.*

Or a John Williams, from England, is listed in the *1890 California Census.* He was a miner living in Magalia and was forty-five at the time he registered in 1888. *Butte County, California, 1890 Great Register, pg. 272.*

Williams, J. A.   east corner
A Joseph Williams left Menard County, Missouri on April 3, 1851 and traveled to Council Bluffs where they crossed the river. He was traveling with his six sons en route to Oregon. They traveled on the north side of the Platte River all the way. They arrived at the Willamette Valley having traveled via the Barlow Road. He left a diary of the trip across. *Mattes, Platte River Narratives, pg. 333.*

Williams, Jo   unknown   **June 22, 1852**
This name was recorded by D. W. Greenburg who did a survey of Independence Rock on August 22, 1926. Locations of inscriptions were not recorded. *Ellison Files, WY State Archives.* We have not found this inscription in recent surveying.

Williams, W. F.   s nr. cave

(*Ellison*, nf) An F. Williams from Wisconsin is listed among those using the Lander Cutoff in 1859. *House of Rep. Exec. Document #63, 1859.* See H. Williams entry.

Or a Wiliam Williams, originally from Wales, is listed in the *1890 California Census*. He was a miner living in Cherokee and was fifty-one at the time he registered for the census in 1884. *Butte County, California, 1890 Great Register, pg. 271.*

Williams, W. S.   net   **July 8, 1853**

(*Ellison*, found) Probably with A. E. Moody, W. W. Gilbert, J. R. Hughes.

A Wellington Williams left a book, *The Traveller's Tourist's Guide through the United States, Containing the Routes of Travel*, published in 1853. *Mattes Diary and Recollection Survey.*

Or a Wallise Samuel Williams, a freighter, went back and forth to the Salt Lake Valley from Nebraska. *Information from descendant.*

Williams, W. V.   nt   **July, 1852**

(*Ellison*, found) Date almost gone. In 1852 a Washington Williams crossed the plains going to the Great Salt Lake Valley as a member of the Sixteenth Company under Captain Urich Curtis. *LDS Crossing the Plains Index.*

Williams ?, J.   s   **June 22, 1864**

Willis, J. I.   mt

Willis, J.   nt   **(?)-L-D-V-C**

(*Ellison*, found)

Willis, L.   nt   **June 21, 1852**

(*Ellison*, found) An L. S. Willis inscription recorded at Register Cliff. *Henderson 1930 Survey of Register Cliff.*

Willo—??, R.   net

Wilso (n?), F.   nt

Last letter of the name gone.

Wilson   R. Pass n

Wilson   nt   **76**

Wilson, C.   s

This C. Wilson must be with J. S. Downs for both are pecked lettering and close together.

A C. Wilson is listed among arrivals in Placerville during the first week of September 1853. *Rasmussen, pg. 164.*

Wilson, C.   s

This second C. Wilson inscription is inscribed, not pecked.

Wilson, C. F.   mt   June 18, 52

(*Ellison*, found) Inscription is in a box with S. P. Beard.

There was a Wilson party who traveled to Oregon in the emigration of 1852. *Comprehensive Index to Oregon Trail Diaries*

Wilson, J. R.   nw   18??

Almost gone. A James Wilson, originally from England, is listed in the *1890 California Census.* He was a fisherman living in Chico and was sixty-five at the time of census registration in April 1884. *Butte County, California, 1890 Great Register, pg. 275.*

A James Wilson is buried in the Chico, California cemetery. He was born August 1, 1817 and died September 19, 1903. His wife and son are buried next to him. It is possible this is the same James Wilson as listed in the California census above.

Or a Joseph Wilson, originally from England, is listed in the *1890 California Census.* He was a farmer living in Gridley and was fifty-three at the time of census registration in 1884. *Butte County, California, 1890 Great Register, pg. 274.*

A John Wilson is listed among those emigrants arriving in Oregon in 1850. *The Oregonian, Dec. 4, 1925.*

A J. R. Wilson, July 20, 60 inscription recorded at Emigrant Springs, WY. *Kelly 1930 Survey of Emigrant Springs.* This inscription still visible at Emigrant Springs, WY in 1969. *BLM 1989 Survey of Emigrant Springs.*

Wilson, L. H.   nt

(*Ellison*, nf)

Wilson, S. K.   mt   Sept

A Samuel Wilson is listed among the arrivals in Oregon in 1851. *Oregon in 1851.*

Wilson, U. A.   nw   June

Wilson(m?), S. R.   e

Wilson?, J.W.H.O.?   se   June 9, 1850

(*Ellison*, nf) Possibly this reading includes two overlapping sets of initials.

Winans, W. K. mt **July 4, 62 Min**
(*Ellison*, found) Winans possibly traveling with A. Balcomb.

Winchell, H. H. mt **1853 Wis**
(*Ellison*, found) Winchell was possibly traveling with O.S. Gibson.

Winet, J. s **1860**
(*Ellison*, found) With S.C. Hitchfield.

Winship, M. & S. s **Aug. 11, 45**
(*Ellison*, found)

Winship, R. L. net **1875**
(*Ellison*, found)

Winter, F. A. unknown
This inscription is in a list of names surveyed June 5, 1927 by an unidentified person. Locations are not given. Although this list is found in the R. S. Ellison files, the name is not included in his book. *Ellison Files, WY State Archives.* We have not found the name in recent surveying.

Wise, H. W. s
Name is boxed in.

Wold, W. se
In crevice east of cave.

Wold, J. D. s **49**
Error in Ellison? Name is definitely **WOLE**.

Wole, J. D. s **July 19**
Possibly the J. D. Wold in Ellison, though the dates are different.

Woldley, M. B. nt

Wolley, J. M. F. cave
(*Ellison*, nf) Could be John Mills Woolley who was born in Pennsylvania in 1822 and moved with his family to Illinois. He lived and worked in Nauvoo and crossed the plains

John Mills Woolley. (L.D.S. Family History Center, Casper.)

in 1847 in George B. Wallace's Fifty. *LDS Biographical Encyclopedia, Vol. I, pg. 782.*

Wong, W.   mt   **July 1**
(*Ellison*, found) Name almost gone.

Wood, A. B. P.   R. Pass n   **June 2 ?, 1852**
M. Neal, Wood, O. Babcox, and J.D. Barnard all together.

Wood, B.   s
(*Ellison*, found)

Wood, I. W.   mt
(*Ellison*, found) We read J. W. Wood.

Wood, R. P.   s
An R. B. Wood inscription recorded at Register Cliff. *Henderson 1930 Survey of Register Cliff.*

Wood, S.   s
Backwards S. A Sarah Wood, married lady, is listed among the emigrant arrivals in Oregon in 1847. *Flora, Emigrants in 1847.*

Wood (Food?), A.T.   se

Woodock, C B   w

Woodruff, C. B.   w   **N J**
N backwards.

Woodson (s), S. R.   net

Woom, S. M.?   nt
Seen with use of B/W technical pan film.

Wordley, M. B.   nt   **May 28, 1895 Wauneta, Nebr**
Seven people all from Wauneta, Nebraska together.

Worth, An??ay   cave
In a digital photo the inscription seems to read **Allan Worth**.

Worth, S.   nt   **52**
(*Ellison*, found)

Worumbaugh?   mt
Some letters hard to read.

Wotzo?, R. M.   s   **May 19**

Wright, A.   mt

Wright, C.S.   mt   **July 4, 59**
(*Ellison*, found) Written **Jy 4**. Box around name.

An E. R. Wright party of eight from Iowa is listed among those using the Lander Cutoff in 1859 en route to California. *House of Rep. Exec. Document #63, 1859.*

Wright, John   cave
(*Ellison*, found) John Wright, a Mormon, first went from Nauvoo to Mt .Pisgah and stayed there until called to the Salt Lake Valley by Brigham Young. *Information from descendant, 1997.*

More on this John Wright: John Fish Wright was born in Yorkshire, England. The family emigrated to America in 1848 arriving at New Orleans and they then went up river to Iowa. They remained on the frontiers until 1852 when they left for Utah in Captain Tidwell's Company arriving in Salt Lake City in September 1852. Could be same as above. *LDS Biographical Encyclopedia, Vol. I, pg. 431.*

John Wright. (L.D.S. Family History Center, Casper.)

Wright, L.   w
(*Ellison*, nf)

Wright, W. W.   s   **1856**
(*Ellison*, found) A William Wright and his wife arrived in the Great Salt Lake Valley on September 26, 1856. They were members of Captain Daniel MacArthur's Handcart Company. *LDS Crossing the Plains Index.*

Wylie, Old Nick   wmt
(*Ellison*, found)

X   R. Pass w
Large X symbol with tails, looks like crossed pickaxes.

XX   R. Pass n
Another set of double **XX**, no line through these.

XX   R. Pass n

Long line through the **XX**, boxed. **XX** Pony Express inscription recorded at Register Cliff. *Scottsbluff Survey List.*

Y (?) attles, P. I.   D Gate   **July 4, 5 (1?)**

Y (o or e)or   w   **Jun**

In tar, almost gone.

Y., W. J.   nw   **7, 4 ??.**

Yager, Wm.   mt

Small inscription, in the vicinity of Hollingsworth & McLain. No date on this one.

Yager, W. A.   smt   **June 13, 62 6th Ohio V.C**

(*Ellison*, found) William Yager seems to have put his name on Independence Rock three times.

This is William A. Yager of Company A of the Ohio Volunteer Cavalry. He was twenty-nine years old when he enlisted on October 23, 1861. In November of 1861 he was appointed Corporal and was later promoted to Sergeant when he transferred to Company E. *Roster of Ohio Soldiers, Vol. XI.* Members of the Ohio Volunteer Cavalry were stationed just east of Independence Rock at Sweetwater Bridge Station. These soldiers of the Ohio Volunteer Cavalry were under the command of Lt. Colonel William Collins. His command was sent to the west to protect the telegraph lines. The Sixth Ohio Volunteer Cavalry later became the Eleventh Volunteer Cavalry so you might see both units in different inscriptions. Several of these soldiers put their name on Independence Rock; some of them more than once.

Yager, Wm. A   mt   **June 9, 62**

(*Ellison*, found) This is William Yager of the Ohio Volunteer Cavalry. See above. He put his name on the Rock in three places.

Yeo, Frank   nt

(*Ellison*, found)

Young, A.   e   **?? 9**

The **9** could be day of month or year. An A. J. Young is among those listed as using the Lander Cutoff in 1859. *House of Rep. Exec. Document #63, 1859.*

Young, C.   nw

Tails on letters. In red rock circle halfway up.

Young, J. B.   D Gate   **MO USD SUR**

He was a member of government surveyors. Several surveyor names together.

Young, J. B.   nt

(*Ellison*, found) A J. B. Young inscription is also at Devil's Gate.

Could be John Young, Mormon, who was born in 1797 in Massachusetts. He crossed the plains with his family in 1850 going by ox teams to Utah. *LDS Biographical Encyclopedia, Vol. I., pg. 187.*

Or two brothers James (1827-1847) and John Quincy Adams Young (1828-1905) are among those emigrants who crossed the plains to Oregon in 1847. They traveled the trail with their parents, Elam and Irene Young. James was delivering wood to the Whitman Mission when the uprising was in progress and although he attempted to turn back, he was killed. John was a survivor of the Whitman massacre. *Flora, Emigrants in 1847.*

A John Young is listed in the *Champoeg County, Oregon Territory, 1849 Census. US Gen Web Archives.*

Young, L.   nmt   **June 25, 1862**

(*Ellison*, found) An L. Young inscription recorded at Register Cliff. *Scottsbluff Survey List.*

The following inscriptions are partial inscriptions. The goal of the surveyors was to record all that was visible at the turn of the century. The inscriptions are included here because they may benefit researchers or some future technology may allow more accurate or complete readings.

                  n   **May, 1854**

Very faint. Midway up.

                  n   **Date of Jy 26, 60**

Could possibly go with B. Bishop.

                  n   **July 6, 1852 ILL**

The name covered by twentieth century Masonic name.

                  ne   **1887**

No name close. Could possibly go with Oster.

                  s   **June, 50.**

Very clear. Not sure what inscription it may be with.

	st	-856

In tar. The rest gone.

	sw	9, 1850

Do not know month.

	sw corner	June 18, 18(?)0

In red paint. Hard to read. Name does not show.

Jim   D Gate

Jim   ne

With J.B. and M.B. On ground.

Mrs.   nt

In black paint, covered by carved names. Rest of name gone.

? , Jason   w

Almost gone. Could be last name.

(Berth?), Lisa	n	74

Right above R. B. Berth, 74.

(W ?)orke, E.   se

—ern?, W. P.   se

—??nger   R. Pass n

In lichen. First part gone.

—??hic, N—   s

Very faint, weathered red paint, below cave.

—??tines   nt

—?, F   R. Pass n

Very hard to see.

—RUAD ???	mt	June, 1852

W. M. Linn wrote name over this inscription. Hard to read.

—?heady, T. M.   s

—? ornd   D. Gate

What remains of name in tar.

—?? astr, W.   n
   almost gone. Midway up.

? M.?   mt
   (*Ellison*, nf)

? (G) ue   R. Pass n

?—upman, B. or K.   w

?—Yon or Yun, W.A.   s   1850

?—ams, L. E.   s   June 29, 1849

??—orut, H—??   mt
   very faint.

??? (big tar name?)   w   25, 4?

????   w   —50
   Name gone, only numbers. In tar.

?????, C. E.   w
   Last name unreadable.

? ? ?, John   s

?????, V. A.   R. Pass n

??????   w   50
   Everything else gone. Seen best on color slide.

??arnes,   s   je 15

??frodd.   D Gate   NEB.

??JAES   D Gate

?e-orge, J.   D Gate   July 4, 1860

?oreaux   e

?Ot?ke, E.   e

?siselois (?)   s
   Could possibly be Reisellis in Ellison.

APPENDIX A:
MATTHEW FIELD'S LIST

A T INDEPENDENCE ROCK in August of 1843, journalist Matthew Field and a companion made a list of some of the names they found. On August 28 he wrote in his diary: "From the numerous names inscribed on the rock Tilghman assisted me copying the following. Many others are obliterated, and many are made in such hieroglyphical mystery that they are wholly illegible. The female names are, many of them, sweethearts of the wanderers, except some of the newest, which may have been left by the ladies of the Oregon Party."

This list is reproduced as Field recorded it in his diary: [1]

Inscriptions copied from Rock Independence.

T. Owen (not Tom, the Bee Hunter)
L. Applegate—1843
Fitzpatrick—L. C. Cooper—1843
Mary Zachary—Jane Mills
T. Campbell—Henry Clay over Clay we found by W. C. K.
Martin Van Buren, in 40 line pica, by Wm. Gilpin
F. Fitzpatrick, again
W. Cruss, 1843—J. T. Talbot, 1843
D. F. Hill—D. Delaney—W. T. Newby, 1843
J. H. Barker—R. H. Thomas, 1841
Wm C. Kennerly—G. E. Hepburn
J. K. Clark—T. Smith
H. Bay—and J. Cromwell
L. C. Menard—Jo Pourier

Wm L. Sublette, with Moses Harris, on express, Jan. 1827,
again on July 4th, 1841 [*sic*]. when the rock was christened
— and again, with us, July 22nd & Aug. 12, [*sic*] 1843.
Antoine Clement — A. Drips 40
M. Harris — M. C. Nye
E. Barnet — G. Predame
T. Smith — 43 — B. H. D. Wall
L. D. Walker (Susan) 43
L. D. Walker 34
Richd. Phelan, 40 — Alex. Goday 43
R. Rowland (in an enormous black margin! never saw such a black mark
around a man's name!) 43
S. W. D. S. 43 — s. H. Lowry
Sid. Smith, Lieut. 4th Infy.
Wm. C. Kennet — G. W. Christy —
C. Kennerly — E. F. Choteau
Virginia
Geo. R. H. Clark 37

The Oregon Co. arrived July 26, 1843
W^m. Wilson
L. W. Hastings — A. L. Lovejoy
A. F. Sanford — Jas Rudford
P. Richardson — B. Savoy
M. M. McCarver — W. Gilpin
T. Fitzpatrick — W. T. Newby
Jos. Carroll — B. Gray
C. F. Klein — J. Boileau
J. Gray — E. Chausse

I.H.S.
E. P. I. De Smett
F. N. Point — F. Mengarini

I. H. S
F. P. Devos, S. J.
F. A. Hoechen, S. J.
Lay brothers
D. Lions — I. McGean
I. Borris

L. Crawford, 38—T. Patterson
J. P. Walker, 40—Wm. P. Clark 38

Indian signs, fresh upon the rock, the vermillion yet wet, their fire yet warm—the following is a close transcript.

in a spot near this the following mark, we also found, done in red paint.

Our Scioux squaw gave us the explanation

M. Greely—B. Tisot, 43
R. C. Nelson—C. Town
T. P. Springer—*Fontenelle* 27—28—30—37—38
T. Fallon—F. Parrow 43
A. Parrow—43—A.-T. Baker 43
Geo. Davis, 40—J. B. Childs
C. B. Beale 41—H. Peyton
A. G. Patton
C. De Forrest, 42
P. Perain

NOTES ON APPENDIX A

1. Field, Matthew, *Prairie and Mountain Sketches*, p. 174–6.

APPENDIX B:
ELLISON'S BIOGRAPHY

ROBERT SPURRIER ELLISON's *Independence Rock* was the first book containing a list of the Rock's inscriptions. Ye Galleon Press published this book in 1930. All historians owe Ellison a debt of gratitude for recognizing the need to preserve a record of this historic site. For years this book was used as a reference by those searching out specific inscriptions on Independence Rock. Readers with a deep interest in history also found this small book useful. At the time that Ellison did his research and surveying of the inscriptions on Independence Rock, he was vice president of the Midwest Refining Company located in Casper, Wyoming. Daniel W. Greenburg, one of the people helping Ellison with the survey, also worked for this company.[1]

Robert S. Ellison was born November 6, 1875, in Rushville, Indiana, the son of Franklin and Mary A. (Krammes) Ellison. He received his basic education in Rushville and later entered Indiana University, receiving a Bachelor of Arts degree in 1900. He immediately began the study of law, moved to Colorado, and was admitted to the Colorado bar in 1903. Soon he became associated with the law firm of Schuyler & Schuyler in Colorado Springs. In 1907 he married Vida Gregory, the daughter of prominent Colorado Springs residents. He served in the Colorado House of Representatives in 1911–1912. The Ellisons moved from Colorado Springs to Casper, Wyoming, in 1919, where he became vice president of the Midwest Refining Company. In 1930 he was transferred to Tulsa,

Oklahoma, where he became president of the Stanolind Crude Oil Purchasing Company; the Midwest Refining Company was purchased by Standard Oil in that year. Ellison retired from active business life in 1940, and he and his wife then moved to Manitou Springs, Colorado. Even though he was retired from the oil business, he remained very active in business and civic affairs. He became president of the Bank of Manitou, vice president of the Industrial Finance Bank in Denver, and for two years was a trustee of the city of Manitou Springs. In 1944 he was elected mayor of Manitou Springs and held that office until the time his death on August 16, 1945.[2]

No matter where Ellison lived, he always took an active interest in local affairs. While living in Casper, he became involved with the work of the Boy Scouts of America, eventually becoming Wyoming's regional director and also serving on the national board. In Tulsa he became president of the Tulsa County Council of Boy Scouts; when he moved to Manitou Springs he became director of the Pikes Peak Boy Scouts. Some of the other civic offices he held while living in Casper included president of the Casper Chamber of Commerce in 1924 and 1925 and president of the Casper Literary Club. Probably his true love was the history of the Old West; he pursued this interest all his life. While in Casper, he became a founder of the Historical Landmark Commission of Wyoming. In this role, he was instrumental in the state's acquisition of Fort Bridger, thus preserving it as a state historical site. Later in life, when living in Colorado, he was active in the Colorado Historical Society.

Of particular relevance to the history of Independence Rock, Ellison was regional director of the Oregon Trail Memorial Association. In that capacity he directed the Covered Wagon Centennial celebration held at the Rock on July 4, 1930.[3] This celebration was a very large undertaking encompassing three organizations. The Boy Scouts of America made it their first national jamboree; more than two thousand Scouts, from nearly every state of the union, participated in the three-day affair. The second group taking part was the Knights of Columbus, who met to commemorate the work

1930 photo showing the approach from the east towards Independence Rock as the emigrants viewed it. Numerous trail swales are still visible in the foreground years after the busy trail years. (Photo courtesy Wyoming Division of Cultural Resources.)

of Father Pierre Jean DeSmet, an early missionary priest in the West. About five hundred members took part, including prominent priests from Saint Louis, Saint Joseph, and Kansas City. The third group was about two thousand members of the Ancient, Free, and Accepted Masons, and their families. The first meeting of Masons at Independence Rock had taken place on July 4, 1862, and the 1930 celebration was in commemoration of that event. A total of four to five thousand people are estimated to have been at that large celebration[4]. Ellison had an enduring interest in Independence Rock, but perhaps this anticipated celebration was the catalyst that spurred him to survey the inscriptions and write the book. The narrative that constitutes part of his book was first presented as a paper to a gathering of petroleum engineers at the Rock on August 30, 1925.[5]

Besides his book on Independence Rock, Ellison also wrote *William H. Jackson: Pioneer of the Yellowstone* (1925), *Fort Bridger, Wyoming: A Brief History* (1931), and *The Red Buttes Indian Fight*. At the time of his death he was writing a history of the early Wyoming country and the Ute Indians.[6]

During the last twenty years of his life, Ellison acquired an extensive library collection of Western Americana. He was particularly interested in the regions of the Plains and the Rockies, but his collection also contained items related to the Southwest and Pacific Northwest. Included in this collection were rare Overland narratives, among them numerous first editions, and several extremely rare works. After his death his vast collection was given to Indiana University by his widow, Vida Ellison. In 1955 there were forty-five hundred titles comprising this collection.[7]

Kathleen Troxel wrote these words in 1955:

> The West knew him as a civic leader, counsellor of young men, a keen analyst of trends in business and political life, and a valued adviser to business associates. A wider circle now honors him as the collector of a large and distinguished library of Western Americana, which is a tribute to his business acumen and, above

all, an enduring monument to his interest in the West and the men who made it.[8]

Ellison was truly committed to recognizing and preserving records of the past. In his 1925 speech at the Rock, he stressed the importance of preserving Independence Rock as a historic site:

> I do not ask for hero worship, for these old pioneers were but of common clay, or that we dwell upon the glories of the past, but I do believe our nation and its people cannot be truly great or long endure unless the worthy deeds of our fathers before us are honored.[9]

Robert S. Ellison left his inscription on Independence Rock in 1930 where it can still be seen today.

NOTES ON APPENDIX B

1. Ellison, Robert S., files at Wyoming Division of Cultural Resources, Cheyenne, Wyoming.

2. Troxel, Kathryn, "Robert Spurrier Ellison—Collector of Western Americana," *Westerner Brand Book*, Vol. II, #4, p. 77.

3. Ibid., p. 77.

4. Mokler, Alfred J., "Resplendent Sunrise at Independence Rock," *Wyoming Pioneer*, Nov.–Dec.,1942, p. 10.

5. Ellison, Robert S., *Independence Rock*, foreword by D. W. Greenburg.

6. Troxel, Kathryn, op. cit., p. 77.

7. Ibid., p. 78. For more information regarding the Robert S. Ellison Collection refer to "The Robert S. Ellison Collection," written by Oscar Osburn Winther, *Indiana Quarterly for Bookmen*, Vol. I. #1, January 1948.

8. Ibid., p. 78.

9. Ellison, Robert S., "Independence Rock and the Oregon Trail," *Midwest Review*, Vol III, #2, p. 7.

BIBLIOGRAPHY

Adams, Cecelia, and Parthenia Blank. *The Oregon Trail Diary of Twin Sisters*. Medford, OR: Webb Research Group, 1990.

Anderson, William Marshall. *The Rocky Mountain Journals of William Marshall Anderson*. Edited by Dale L. Morgan and Eleanor Harris. San Marino, CA: Huntington Library, 1967.

Archambault, Amanda Z. "Historic Document Tells Early Day Drama of the West." *Annals of Wyoming* Vol. 15: #3. July 1943.

Arms, Cephus. *The Long Road to California*. Mount Pleasant, MI: John Cumming Press, 1985.

Beebe, Ruth. *Reminiscing Along the Sweetwater*. Casper, WY: House of Printing, 1973

Belden, L. Burr. *Goodbye Death Valley*. Publication No. 5. Death Valley 49er's, Inc.

Bennett, Richard F. *We'll Find the Place*. Salt Lake City, UT: Deseret Book Company, 1997.

Bollinger, Gene. "When You Don't Pay Attention." *The Institute News Magazine* Vol. 1: #5. Hatch, NM: 1997.

Brown, Randy. *Emigrant Inscriptions of the Oregon, California, Utah Trails.*

Brown, Randy. "Millie Irwin Story." *Wyoming Trails Newsletter*. April, 1998.

Bryant, William. *What I Saw in California*. Lincoln, NE: University of Nebraska Press, 1985.

Bullock, Thomas. *The Pioneer Camp of the Saints*. Edited by Will Bagley. Spokane, WA: The Arthur H. Clark Company, 1997.

Burton, Richard F. *The City of the Saints*. Edited by Fawn N. Brodie. New York, NY: Alfred A. Knopf, 1963.

Butte County, California, 1890 Great Register. Paradise, CA: Paradise Genealogical Society, Inc.

Chittenden, H. M. *A. Western Epic*. Edited by Bruce LeRoy. Tacoma, WA: Washington State Historical, 1961.

Clark, Thomas D., editor. *Off at Sunrise, The Overland Journal of Charles Glass Gray*. San Marino, CA: Huntington Library, 1976.

Clyman, James, *Journal of a Mountain Man*. Linda Hasselstrom, editor. Missoula, MT: Mountain Press Publishing Company, 1984.

Coutant, C. G. *The History of Wyoming, Vol. I*. Laramie, WY: Chaplin, Spafford, Mathison, Printers, 1899.

Crosby, Jesse W. "The History and Journal of the Life & Travels of Jesse W. Crosby." *Annals of Wyoming* Vol. II: # 3. July 1939.

Crossing the Plains Index, 1847-1868. Microfilm index. Casper, WY: LDS Family History Center.

Crossroads Vol. 8, #4. Newsletter of the Utah Crossroads Chapter. Oregon California Trails Association, Fall 1997.

Crumb, John H. Manuscript. "Statement Regarding Fight at Platte Bridge and Red Buttes, July 26, 1865." R. S. Ellison files. Wyoming Division of Cultural Resources, Archives, Cheyenne, WY.

Cutler, William C. *History of the State of Kansas*. Eleventh Regiment Kansas Volunteer Cavalry. Kansas Collection Books: Kansas State Historical Society, www.kshs.org/archives.

DeVoto, Bernard. *Across the Wide Missouri*. Boston, MA: Houghton Mifflin Company, 1947.

Draper, Delbert M. *The Mormon Drapers*. Family record furnished by descendant Joy Thomas.

Drury, Clifford. *First White Women Over the Rockies, Vol II, III*. Glendale, CA: Arthur Clark Company, 1966.

Ebey, Winfield Scott. *The 1854 Oregon Trail Diary of Winfield Scott Ebey*. Edited by Susan B. Doyle. Independence, MO: Oregon CaliforniaTrails Association, 1997.

Elgin, James Henry. "Over the Plains 50 Years Ago." *The Oregonian*. 1902. Courtesy Susannah Elgin Lingross.

Ellison, Robert Spurrier. *Independence Rock*. Fairfield, WA: Ye Galleon Press, 1931.

Ellison, Robert S. "Independence Rock and the Oregon Trail." *Midwest Review* Vol. VIII, #2. February 1927.

Executive Document No. 63. House of Representatives, 36th Congress, 2nd Session. Printed 1861.

Field, Matthew. *Prairie and Mountain Sketches*. Edited by Kate Gregg and John F. McDermott. Norman, OK: University of Oklahoma Press, 1957.

Flora, Stephanie. *Emigrants to Oregon*. Internet source sflora@teleport.com.

Franklin, William Riley. "Journal of William Riley Franklin to California from Missouri in 1850." *Annals of Wyoming* Vol. 46, #1. Spring 1974.

Fremont, Brevet Capt. J. C. *The Exploring Expedition to the Ro Mountains in the Year 1842*. Printed by order of the Senate United States. Washington, D. C.: Gales & Seaton Printer'

Gordon, Mary McDougal. *Overland to California with ' Line*. Champaign, IL: University of Illinois Press, 19'

Greenburg, D. W. "Survey List of Independence Rock, August 22, 1926." Robert S. Ellison files: Wyoming Division of Cultural Resources, Cheyenne, Wyoming.

Hafen, Leron R. and Francis Marion Young. *Fort Laramie and the Pageant of the West, 1834-1890*. Lincoln, NE: University of Nebraska, 1938.

Haines, Aubrey. *Historic Sites Along the Oregon Trail*. St. Louis, MO: The Patrice Press, 1981.

Hannon, Jessie Gould. *The Boston Newton Company Venture*. Lincoln, NE: University of Nebraska Press, 1969.

Hastings, Lansford W. *The Emigrants' Guide to Oregon and California*. Bedford, MA: Applewood Books.

Henderson, Paul, and George House. "Register Cliff." Survey of emigrant names, about 1930.

Hill, John B. "Gold, The Story of the Plains in 1850." *Annals of Wyoming* Vol. 9 #4, September 1930.

Hill, William E. *Writing & Riding Along the Oregon California Trails*. Independence, MO: Oregon California Trails Association, 1993.

Holliday, J.S. *The World Rushed In, The California Gold Rush Experience*. New York, NY: Touchstone Books, Simon & Shuster, 1983.

Holmes, Kenneth L., editor. *Covered Wagon Women, Diaries and Letters from the Western Trail*. Vol. 1, 3, 7. Lincoln, NE: University of Nebraska Press; Vol. 4, 5, 6, 8. Arthur H. Clark Co.

House of Representatives Executive Document No. 63. 36th Congress, 2nd Session. 1861.

Index to Kansas Volunteer Regiment Enlistments, 1861-1863. Kansas State Historical Society. www.kshs.org/archives.

Inman, Colonel Henry L. *The Great Salt Lake Trail*. Topeka, KS: Crane & Company, 1913.

Jackson, William H. *Picture Maker of the West, William H. Jackson.* New York, NY: Charles Scribners Sons, 1947.

Jacob, Norton. *Diary of Norton Jacob.* Provo, UT: From a microfilm typed copy of the original diary now in possession of BYU Library, LDS Family History Center.

Jensen, Andrew. "Day by Day With the Utah Pioneers." *Salt Lake Tribune.* Revision, St. George, UT: American Graphics Printing, April 5, 1897 to July 24, 1897.

Jensen, Andrew. *LDS Biographical Encyclopedia.* Salt Lake City, UT: Western Epics.

Junge, Mark, and Ned Frost. *Prospectus on Independence Rock.* State of Wyoming: Wyoming Recreation Commission, Central Duplication Plant, 1973.

Keller, George. *A Trip Across the Plains.* Oakland, CA: Bio Books.

Kelly, Charles, and Paul Henderson. "Names Recorded at Emigrant Springs in 1930."

Kimball, Stanley. *Historic Resource Study, Mormon Pioneer National Historic Trail.* National Park Service, May 1991.

Mansfield, George, C. *History of Butte County.* Los Angeles, CA: Historic Record Company.

Mattes, Merrill J. *Diary and Recollection Survey.* Independence, MO: Merrill J. Mattes Research Library, National Pioneer Trails Center.

Mattes, Merrill J. *Platte River Road Narratives* Urbana, IL: University of Illinois Press, 1988.

McDermott, Jack. "Guinard's Bridge and Its Place in History." Mills, WY: CLG Oregon Trail Sesquicentennial Newsletter, Summer 1993.

Mintz, Lannon W. *The Trail, A Bibliography of the Overland Trail to California, Oregon, Salt Lake City, and Montana during the Years 1841-1864.* Albuquerque, NM: University of New Mexico Press, 1987.

Mokler, Alfred J. "Devil's Gate, A Prominent Wyoming Landmark." *The Wyoming Pioneer.* Casper, WY: published by A. J. Mokler, July-August 1941

Mokler, Alfred J. "John Charles Fremont Was Not a Glory Hunter." *The Wyoming Pioneer.* May-June 1942.

Mokler, Alfred J. *History of Freemasonry in Wyoming, Vol I.* Wyoming: Grand Lodge of A. F. and A. M., August 28, 1924.

Mokler, Alfred J. *History of Natrona County Wyoming.* Chicago, IL: The Lakeside Press, 1923; reprinted, Casper, WY: Mountain States Lithographing, 1989.

Mokler, Alfred J. "Resplendent Sunrise at Independence Rock." *Wyoming Pioneer.* Nov.,Dec.,1942.

Morgan, Martha M. *Martha M. Morgan, Trip Across the Plains.* National Frontier Trails Center, Independence, MO: Newbury Microfilm 2-2, Merrill J. Mattes Research Library.

Munkres, Robert L. "Independence Rock and Devil's Gate." *Annals of Wyoming* Volume 40 #1. April 1968.

Murray, Robert. *Military Posts of Wyoming: 1865-1894.* Lincoln: University of Nebraska Press, 1968.

Myres, Sandra L., editor. *Ho for California!, Women's Overland Diaries from the Huntington Library.* San Marino, CA: Huntington Library, 1980.

"Names Recorded at Emigrant Spring in 1989." Bureau of Land Management.

"Names Recorded at Register Cliff." Scottsbluff, NE: Scottsbluff National Monument Survey List.

Paden, Irene D. *The Wake of the Prairie Schooner.* New York, NY: The MacMillan Company, 1947.

Page, Elizabeth. *Wagons West, A Story of the Oregon Trail.* New York, NY: Farrar & Rinehart, Inc. 1930.

Parke, Charles Ross. *Dreams to Dust*. Edited by James D. Davis. Lincoln, NE: University of Nebraska Press, 1989

Phillips, Jeannie Sharp. *Reflections of Oregon Pioneer Families*. Milwaukie, OR: AlphaGraphics Printshops, 1994.

Porter, Mae Reed, and Odessa Davenport. *Scotsman in Buckskin*. New York, NY: Hastings House Publishers, 1963.

Potter, David M., editor. *Trail to California, The Overlant Journal of Vincent Geiger and Wakeman Bryarly*. Yale University Press, 1945.

Prevost, Nancy. *USGenWeb Archives*. prevost@ieway.com.

Pritchard, Earl H., and Phil, editors. *Journal of William Fowler Pritchard*. Fairfield, WA: Ye Galleon Press, 1995.

Rasmussen, Louis J. *California Wagon Train Lists, Vol. 1*. Calma, CA: San Francisco Historic Records, 1994.

Read, Georgia Willis, and Ruth Gaines, editors. *Gold Rush, The Journals, Drawings, and Other Papers of J. Goldsborough Bruff.* NY: Columbia University Press, 1949.

"Regimental History of the 11th Kansas Volunteer Cavalry." Kansas State Historical Society, web site.

Richardson, Larry, Paradise, CA: private interview.

Robrock, David P. "The Eleventh Ohio Volunteer Cavalry on the Central Plains, 1862-1866." *Arizona and the West* Vol. 25 pp. 23-48. University of Arizona Press, Spring 1983.

Roster of Ohio Soldiers, 1861-66, During War of Rebellion, Vol. XI. Fort Casper, WY: Fort Casper Museum.

Sage, Rufus. *Rocky Mountain Life; or Startling Scenes and Perilous Adventures in the Far West*. Boston, MA: Wentworth & Company, 1858.

Scamehorn, Howard L., editor. *The Buckeye Rovers in the Gold Rush*. Athens, OH: Ohio University Press, 1965.

Spring, Agnes Wright. *Casper Collins, The Life and Exploits of an Indian Fighter*. NY: Columbia University Press, 1927.

Stewart, George R. *The California Trail*. Lincoln, NE: University of Nebraska Press, 1983.

Talbot, Theodore. *Journals of Theodore Talbot, 1843 and 1849-52*. Portland, OR: Metropolitan Press Publishers, 1931.

Todd, Edgeley Woodman, editor. *The Diary of Dr. John Hudson Wayman, 1852*. Denver, CO: Old West Publishing Company, 1971.

Troxel, Kathryn. "Robert Spurrier Ellison—Collector of Western Americana." *Westerner Brand Book* Vol. II #4 p. 77.

Unrau, William E. *Tending the Talking Wire, A Buck Soldier's View of Indian Country, 1863-1866*. Salt Lake City, UT: University of Utah Press, 1979.

Watson, Jeanne Hamilton, editor. *To the Land of Gold and Wickedness*. St. Louis, MO: The Patrice Press, 1988.

Webber, Bert. *Comprehensive Index to Oregon Trail Diaries*. Medford, OR: Webb Research Group, 1991.

Wilkins, Edness Kimball. "Sweetwater Station." *Annals of Wyoming* Vol. 43 p. 286.

Williams, Jacqueline. *Wagon Wheel Kitchens*. Lawrence, KA: University Press of Kansas, 1993.

Winther, Oscar Osburn. "The Robert S. Ellison Collection." *Indiana Quarterly for Bookman* Vol. IV #1. January, 1948.

Wyoming, A Guide to Historic Sites. Wyoming Recreation Commission. Basin, WY: Big Horn Publishers, 1976.

For additional reading about Independence Rock and Devil's Gate refer to:

Independence Rock by Robert Spurrier Ellison, Ye Galleon Press, Fairfield, Washington, 1930, reprint 1995 by the City of Casper Historic Preservation Commission and the Natrona County Historical Society.

"Independence Rock and Devil's Gate" by Robert Munkres, *Annals of Wyoming*, Volume 40, #1, April, 1968.

ACKNOWLEDGMENTS

A debt of gratitude is extended to all those listed below, for without them this book could never have been completed. I have met many wonderful people during the past six years who have all had an influence on this book.

1. The small group of dedicated members from the Natrona County Historical Society and the Wyoming Chapter of OCTA who spent long cold hours in the fall of 1994 starting this survey work on Independence Rock. Little did I know at the time that this project would start me on an exciting continuing journey into the past. I wish I could name them all but if I try I'd leave someone out inadvertently. The group changed from week to week.

2. Norman and Gaynell Park of the Dumbell Ranch for their unselfish contribution to the preservation of this historic landmark and for their encouragement of my work.

3. Riggie and Irene Long, caretakers of the Independence Rock rest area until the fall of 1999. I spent many winter and early spring hours alone on Independence Rock, yet I always knew I could rely on them to know if I should be in trouble on the Rock. Their continued support, assistance, and their welcome glasses of special lemonade during our hours of summer volunteer work at Independence Rock will always be appreciated. They are true caretakers of the past.

4. Dear, dear Leneigh Schrinar of Riverton, WY. Somehow she always had that special spark at just the right time to keep me going in this project. She spent more hours with me than anyone else searching out inscriptions and furnishing me with diary information. Those hours spent together will never be forgotten. She is an important part of this book.

5. Randy Wagner for writing the introduction.

6. The numerous descendants to whom I spoke and with whom I had correspondence. I am especially grateful to the different Internet sources that supplied me with valuable information.

7. Jerry Saunders at Saunders Camera, Casper, my technical advisor on photography work.

8. Pat Thompson, Wyoming Department of State Parks and Cultural Resources, past Superintendent of Independence Rock. I especially want to thank him for the opportunity to get my aerial photos of the trail in Natrona County and of Independence Rock and Devil's Gate. He supported me in this project in every way he could.

9. Kevin Anderson, Western History/Automation Specialist, Special Collections, Casper College Library. Kevin spent hours digging out random bits of information helping with my research.

10. Kathy and Al Orr for their help, support, and advice. Kathy especially for her enthusiasm doing survey work.

11. Amy Murphy, Ray Bender and Dr. Ronald Lund for proofreading my manuscript and furnishing advice and support. Deep gratitude to Amy for offering me technical assistance and a special thank you to Dr. Lund for his kind endorsement of the book.

12. The very helpful volunteer ladies of the Family History Center, LDS Church, Casper.

13. Don Buck, for giving me an encouraging word when I was ready to abandon this project.

14. Doug Jensen, for his interest in the saleratus. His testing of the saleratus furnished me with heretofore unknown information about the substance.

15. BLM Office at Pinedale, WY for supplying me with the list of inscriptions found at Emigrant Springs.

16. Jude Carino, BLM Office, Casper, for support and advice.

17. Shaun Hogan for use of his photographs and assistance during surveying.

18. Charles Germain for furnishing information on the Masonic celebrations.

19. The staffs at Scottsbluff National Monument, Chimney Rock Historical Site, and the Harold Warp Pioneer Village, Minden, NE.

20. The Wyoming Department State Parks and Cultural Resources, Edness Kimball Wilkins State Park and Guernsey State Park for supplying me with lists of emigrant inscriptions and related materials.

21. Archivists Gary Gillespie, William Slaughter, and Melvin Bashore of the LDS Historical Offices, Salt Lake City, Utah.

22. Joy Thomas, descendant of Bishop W. Draper for furnishing a photo and information on Bishop Draper.

23. Rick Young, Director, Fort Caspar Museum for his help with the 11th Ohio Volunteer Cavalry.

24 Lee Underbrink, Casper, for the use of his trail library.

25 Randy Brown for furnishing the initial survey group with a database copy of the R. S. Ellison names in 1994.

26. Museums and Libraries:

American Heritage Center, University of Wyoming. Laramie, WY, contact: Carol Bowers.

Denver Public Library, Denver, CO, contact: Brian Kenny.

Family History Center, LDS Church, Casper, WY.

Fort Caspar Museum, contact: Rick Young, Director.

Goodstein Library, Casper College, Casper, Special Collections, contact: Kevin Anderson.

Island County Historical Museum, Coupeville, WA, contact: Janet Engmann

LDS Historical Department, Salt Lake City, Utah.

Merrill J. Mattes Research Library, Independence, MO, contact: John Mark Lambertson.

Morgan Library, Colorado State University, Archives, Fort Collins, contact: Pat Vandeventer.

Natrona County Public Library, Casper, Wyoming.

Santa Clara University, Santa Clara, CA, contact: Anne Mc-Mahon.

Wyoming Division of Cultural Resources, Archives, at Cheyenne, WY, contact: Lavaughn Breshnahan.

And a special thank you to my publisher and editors, Nancy Curtis, Mindy Keskinen, and Tracy Eller for taking me by the hand and patiently guiding me through the process of making this book a reality.

INDEX

The list of inscriptions in Chapter Eight is alphabetical and is not included in this index. Only the items in the text chapters are indexed here.

The list of inscriptions in Chapter Eight is alphabetical and is not included in this index. Only the items in the text chapters are indexed here.

The list of inscriptions in Chapter Eight is alphabetical and is not included in this index. Only the items in the text chapters are indexed here.

The list of inscriptions in Chapter Eight is alphabetical and is not included in this index. Only the items in the text chapters are indexed here.

The list of inscriptions in Chapter Eight is alphabetical and is not included in this index. Only the items in the text chapters are indexed here.

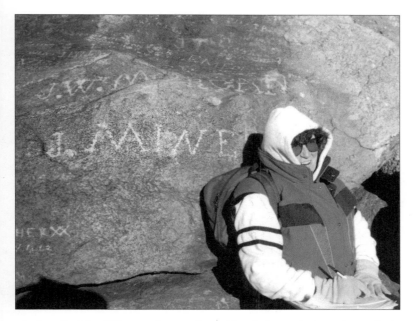

Author Levida Hileman braves the cold winds at Independence Rock. (Courtesy Nona Kimball)

LEVIDA HILEMAN HAS BEEN a member of the Oregon California Trails Association since the Wyoming Chapter was founded in 1987, having served both as secretary and as president of this group. She is a past member of the National Board of Directors of the Oregon California Trails Association and is also a past member of the Board of Directors for the National Historic Trails Interpretive Center in Casper.

Levida is a retired teacher and enjoys going into local class-rooms to talk about the trails across Wyoming. She is also a frequent speaker for community groups. For three years she was the Trails instructor for the summer Elderhostel Program held at Casper College, and she taught a class, The Emigrant Trails, for two years at Casper College in the evening program. Her true joy is accompanying large or small groups to trail sites in the Casper area.